MORE ADVANCE PRAISE FOR ALPHA GIRLS

"An intimate and addictive homage to the fearless female pioneers who made Silicon Valley blossom. Julian's vivid portrayals of once-hidden risk takers and mavericks will leave you heartbroken, hopeful, and hungering for more."

—*Brian Keating, professor of physics at the University of California, San Diego, and author of* Losing the Nobel Prize

"ally, it's here: a book about Silicon Valley as seen through the accomplishments e powerful women who, against all odds, made their mark there. *Alpha Girls* rs an inside look at the true meaning of grit and drive and upends the myth it is only men who create and build tech companies. For any young woman in search of a role model, or any young man too, *Alpha Girls* is a must-read."

—*Caroline Paul, author of* The Gutsy Girl: Escapades for Your Life of Epic Adventure

"*Alpha Girls* is about four women in a high-stakes, high-drama world. Each of the women's stories is gripping, treacherous, heroic, and entertaining. They are being pulled out from behind the gender curtain and given their rightful place in contemporary history."

—*Cathy Schulman, president of Welle Entertainment, Academy Award–winning producer, and women's activist*

"Julian Guthrie is the best author writing about Silicon Valley today, and *Alpha Girls* is the book that the world needs right now. It's the real story behind the largest legal creation of wealth in the history of the planet. If you are a woman who works, or simply work with women, *Alpha Girls* is essential reading."

—*Adam Fisher, author of* Valley of Genius: The Uncensored History of Silicon Valley (As Told by the Hackers, Founders, and Freaks Who Made It Boom)

"A revelatory, riveting journey into a part of Silicon Valley's history that has been overshadowed for far too long. Through vivid prose and artful story-telling, Julian Guthrie brings to life the nuanced tales of the struggles and success of women in the technology industry."

—*Ashlee Vance, bestselling author of* Elon Musk

"The story of four women who entered the tech industry to follow their dreams and managed through hard work and creativity to make those dreams come true. I'm glad Julian has written this book; we need to tell the success stories of women in tech."

—*Reid Hoffman, co-founder of LinkedIn and investor at Greylock Partners*

"If you read one book about women in business, *Alpha Girls* should be the one. Julian Guthrie has written another dazzler."

—*Peter Diamandis,* New York Times *bestselling author, founder and executive charman of XPRIZE*

"Julian Guthrie is a mesmerizing storyteller, weaving the life stories of four dynamic women into a page-turning yarn. We don't just read of but feel the outrageous and often clueless male slights and insults, the double standards and blatant sexism endured by women in the blustery, male-dominated world of Silicon Valley. Yet *Alpha Girls* leaves you awed by their resilience and their professional feats. A stirring tale of triumph."

—*Ken Auletta, acclaimed author and* New Yorker *staff writer*

"The women of *Alpha Girls* had to grow some thick skin to survive and succeed. And succeed they did. *Alpha Girls* will reshape how you look at women in finance. A must read for women and girls interested in changing the world."

—*Sallie Krawcheck, CEO and co-founder of Ellevest*

"An extremely important addition to the literary canon of Silicon Valley, told through the honest and specific stories of a handful of individual women. Beautifully done."

—*Po Bronson,* New York Times *bestselling author of* What Should I Do with My Life?

"Once I started reading *Alpha Girls*, I couldn't put it down. The story of these VC women trailblazers must be told, and Julian tells it brilliantly. The book stimulates reflections on how we must accelerate changes in ourselves, at home, and in the workplace."

—*Judy Vredenburgh, president & CEO of Girls Inc.*

ALPHA
GIRLS

The Women Upstarts Who Took On
Silicon Valley's Male Culture and
Made the Deals of a Lifetime

JULIAN GUTHRIE

piatkus

PIATKUS

First published in the US in 2019 by Currency, an imprint of the Crown
Publishing Group, a division of Penguin Random House LLC, New York

First published in Great Britain in 2019 by Piatkus

1 3 5 7 9 10 8 6 4 2

A CIP catalogue record for this book
is available from the British Library.

ISBN 978-0-349-42025-7

Printed and bound in Great Britain by Clays Ltd, Elcograf S.p.A

Papers used by Piatkus are from well-managed forests and
other responsible sources.

Piatkus
An imprint of
Little, Brown Book Group
Carmelite House
50 Victoria Embankment
London EC4Y 0DZ

An Hachette UK Company
www.hachette.co.uk

www.improvementzone.co.uk

To my mother,
Connie Guthrie,
an original Alpha Girl

CONTENTS

PROLOGUE

Mary Jane Elmore was giddy as she looked down at the rusted-out floorboards of her old green Ford Pinto. She could see the road rushing by below. But she wasn't driving on just any road. She was making her way up Sand Hill Road, in the heart of Silicon Valley, about to start a new life intent on changing the world.

A pretty young woman with brown hair and brown eyes, Mary Jane had graduated from Purdue University in 1976 with a degree in mathematics. She paid for her car by waitressing during college summers, wearing a small orange romper that prompted oversize tips. Her beat-up Pinto, which leaked radiator fluid and still had its original Firestone 500 tires, had taken her nearly two thousand miles, from Kansas City to northern California, where she had landed a job at an eight-year-old technology company called Intel.

Although Sand Hill Road was the center of the venture capital world, no bronze statue of a charging bull, no Gilded Age architecture, and no artificial canyons towered over by gleaming skyscrapers commemorated it. At that time it was a stretch of rolling land laced with scrub brush, sprawling oak trees, big pink dahlias, and buildings that stretched long and low like an old Lincoln Continental. The midcentury modern structures, with outer skins of cedar, redwood, and masonry, featured numbers but no names. Unlike other centers of commerce, Sand Hill

1

Road is intentionally inconspicuous; it consciously resists contemporary symbols of money and power. Instead, it is country club hush. To Mary Jane, it was a world away from the tall cornfields where she had skittered about as a child, playing hide-and-seek, moving three rows up and four rows over, strategic and mathematical in her decision making even then.

Her aptitude in math—not to mention a prescient feel for the markets—would make Mary Jane particularly well suited for this new California frontier. And in the 1970s, that was exactly what Silicon Valley felt like, a frontier, steeped in the aggressive and hungry spirit of the Gold Rush, of adventurers and fortune seekers risking everything for a glimmer of gold, aware that only a lucky few walked away winners. The original Gold Rush days of 1849 were dominated by mining companies and merchants hawking overpriced goods. It was ruled by men: Samuel Brannan, Levi Strauss, John Studebaker, Henry Wells, and William Fargo. Women, outnumbered and overmatched, were mostly reduced to entertainers, companions, wives, or housekeepers. Things were not that different in the more recent gold rush. The Valley was always a region dominated by men, from William Hewlett, Dave Packard, Bob Noyce, Gordon Moore, Andy Grove, Larry Ellison, Steve Jobs, and Steve Wozniak to, decades later, in the twenty-first century, Larry Page, Sergey Brin, Mark Zuckerberg, Elon Musk, Tim Cook, Travis Kalanick, and Marc Benioff.

Mary Jane, fueled by peanut butter sandwiches packed in wax paper for the two-day journey, was under no illusion that it would be easy to navigate the old boys' club of Sand Hill Road and Silicon Valley. Even today, decades after Mary Jane first arrived, 94 percent of investing partners at venture capital firms—the financial decision makers shaping the future—are men, and more than 80 percent of venture firms have never had a woman investing partner. Less than 2 percent of venture dollars go to start-ups founded by women (less than 1 percent to women of color), and roughly 85 percent of the tech employees at top companies are men. Yet technology is pervasive, and it is changing our lives. When Mary Jane first drove up Sand Hill, women made up barely

40 percent of the overall American workforce. Less than a handful of those women were venture capital partners.

But Mary Jane Elmore, the unflappable, fresh-faced girl next door, would go on to become one of the first women in history to make partner at a venture capital firm. Like the bold pink dahlias flourishing in one corner of Sand Hill Road, she and the other pioneering women venture capitalists, the "Alpha Girls," would figure out a way to take root and thrive.

They made their way west like early-day prospectors during Silicon Valley's headiest days, as enormous mainframe computers gave way to minicomputers, personal computers, and the Internet, just as punched computer cards had at one time set the stage for computation. Through the start-ups they would discover, fund, and mentor—financing the ideas of entrepreneurs—these women venture capitalists would play a critical role in shaping how people around the world work, play, communicate, study, travel, create, and interact. Venture capitalists influence many of the most important new inventions in drugs, medicine, and technology.

In addition to Mary Jane, there is Sonja Hoel, a blond, blue-eyed, doggedly optimistic southern belle whose investments at the white-glove Menlo Ventures on Sand Hill Road would focus on making the Internet safer and more reliable; Magdalena Yeşil, a feisty Armenian outsider reared in Istanbul, who loved getting in where she wasn't invited; and Theresia Gouw, an overachieving daughter of Chinese immigrants, who went from flipping burgers at Burger King to chasing down some of the hottest deals in Silicon Valley history. There are other Alpha Girls, too, such as the first investor and board member of Tesla; the woman who started the first venture fund in India; the first woman to take a tech company public; the first women to build an online beauty site; and today a whole new generation of young women financiers and entrepreneurs. These women share a determination with Alpha Girls everywhere, transcending vocation and location, working in Hollywood, academia, economics, advertising, politics, the media, sports, automobiles, agriculture, law, hospitality, restaurants, and the arts.

History is rich with women rebels who have shined a spotlight from the outside—women such as Rosa Parks, whose one defiant act became synonymous with the civil rights movement. But it is also rife with what one academic calls "tempered radicals," those who learn to play the game to perfection—whatever the game is—before trying to change the rules. Margaret Thatcher took elocution lessons to deepen her voice, to better be heard. Georgia O'Keeffe painted "low-toned dismal-colored" paintings like male artists, to show she could, before turning to the bright desert flowers that made her a giant of American modernism.

As Mary Jane drove up Sand Hill Road on that perfect fall day, she had little sense of the hard realities ahead. She could never have imagined juggling a high-stakes job, three children, a husband aggressively pursuing his own Silicon Valley dreams, and a junior partner with outsize ambitions. But she knew intuitively that this was the right place for her: Silicon Valley was the embodiment of breathtakingly bold ideas and inventions, a region awash in unparalleled ingenuity, originality, tenacity, optimism, and opportunity. It had given rise to more new companies and industries than anywhere else in the world, including such technology giants as Hewlett-Packard, Fairchild Semiconductor, Intel, Teledyne, ROLM, Amgen, Genentech, Advanced Micro Devices, Tandem, Atari, Oracle, Apple, Dell, Electronic Arts, Compaq, FedEx, Netscape, LSI, Yahoo!, Amazon, Cisco, PayPal, eBay, Google, Salesforce, LinkedIn, Tesla, Facebook, YouTube, Uber, Skype, Twitter, and Airbnb.

But Mary Jane and the other Alpha Girls would need steel in their spines to stay the course, and they would pay a steep emotional price along the way. They would be betrayed when they least expected it. Silicon Valley, teeming with youthful testosterone, is a deceptively rough arena, where bullying, bias, dysfunction, and subjugation are part of the rules of engagement. In the end, the Alpha Girls—these resilient daughters of merchants, teachers, dentists, and immigrants—would come to realize there was only one way to shake up the industry they loved: by breaking and remaking its rules.

PART
ONE

The Valley of Dreams

1980–1994

MAGDALENA YEŞİL

Breathless from her bike ride across campus, Magdalena Yeşil arrived for work at the Stanford computer center wearing a white floor-length gown and yellow daisies in her hair. It was ten P.M., and the room was full of men playing *Dungeons & Dragons* and working on their engineering theses and dissertations. Magdalena smoothed her dress, unpacked her bag, and sat at her desk. The sign on the wall behind her read COMPUTER CONSULTANT.

It was late spring 1980. Magdalena worked the night shift at LOTS, Stanford's Low-Overhead Time-Sharing center, where she fielded predictable questions and laments from students: "I ran out of allocated memory"; "My software keeps running in an infinite loop"; and "I can't log into my account."

Magdalena herself was anything but predictable. Already striking with her long, thick, reddish-brown hair and hazel eyes, she attracted even more attention wearing ballgowns and tiaras to work, or Sixties-inspired fashion; she loved geometric dresses, patterned tights, paisley pantsuits, and anything with daisies. If she had to endure the boredom of these graveyard shifts, she was determined to keep herself, at least, if not those around her, entertained with her whimsical costumes.

As Magdalena logged in, username Y.Ynot, one of the regulars took a seat next to her. He'd printed out a long sheet showing the software he was using and the code he'd written. Pencil in hand, Magdalena studied the printout, and like a forgery expert searching for anachronisms in a painting, she zeroed in on a line created with the wrong command. The satisfied graduate student, his mistake corrected, returned to his table.

As the lights flickered and buzzed, many of the regulars stole glances at Magdalena in her latest ensemble. She bought most of the costumes for a dollar or two at a secondhand clothing store just off campus on California Avenue. But before long their attention was pulled back to the Digital Equipment 2040, a massive mainframe computer that gave users the illusion of having its undivided attention. The DEC was housed in its own cooled room behind glass. The LOTS regulars tended to fit into three categories: students still working on their dissertations, sometimes a decade after graduating; the graduate students in engineering or computer science who came in to do research or play *Dungeons & Dragons, Pong,* or *Asteroids;* and the social sciences graduate students—often the only women—who used the center's statistical analysis tool, SPSS.

Many of the regulars, she knew, were brilliant; she affectionately referred to them as her "colorful weirdos." She also knew that they were kindred spirits—people who, like her, considered engineering akin to a religion, artfully assembling complex puzzles. And despite the night-owl hours, she appreciated a place where she could both stand out and fit in at the same time.

Growing up in Turkey, she learned that fitting in had consequences. From an early age, she had been taught the importance of guarding her Armenian ethnicity. She went by Lena instead of her Christian name, Magdalena. Armenians in Turkey were both cursed and harassed in Magdalena's time. In her grandparents' time, they had been jailed and executed, just as Jews were decades later by the Germans.

There were moments even now, nearly seven thousand miles from home, when she couldn't shake images of sunny days that suddenly darkened, beautiful afternoons on the public beaches in Istanbul, laughing, running, and swimming, until she was singled out as an Armenian. The other kids at the beach would turn on her, throwing sand in her face and chasing her away. Their rejection, however, made her even more determined to fit in, to play with them, to challenge Turkey's rigid social boundaries. She would return home and plot out what she could do to get herself invited back. A strong swimmer, she would show off her swimming strokes. She would use the change she'd saved to win favors by buying the other kids candy or ice cream.

Her father had raised her to dress like a lady but think like a man. As a young girl, she wore frilly dresses and white gloves and pushed a play stroller with a baby doll in it. Growing up in Turkey, being well mannered was even more important than being well educated. But when people asked her what she wanted to be when she grew up, she replied without hesitation, "A carpenter," a profession that wasn't considered appropriate for girls in Turkey. One of Magdalena's favorite pastimes as a child was hammering nails into the walls of her family home. When her parents took away her hammer, she used wooden hangers to strike the nails.

Magdalena arrived in America to attend college in 1976, with forty-three dollars in cash and nine gold bracelets that her parents told her she could sell when she needed extra money. She hadn't sold one yet, thanks to the two jobs that she held down while attending Stanford, including the graveyard shift at the computer center. She was fluent in Turkish, Armenian, French, and English.

As the center's computer expert, Magdalena was able to access the student's work. In the early-morning hours, to stave off boredom, she perused files. She found that the men wrote a great deal about movies (*The Empire Strikes Back* and *The Deer Hunter*), basketball (Michigan State beat Indiana State in the NCAA championship), music (Donna Summer's "Bad Girls," the Knack's "My Sharona"), and politics (whether President Jimmy Carter could defeat Hollywood actor and Republican candidate Ronald Reagan). But mostly the men working through the night at the computer center came across to her as lonely, fixated on fellow classmates and unrequited love, or caught up in the gossip surrounding stars like Carrie Fisher, Sigourney Weaver, Farrah Fawcett, Jacqueline Bisset, and Debbie Harry.

Besides offering computer assistance, Magdalena helped the students with their research on everything from writing basic software to writing machine language. She had enrolled at Stanford thinking she would become a doctor but found the premed classes tedious. She was now about to graduate with her bachelor's degree in industrial engineering, while simultaneously earning a master's in electrical engineering—the only woman in the "double e" master's program. Electrical engineering and digital computer design, unlike medicine, opened her mind in unexpected ways and taught her the flaws in her own deductive reasoning. As she learned about the absolute logic of electrical circuits and digital computers, she began to debug her own logic.

To her surprise, designing computer software brought her back to her faith. Growing up in Turkey, religion had been everything: tribe and identity, more important than race. As a young woman on her own in America, Magdalena had moved toward agnosticism. But as she worked on problems in engineering classes, designing logic gates, end gates, outputs, inputs, and registers, she saw the faultiness of her logic, at times, and reveled in the finding. She was a member of the first class at Stanford to design the complex VLSI (Very Large-Scale Integration) circuit. She designed with precision and care, reviewing her work over and over, until she was confident she had got it right. But inevitably something would fail. Eventually, she would see—or someone would point out—a blind spot in her thinking. *Individual logic is not absolute,* she came to realize. She could not rely on her brain alone to know with certainty. Her engineering and computer classes made her realize: *There is so much above and beyond my brain, my logic.* She found the same thing in others at the computer center. Even the most brilliant students had blind spots.

Her attention was drawn to an unkempt couple who came to the center almost every night to play multiuser games. They usually screamed and carried on as they played, oblivious to those trying to study. But one of her favorites was here tonight, as well, a considerably older female PhD student, impeccably dressed, in pants (never skirts). The woman had straight brown hair and smoked a pipe. Magdalena admired the woman's theatrical sense of self.

Everywhere she went in America, Magdalena had found herself sur-

rounded by men. In many ways, it was the world she knew and preferred. She was the son her father had never had. Her older sister had
been claimed by their mother, and there would not be another child
after Magdalena. Her father, a merchant, took Magdalena to business
meetings and even got her enrolled in one of the top all-boys schools
in Turkey.

As the night wore on, Magdalena surveyed the dozen or so students who remained in the computer center, pondering which of them
would go on to become successful inventors, entrepreneurs, or even
household names. There was little hint at Stanford, or in Silicon Valley,
of how hard it was to make money in business. Instead, the presence
of money felt persistent, taken for granted even. Her friends at Stanford had money; their parents paid their tuition. Millionaires seemed to
be minted throughout the region overnight. Magdalena, on the other
hand, had to make every penny count. She had a practice of calculat-
ing how many hours she needed to work to pay for a meal with friends.
Afterward she would say ruefully to herself, "That meal cost me four
hours!" She looked at the accumulation of money as a report card. If it
was, she intended to get all A's in her life after school.

The computing landscape had been morphing rapidly, from month to
month, as massive mainframes transitioned to desktop computers. Word-
processing applications, digital spreadsheets, and relational databases
were becoming available. They in turn would require stable hardware
platforms and, even more important, reliable software systems.

Finally, the clock in the Stanford computer center reached five-
thirty A.M.—quitting time. Magdalena rustled in her bag for her sunglasses, smiled at her fellow night owls, and headed outside. Her gown
made a swishing sound as she walked. She gathered up the layers before
hopping onto her bike.

The early-morning light was her reward for the long night spent
in the center. The smell of fresh-mown grass and the sound of the
sprinklers watering the Stanford campus grounds were as soothing as a
metronome. Fueled by the fresh air, Magdalena—gown hiked around

her, daisies in her hair—accelerated down the soaked paths, spraying water behind her in an aerial wake.

Back in her dorm room, she left a trail of clothing from the door to her bed, then dove under the covers. She had class in a few hours, and job interviews in a few days, including one with the bearded boys of Apple Computer—two guys named Steve.

MARY JANE "MJ" ELMORE

The present was so different from MJ's past. Her past was a small house in the Midwest surrounded by cornfields. It was her mother on her knees scrubbing floors, working nights at JCPenney, taking care of a husband and five children. It was her father driving fifty miles to teach middle school. MJ spent summers roaming unsupervised, with a bike, a paper sack lunch, and jars of Kool-Aid. The past was the occasional family dinner when everyone else got steak, but Mom opted to eat hamburger to save money.

Now in 1981, MJ, after working several years at Intel, had left the company to pursue her MBA at Stanford. One of her professors, Jack McDonald, regularly invited prominent businesspeople to speak to the class. MJ had been given the honor of choosing today's speaker, Sandy Kurtzig, the first woman to take a tech company public.

Kurtzig, thirty-four, dressed in cobalt blue with matching high heels, had started ASK Computer Systems in her spare bedroom with $2,000 in savings. Her personal fortune was now worth $67 million. Sporting long and perfectly manicured nails and carrying a pink brief-case, she arrived at Stanford in a new Ferrari.

"The reason I studied math is that I'm a slow reader," Kurtzig told the students. "I like things with a right and wrong answer. And I was probably more of a tomboy growing up. My mom gave me a Girl Scout doll, and I put the doll aside to play with the box."

MJ smiled in recognition. Math had taken her to Purdue, then on to Intel, where she worked on one of the most important campaigns in the company's history, a marketing crusade called Operation Crush to establish dominance in the chip industry. MJ's math background had enabled her to understand Intel's sophisticated chip technology, despite the fact she was not an engineer. Like Kurtzig, MJ had been something of a tomboy, schooled by the neighborhood boys in how to stand up on her bicycle seat as she rode by her house. The boys had also coached her in some of their colorful vocabulary. When her dad told a story over dinner one night about something unfortunate that happened at school, MJ piped up, "Tough titties!" Everyone burst into laughter.

Kurtzig said she knew she wanted to do something beyond changing the "thousandth diaper." "I felt if I wasn't happy in what I was doing, I would have a hard time making a happy life for my boys."

MJ thought of her own mother, who had married her father in 1950 at nineteen instead of going to college, despite being offered a four-year scholarship. MJ's family of seven had lived in Arcola, Illinois, then Terre Haute, Indiana, where they shared a single bathroom. Her mother spent hours baking their favorite foods and sewing outfits from patterns. In another place and time, given opportunities, MJ knew that Dorothy Hanna could've been a Sandy Kurtzig.

In Arcola, opportunity was the vending machine at the laundromat that regularly dispensed extra candy bars when MJ only paid for one. It was the huge cement drainage pipes in the summer, where the cool interior walls echoed back her shouts and songs. It was the freedom to roam the town, unsupervised, with adults expecting that she would do what was right. MJ admired Silicon Valley's spirit of invention, but she revered its spirit of reinvention. Stanford business school was another step from her past to the future, where the girl next door could be whatever she imagined.

MJ had researched the facts about Kurtzig's company and asked a series of questions. What was it like to be a female CEO in technology? How did she juggle being a mother and a CEO? What did she look for in building a team? Few of MJ's classmates shared her interest in technology; most wanted to become management consultants or investment bankers. Silicon Valley had not yet become a household name.

Kurtzig talked about the development of ASK and its software, MANMAN (short for manufacturing management). Kurtzig originally intended to call it MAMA, until a CEO she knew said, "Can you imagine an executive getting in front of a board of directors and saying he wanted approval to run the company's manufacturing operations with 'the MAMA system'?"

Wanting to stay with the same construction, Kurtzig began jotting down a few potential names. Suddenly it dawned on her: "You often need two men to do the work of one mama!" So, she renamed the software MANMAN, and both the company and the product became hits.

Kurtzig told the class that she had never had a single female employee come in and ask for a raise, an observation that surprised MJ. "Men will come in and ask whether they're qualified or not," Kurtzig said. "Women will expect to have every qualification and skill and years of experience. Men are promoted based on potential, women on performance."

Kurtzig went on to tell the class some of the more memorable stories from her career. In one, she walked into a business meeting late, the only woman in the room. A potential client sitting at the table assumed she was the secretary and asked for coffee. "Sure! Cream or sugar?" Kurtzig replied without missing a beat. When Kurtzig returned with coffee, the man, having realized his mistake, hemmed and hawed and apologized. Kurtzig told him, "I don't mind. If you sign the contract, I'll bake you cookies!"

"If you look for sexism," Kurtzig told the Stanford class, "you'll never get where you want to go." When a client or potential client hit on her, she learned to deflect it with humor. "Hey, I'm busy this quarter. Maybe next fiscal year." She found ways to dispatch men's advances without making them so uncomfortable that they didn't want to do business with her.

Listening to Kurtzig, MJ realized she had adopted a similar approach to dealing with slights. Humor—coupled with a change of subject—went a long way toward quelling questionable behavior. When men in her class made jokes about a campus women's networking club, MJ learned to shrug it off. Twenty-four percent of MJ's MBA class at Stanford—75 out of 305 students—were women. Since 1976, every MBA class had had a women's group to facilitate networking. MJ was "captain" for the 1982 GSB class. The club, called Women in Management (WIM), met regularly. When they returned from their meetings, the guys in their class would yell out, "Oh the WIMs—'Women Impersonating Men'—are back!"

Kurtzig told the Stanford class that she'd made it a policy of never talking to women-only groups—she had no patience for a "can't-do-it attitude." She concluded her presentation with one of her favorite credos, targeted specifically at the women in the class: "You can't play the game if you're not in it."

MJ nodded; she too had a history of finding her way around walls. She'd enrolled at Purdue, a highly respected public university, instead of Indiana State, paying her own way. When she graduated from Purdue, she discovered that job recruiters were not interested in math majors. Companies listed the majors or specialties they were looking for, and only those students could sign up for interviews. MJ had to figure out who was coming to campus and wait outside the interview room door—or follow the recruiters on their way to the bathroom—to make her case for why she should be interviewed.

A year into her job at Intel, MJ hit another wall. She had spent her first year trying to expedite memory chip deliveries to impatient customers—it was frustrating. MJ was determined to switch to product management, where she could help bring something new to market. She found an ally in Susan Thomas, a computer scientist and electrical engineer trained at MIT. Thomas had joined Intel in 1976 and worked in marketing for microprocessors, traveling with the salesmen to explain how the microprocessor worked. Thomas helped MJ transfer to the division that made the tools for making microprocessors.

The timing could not have been better. Within a few months, MJ became part of Operation Crush, the make-or-break companywide race to win the microprocessor war with Motorola. Intel needed its new 8086 sixteen-bit microprocessor chip to "crush" the competition, Motorola's sixteen-bit 68000 chip. MJ flew around the country with one of Intel's so-called SWAT teams, hosting seminars and meetings to sell customers on how Intel's microprocessors would automate manufacturing, run assembly lines and satellites, and change the way businesses operated.

Intel, from founders Gordon Moore and Bob Noyce to COO Andy Grove, poured everything into Operation Crush. Media strategist Regis McKenna—who also handled marketing for Apple—ran a $2 million advertising campaign, using images from artist Patrick Nagel. Intel offered trips to Tahiti to the top salespeople. A young man named John Doerr, brimming with competitive energy, sold the microprocessors as if his life depended on it, employing such then-novel techniques as videos to help him sell. Employees wore OPERATION CRUSH T-shirts—until Intel's attorney decided a "crush the competition" mantra might stir unwanted antitrust concerns.

MJ, Sue Thomas, John Doerr, and Ann Howland, an electrical engineer who later became Doerr's wife, socialized at company picnics, volleyball games, and Christmas parties. The Hungarian-born Grove, blunt and demanding, expected employees to sign a tardy sheet if they came in after eight A.M. Some employees who arrived late signed in with aliases, including "Chuck Roast" and "Luke Warm."

MJ felt like she had landed at the center of the universe. IBM was working on its 5150 personal computer and had narrowed the microprocessor that would power the PC down to Motorola and Intel. When MJ decided to leave Intel to pursue an MBA, to advance her career, she asked Grove for a letter of recommendation. Grove told her he was ambivalent about the value of an MBA—but agreed to write the letter anyway.

Now, just a few months shy of graduating from Stanford, MJ helped Kurtzig field final questions, and afterward, she walked Kurtzig out. MJ admired Kurtzig for her boldness. She was strong and confident, and she *owned* her success. As Kurtzig stepped into her Ferrari, she urged MJ to think big: "Why sit at the table when you can buy it?"

MJ soon began to interview with start-ups and venture capital firms. This time she had the qualifications recruiters were looking for, given her background at Intel. Intel had won the war with Motorola, and Operation Crush marked the company's move away from memory products and into the microprocessor world, Intel's future. MJ had seen firsthand the power of small and highly motivated teams.

MJ told a few of her business school classmates that she had an interview with Reid Dennis, one of the founding fathers of venture capital, at Institutional Venture Partners. Her classmates warned her, "Reid Dennis is *not* going to hire a woman."

Arriving at 3000 Sand Hill Road, she parked in the back lot and walked through a quiet courtyard with a sprawling oak tree. The fifty-six-year-old Dennis had white hair and thick glasses, wore pleated slacks, a button-down shirt, and a belt with a big buckle. As the two sat down in his corner office, MJ tried not to let her nervousness show. His office was full of historical San Francisco lithographs, and several of his brass scale-model trains—including a four-foot tinder—were on display. He told MJ that as a child, he'd loved watching the trains go over the Donner Pass.

MJ told Dennis about growing up in Terre Haute and about her time at Purdue, Intel, and Stanford. She talked about her strong mother, her father's teaching career, and her large family.

As she talked, she kept her hands loosely clasped on her lap, composed. Her sister often told her she had a knack for remaining calm amid chaos.

"I've always been interested in solving problems," MJ told Dennis. "Math gave me a way of looking at the world. It taught me how to find the right answer, but also how to avoid the wrong answer, to avoid misleading probabilities and percentages."

As the two talked about microprocessors and the changing landscape of computers, it was clear that Dennis appreciated MJ's grasp of technology and liked that she was more of a generalist than an engineer. He was an electrical engineer by training, he said, and had enough engineers working for him already.

"I used to change power tubes and radio transmitters in the navy," he said. "I have to admit I've been surprised by this incredible miniaturization of electronic circuits. The smallest little deposit of conducting material can make all sorts of things happen."

"But technology is only as good as the people behind it," MJ pointed out. "Intel showed me that. The Motorola microprocessor was just as good as—if not better than—ours, but we had amazing people on a warpath to win. I think I'd say I'm most interested in people, relationships, and solving problems." Then she added, "I want to accomplish something lasting in my lifetime."

He told her that IVP was in the second year of a new $22 million fund. "We invest in both people and the product," he said. "But I would agree that *people* are more important than the product. If the product fails, the right people find something else to do."

Dennis offered to give MJ a tour of the IVP offices. He told her that when he hung his shingle on Sand Hill Road in 1973, he would arrive at work to silence. The phones didn't ring. Entrepreneurs were not beating down the doors, he said with a laugh. "I used to get in my car and drive around South Palo Alto and look at names on doors," he said. "If something said 'electronics,' I would knock on the door and see if they needed money. That was how investments were made. Venture was not an industry; it was an activity."

Even earlier, in the 1950s, Dennis said, when he worked at Fireman's Fund Insurance Company, he and a small group of friends—Bill Bowes, John Bryan, Bill Edwards, and Brooks Walker Jr.—would invite entrepreneurs to Sam's Grill in San Francisco for lunch. The men would listen to the entrepreneur make a pitch, then tell him to wait outside for five minutes so they could talk it over.

"We could raise around a hundred thousand dollars between us,"

Dennis said. "Over a period of eight to ten years—remember, we all had day jobs—we probably helped start twenty-three or twenty-four companies. Of those, I'd say eighteen were wonderfully successful."

He continued, "What makes you successful is your ability to judge people. You get in these meetings with entrepreneurs and listen to their stories. You have to figure out whether you believe their business model or not, and whether it makes sense."

Looking at his watch, Dennis said to MJ, "Why don't you stay and sit in on the meeting coming up? We have a company coming in to pitch." Then he added half-jokingly, "One of your responsibilities will be to stop me from investing in my hobbies: boats, classic cars, trains, and planes."

MJ stayed and listened to the pitch. She felt less nervous, observing, taking mental notes, even asking a few questions. Sandy Kurtzig's advice echoed in her head: "You can't play the game if you're not in it."

Later, as MJ gathered her things, Dennis turned to her, extended his hand, and asked when she could start. She stared at his outstretched hand in disbelief. *I have a job at IVP? On Sand Hill Road?*

As she drove away in her aging Pinto—now truly on its last legs—MJ had the same feeling of excitement she had when she first arrived in California. She didn't mind being the girl next door with the midwestern values. She would always respect her mother, who loved to say, "It doesn't cost anything to be nice." And she was proud of her family. But as she again thought of Sandy Kurtzig, with her pink briefcase and red Ferrari, MJ knew she wanted more. She wasn't settling for hamburger. She wanted steak.

THERESIA GOUW

At Oliver's, a popular watering hole in Providence, Rhode Island, Theresia Gouw ordered a beer, greeted the blue-collar and student regulars, and headed to the foosball table. It was time to kick some butt.

Theresia hated to lose—whether at foosball or anything else. At the foosball table, with her best friend Sangeeta Bhatia playing defense, Theresia went quickly on offense. Her unwitting opponents saw her permed and teased hair, stirrup pants, and oversize sweater and thought she'd be a patsy. But she had a killer spin shot, a great pull shot with the middleman on the rod, and a surprise bank shot. In short order, cocky contenders came and went, dispatched with ease before they knew what had hit them.

Standing five foot three and still looking like a teenager, Theresia was constantly being underestimated. It had been no different at the bar a few blocks from Brown University, where she arrived in 1986 to study engineering. Theresia had grown up in the tiny working-class town of Middleport, an agricultural crossroads about forty miles northeast of Buffalo, where many students dressed for school in camouflage, read *Soldier of Fortune* magazine, and skipped school on the opening day of deer hunting season. Graduating seniors typically enlisted in the military or went to work in the local General Motors factory or at the sprawling Farm Machine Corp. plant that manufactured pesticides.

For the Gouw family, however, education was everything. When Theresia got an A minus in Spanish, her father was furious, telling her, "I know you're smart enough to get A's in everything you do." He did not believe in the concept of extra credit. "It's not extra credit for you. Anything your teacher gives you is required." Theresia lost sleep over tests and became depressed if she got anything less than 100 percent. Her mother, more relaxed than her father, would tell her, "Ninety-five is an A—it is enough. One hundred is for the good Lord."

The Gouws didn't have it easy. For many years, they were the only Asian family in town. They had emigrated from Jakarta, Indonesia, in 1971, to escape persecution as ethnic Chinese and to make a better life for Theresia and her younger sister, Andrea. In Middleport, some of the kids in school made slant-eye gestures at Theresia; the family came home from spring break to find a swastika on their mailbox and GO HOME CHINKS spray-painted on their driveway. One night when they went out to dinner in a neighboring town, locals stared at them, seemingly startled to see Asians among the patrons.

Theresia's father declared that cheerleading was out; sports, however, were in. Theresia became captain or co-captain of the high school field hockey, volleyball, and track teams. She was elected homecoming queen and prom queen. She and her dad had season tickets to the Buffalo Bills, and Theresia memorized the stats on all the players. Oblivious to the freezing temperatures, father and daughter rooted for running back Joe Cribbs in his breakout rookie season and later Hall of Fame quarterback Jim Kelley and wide receiver Andre Reid. Theresia's favorite player was defensive end Bruce Smith, perennially one of the best in the league.

Theresia's first paying job, outside of babysitting and cleaning instruments at her dad's dental office, was working at Burger King. She was responsible for putting the patties on a conveyor belt and adding the ketchup, mustard, pickle, and cheese. From her spot at the back of the fast-food restaurant, she plotted her move to the better positions— working the cash register or the drive-through. Only the girls who had seniority got those jobs.

Over time Theresia's parents worked their way up from waitress and dishwasher to nurse and dentist, and the community of Middleport came to accept them. Steve Gouw's dream had been to be a family dentist in a small American town, where he would know his patients by their first names. His wife, Bertha, became his office manager. Determined to assimilate, Theresia grew up speaking English; for a long time, she refused to eat rice or ethnic food, especially in public. She ate so much American food—Hostess Ding Dongs and Sno Balls were her favorites—that she ballooned from petite to hefty, and other kids started calling her Theresia *Souw*.

When it came time for college, Theresia applied to Brown, Cornell, Carnegie Mellon, Princeton, the University of Rochester, and Rochester Institute of Technology. She was elated when her acceptance letter came from Brown. But soon after she mailed her commitment letter back to Brown, she got an acceptance letter from Carnegie Mellon, offering her a presidential scholarship of $10,000 a year in financial aid. That night Theresia showed her father the letter. "This is worth forty thousand dollars over four years," she explained, "and it's a great school. We'll lose our deposit at Brown, but we'll save a lot of money." Her father looked at her and said, "No. You were clear that Brown was your first choice. We will take out a second mortgage on the house and make it work. This is your dream."

Theresia was one of the first Middleport graduates to attend an Ivy League school. But at Brown, she felt like a "country bumpkin" compared with her elite prep school classmates. Theresia's father told her, "You can beat everyone in Middleport, but not at Brown. If you try to be the best, you're going to drive yourself crazy. Just be *your* best."

But to be her best, she had to overcome another disadvantage: The male students refused to invite her into their study groups, assuming that she wouldn't do as well as the guys. Theresia found solace with her best friend, Sangeeta, who was also an engineering student, and the two women formed their own study cabal. Theresia's engineering focus was in material science, while Sangeeta's was in biomedical engineering.

The women became roommates in Perkins Hall, a dorm located on the outskirts of the campus. Students who lived in Perkins Hall were said to develop especially close friendships, as visitors to the residence hall were few and far between. Theresia and Sangeeta shared their stories of being first-generation immigrants and dutiful daughters to exacting fathers. Each had a younger sister. And for both, their fathers had set them on their engineering path.

The two friends loved rock 'n' roll—U2, the Clash, the Eagles, Van Halen, Bowie—and were karaoke fanatics. (Theresia secretly dreamed of being a rock star.) But they were also clear on their priorities, making sure to do their studying before any partying began. They spent Wednesday nights at a fraternity where they had friends; they spent other nights at Oliver's, drinking beer and destroying the opposition in foosball.

When Theresia started at Brown, the campus was engulfed in protests, sit-ins, hunger strikes, and marches around the anti-apartheid movement. Students demanded that trustees divest their stocks in South African companies. There were massive pro-choice rallies in Washington as well, which Theresia and Sangeeta attended. But they found plenty of inequality closer to home. As freshmen, they had been heartened to see that almost half the students in engineering were women, but by their senior year, there were around a dozen women left in a class of one hundred. They looked into the drop-off and discovered that the academic performance of the women who had left was just as strong as that of the women and men who remained in the program. The female students had left because they didn't know any women who were engineers in the real world. They had trouble seeing what they would do with their hard-earned degrees. Time and again Theresia and Sangeeta heard the women who'd dropped out say they didn't feel as if they *belonged*. Conversely, the women who stayed in the program had one thing in common: a mentor in the field, or a parent, to encourage them. So the two friends joined the Brown chapter of the Society of Women Engineers, which they served as co-presidents.

Theresia and Sangeeta recognized other impediments for women at Brown as well. The men in the engineering department were often members of fraternities that archived engineering tests and study guides from previous years. Nothing like that existed for women. So Theresia and Sangeeta assembled engineering problem sets, tests, and homework for future classes of women engineers. They set up peer mentoring for women, matching juniors and seniors with underclasswomen.

And at the end of the day, Theresia and Sangeeta had each other. When they had to pull all-nighters and were afraid they would fall asleep and miss an exam, they took turns studying, napping, and waking each other up. During finals week, Theresia and Sangeeta set themselves up on the mezzanine level of the science library. They shared everything, from stories of their internships to stories of dates and obnoxious men they encountered.

During a summer internship at General Motors, Theresia worked in an engineering research and design facility. Of the one thousand full-time engineers, only two were women. As she walked through the rows of cubicles, the men assumed she was a secretary and asked her to get them coffee and their mail. One day her manager, who was only a few years older than she was, took Theresia and another intern, a man, out to lunch—to a topless bar. Theresia found the experience sad more than anything. "It was just kind of uncomfortable to have lunch with boobs in your face," she later told Sangeeta.

As graduation approached, Theresia landed a job with Bain, the prestigious management consulting firm in Boston. She owed $42,000 in student loans and needed a job. Sangeeta headed to MIT for a joint MD/PhD program in biomedical engineering. On graduation day, Theresia, the former country bumpkin, learned that she was graduating at the top of her class, magna cum laude, the only honor Brown granted at commencement.

The two friends remained in contact with each other, as Sangeeta began school across the Charles River. Theresia made friends with analysts who were a year or two ahead of her at Bain: Dave Goldberg, Jennifer Fonstad, and Tim Ranzetta, whose desk was right across from hers. Tim was tall, blond, and blue-eyed, and had played varsity baseball at the University of Virginia. Theresia arrived at work each day reading the *National Sports Daily,* and the two soon got into debates over whether the University of Virginia football team could hold on to its No. 1 ranking for the season. (Theresia said no, Tim said yes. Theresia was right.) Before long, Theresia and Tim were involved romantically.

· · ·

n 1992 Theresia applied to business school at Harvard and Stanford. Accepted at both, she chose Stanford because of the school's location in Silicon Valley, the heart of tech. Some of the men at Bain who had been turned down by the schools told her she only got in because she was a woman. She said little but quietly fumed. She had worked twice as hard as most to get where she was.

Theresia had grown serious in her relationship with Tim, as they bonded over sports, a devotion to their families, and their shared goals in life. They both wanted to live in California. Tim hoped to work in banking, like his father. Theresia knew from her stint at GM that she didn't want to be an engineer sitting behind a computer, creating CAD designs. She was more interested in being a product manager. She figured that with a Stanford MBA, she could one day earn good money in Silicon Valley—maybe even a six-figure salary.

SONJA HOEL

In 1989 twenty-two-year-old Sonja Hoel had been working as an analyst at the venture capital firm TA Associates in Boston for several weeks—yet she still didn't have a chair for her desk. The secretary wouldn't order her one.

Sonja didn't dwell on it—she was just glad to be there. Before starting at TA, she had heeded her mother's advice to cut her hair and wear glasses. "You will be treated with more respect," her mother advised. In the same way, when she heard that her fellow analysts were getting together for scotch after work, she quickly joined, feigning delight at what she found to be an awful-tasting drink. Nothing was going to dim her love affair with the venture capital industry. It was the perfect place for the cheerful blue-eyed southerner who liked to say "My obstacles are my allies."

But before long, Sonja's naturally sunny disposition took a hit. Standing upstairs in TA's gorgeous wood-paneled offices, she looked down the spiral staircase and realized she was the only female investor in the Boston office. *Am I here just because I'm a woman?* she wondered. After a few days of sulking and second-guessing herself, she looked in the mirror and said, *Snap out of it.*

There was no point in looking for discrimination, she realized; life was too full of opportunity. Her firm's downtown Boston office was less than a mile's walk from her fashionable Beacon Hill apartment. She relished nights when it snowed, erasing her steps almost as fast as she made them. As boughs of trees became heavy with snow, the sounds of the city softened, and even the streetlight grew paler, turning the color of butter. She wore long underwear under her suits, purchased in the bargain basement of Filene's department store. When she started at TA Associates, she'd had only one black suit and one navy suit, with a few extra jackets, and she would mix the pieces to get through the week. She laughed when a fellow analyst told her, "Sonja, your long johns are showing." She encountered the same homeless man, Michael, on her commute to work every day and eventually struck a deal with him: She would give him a dollar a week, but he was not allowed to ask her for money on any other days. Michael was friendly and made her laugh, and he was grateful when Sonja gave him warm winter clothes.

Sonja shared a two-bedroom apartment with Anne Heese, a woman she'd met while shopping at Filene's Basement. The two had been trying on clothes over their clothes, as the store didn't have dressing rooms. They now shared an apartment on the top floor of a three-unit building, furnishing their flat with chairs and tables that their wealthy neighbors had left at the curb. The top floor was old, and the floor was slanted—a marble would roll from one end of the kitchen to the other—but it had a treasured view of the landmark CITGO sign near Fenway Park. They each paid $500 a month, and often did the dishes while singing along to their favorite song, "Push It," by Salt-N-Pepa. Sonja had taped a picture of Apple Computer founder Steve Jobs up on the fridge. She thought he was "the cat's meow."

Her father had been right—there was life after high school. During her teenage years in Charlottesville, Virginia, some of the girls had her disinvited to prom because she was "too straight." She didn't drink or do drugs and didn't believe in casual sex. She didn't make the cheerleading squad because the dance moves were too fast for her. She was cut from the basketball team as well but volunteered to be the team statistician. She tried out for field hockey and volleyball but didn't make the squads—her high school was big and boasted a strong sports program. She joined the lacrosse team and the school choir because she loved both, and tryouts were not required. She grew up with two sisters, including a twin, and had a Marie Antoinette–style canopy bed.

A graduate of the McIntire School of Commerce at the University of Virginia, Sonja had been hired at TA Associates after a stint at the London Stock Exchange. She had impressed TA management with her self-taught computer skills and the computer jobs she held at UVA. Now an analyst, her job was to find auspicious companies for investments, interview the founders and executives about their business models, and then—when she had enough compelling information—pull in the TA partner best suited to land the deal.

Sonja was a quick study. She knew how to seek out companies that solved problems for businesses with products that were ten times more efficient at one-tenth the cost. She understood intuitively that learning about the problem a company intended to solve, its market size, and its business model was just as important as learning about its core technology. Within two years of her arrival at TA Associates, Sonja landed two hugely lucrative deals by cold-calling companies she'd found in computer magazines—OnTrack, a data recovery software company, and Artisoft, which connected PCs to a network. Both went public.

But to rise through the ranks of the financial world to become a partner, she realized, she would need an MBA. It was the partners who made investments and received the all-important and closely held "carry"—a share of the profits. Venture partners took board seats and worked in lockstep with entrepreneurs, So she applied to the business schools at Stanford, Dartmouth, and Harvard and was accepted at Harvard. Dimming her excitement, her longtime boyfriend was accepted to the business school at the University of Michigan. The two talked about getting married. Sonja was heartbroken that they would be apart. But she was thrilled about attending Harvard. "I want to become a venture capital partner!" she told her roommate Anne.

When Sonja informed TA Associates that she would be leaving at the beginning of the summer, the firm's managing partner, Kevin Landry, offered to double her salary if she stayed. But she was set on becoming a venture capitalist, knowing they played a key role in launching and shaping revolutionary companies. They were the futurists, hand holders, and risk takers in the financial world. Moreover, venture capitalists and entrepreneurs were her favorite type of people: optimists.

Sonja had proved that she had a nose for deals. Now she wanted to help build companies that would make the world a better place.

A few months before leaving for Harvard, Sonja, sitting at her desk at TA, studied an ad in *PC* magazine. A company piqued her interest. She had by now cold-called more than one thousand companies. She dialed the number in the ad but got a busy signal. She tried again a few minutes later. Busy still. So she read the Dun & Bradstreet research report on the software company, which was based in Silicon Valley. The company sold antivirus software and was growing quickly. It had a good product and apocalyptic viruses were predicted to take down computers across the globe.

In the ad, the company was seeking agents to sell its software. Sonja went over the D&B report more closely. She took notes: "Hot co; antivirus products; 2.5mm users; shareware; $7mm 1990 with $6mm pretax; 4,000 major corp users; excellent prospect; doing due diligence."

Sonja picked up the phone again, eventually reaching a man named Jim Lynch in Santa Clara, California, who was creating a network of international agents to sell the antivirus software. She introduced herself, described TA Associates, and said she had money to invest. To her surprise, Lynch gave her the car phone number of the company founder.

She looked at her watch. It was midmorning in California. She reviewed her notes one more time and dialed.

"John McAfee," the man answered.

Sonja again introduced herself and began her pitch. McAfee listened for a moment before saying, "I'm sorry, but I've just agreed to sell my company to Symantec." Symantec was a $460 million company that was the largest supplier of packaged utility software. It had been unsuccessful so far in taking over the antivirus market.

"How much did they offer?" Sonja asked.

"Twenty million," McAfee replied.

Sonja ran the numbers in her head. Over a few years, starting with a handful of employees working out of a home office, McAfee Associates had captured more than 60 percent of the antivirus market. The personal computer revolution of the 1980s and the dominance of the open system IBM personal computer had created the perfect environment for viruses to thrive. McAfee, a programmer who had worked at NASA and Lockheed, had seized the opportunity and developed VirusScan, a product that countered a virus's basic replication techniques.

Drawing on her sales experience, Sonja kept McAfee engaged on the phone. He mentioned that he wanted to hire a new president and move with his wife to three hundred acres in the shadows of Pikes Peak, Colorado. Sonja told herself, *Go after it like a bird dog.*

So she laid out an alternative deal: "We'll value your company at twenty million dollars, and you keep half. You sell half the company for the same valuation, hold on to the upside, and still get money up front."

McAfee said, "I'd love that. I hadn't even thought of it."

It was a gutsy move. Sonja, as a $28,000-a-year analyst, didn't have the authority to offer $20, much less $20 million. She quickly called Jeff Chambers, a managing director who had been with TA Associates for almost two decades and had opened the firm's Silicon Valley office. She left him a voice mail, saying, "Jeff, you *have* to look at this business. Its forecasted revenue growth rate is more than ninety percent, and its pre-tax margins run between eighty and ninety percent of sales. The problem is that John is seriously considering selling McAfee to Symantec."

Jeff Chambers wasted no time in scheduling a meeting with McAfee and working through the due diligence. He pulled in another firm, Summit Partners, and the two jointly offered first-round funding of $10 million ($5 million each) to buy half of McAfee Associates, which had seven employees. McAfee went public a year later, raising $42 million. It grew from there, licensing its antivirus software to more than fifteen thousand corporations and boasting an astounding after-tax profit margin of about 45 percent, far higher than the industry average.

But by that time, Sonja was ensconced at Harvard Business School, studying hard and networking even harder. She had become president of Harvard's venture capital club, which gave her access to industry pioneers. She flew to California for in-person meetings and invited the legends of venture to Harvard to talk to students, including John Doerr, who had left Intel to join the venerable venture firm Kleiner Perkins Caufield & Byers; Reid Dennis of IVP; and MJ Elmore, who worked closely with Dennis.

After graduating from Harvard, Sonja, at twenty-seven, was hired at Menlo Ventures, whose firm had offices adjacent to the Reid Dennis–founded IVP on Sand Hill Road. While Sonja could have remained on the East Coast, Sand Hill was her yellow brick road. It was here that the "traitorous eight" had left the manic but brilliant William Shockley to start Fairchild Semiconductor and later Intel. Here a marijuana- and hot-tub-loving Nolan Bushnell had met Sequoia Capital founder Don Valentine to fund Atari. Here Arthur Rock, at first reluctantly, had provided funds and advice to a scruffy and "very unappealing" Steve Jobs to build Apple. Here venture capitalist Tom Perkins and scientist Bob Swanson had started Genentech. It was on Sand Hill Road that Dave Marquardt's early investment in Microsoft had yielded a bonus of a new red Ferrari, and where Larry Ellison incubated a start-up called Oracle, getting a loan from VC Don Lucas to keep the relational database company going. It was here that Arthur Rock had defined venture capital as "taking adventures with capital."

The day Sonja arrived in California, in July 1994, *Time* magazine hit the stands with a cover story titled "The Strange New World of the Internet." The Internet was moving out of the hands of the military and academia and into civilian life. The cover story raised a question that was on the minds of VCs and entrepreneurs alike: "The world's largest computer network, once the playground of scientists, hackers and gearheads, is being overrun by lawyers, merchants and millions of new users. Is there room for everyone?"

Sonja thought there certainly was room for her. With her mother by her side, she set out in search of an apartment, driving from neighborhood to neighborhood looking for FOR RENT signs on buildings. But this being the Bay Area, housing was difficult to find.

With Sonja's start date at Menlo Ventures fast approaching, one of the partners at Menlo stepped in and offered her his guesthouse; Sonja could stay there while she searched for a flat. There was one caveat. The partner and his wife, an ob-gyn, had just had triplets; they would need Sonja home at five—to babysit.

Sonja didn't pause to consider whether a man with her credentials—a Harvard MBA, deals at TA that had netted the firm tens of millions of dollars—would have been asked to *babysit*. She was just thrilled to have a place to stay. If she had to babysit the triplets, as well as the couple's two other young children, that's what she would do. It was a small price to pay on her path to success. And as she constantly reminded herself, obstacles were her allies.

PART

TWO

Getting in the Game

1994–1999

MAGDALENA

Magdalena thought she was onto something big, a revolution that was about to pay off in a huge way. But there was a problem: What seemed obvious to her came across as fantastical to everyone else.

It was 1994, and Magdalena had been working for several years without a steady income. She'd devoted most of her time to co-founding a start-up called CyberCash, one of the first secure payment systems for online shopping. At the time, though, the Internet barely existed. It consisted of modems that cacophonously—and slowly—sent data over telephone lines. Buying things online would require a seismic cultural shift in everyday life.

Only three years earlier, when the Internet was first opened to commercial uses, it had been *illegal* to sell things online. Today Pizza Hut was making a big deal of selling its very first pizza online. The time to move, Magdalena knew, was now. She believed with every fiber of her being that e-commerce was the wave of the future.

Her career after graduating from Stanford, more than a decade before, had started off so promising, and then she took a detour.

Even before she finished her master's degree, Magdalena had gone to seven job interviews and received seven offers. Her first interview had been with Steve Jobs and Steve Wozniak of Apple. The founders invited double-e students to the LOTS computer center to hear a pitch about their three-year-old company. If the students liked what they heard, they could stay and be interviewed. Jobs, wearing wire-rimmed glasses and jeans, told Magdalena and the other double-e students that working for Apple would be like "an extension of college."

Magdalena was one of sixteen students who showed up for the interview. She loved the idea of working for Apple. Jobs had dropped out of college and spent time studying Hinduism and Buddhism in India. He was a technologist but also a student of the mind. Magdalena had a window opened to her own mind through her love of technology. Five of the sixteen students interviewed that day received job offers—including Magdalena.

When Magdalena told her adviser the exciting news, however, he said, "Why would you go to work for a company that has a fruit for its name?" He urged her to look for something "stable and solvent" and suggested the ten-year-old semiconductor company Advanced Micro Devices. AMD had recently listed shares on the New York Stock Exchange, had extraordinary growth, and was becoming a recognized leader in research and development. On his advice, she took the AMD job.

AMD's co-founder, Jerry Sanders, kept a poster on his office wall that read, "Yea, though I walk through the valley of the shadow of death, I shall fear no evil—for I am the meanest son of a bitch in the valley." At AMD, Magdalena was responsible for getting local area networking chip sets designed into computers.

Early in her job at AMD, Magdalena was invited to attend a sales conference at the Hilton Hawaiian Village in Honolulu. The conference kicked off with what was billed as a "breakfast eye-opener." Magdalena settled in, anticipating a festive Hawaiian dance performance, but instead of a hula, she got a striptease. *At eight A.M.!* The women onstage shimmied around with their tops off. When the performance was over, Sanders and his top sales executive, Steve Zelencik, took to the stage to rally the troops. *What is the message here?* Magdalena wondered. *That topless women are the reward for top sales?* The next night's entertainment was even more jaw-dropping. Before dinner was served, a coterie of dancers appeared, dancing and slowly stripping down to nothing. Then the women performed explicit sex acts on one another.

Magdalena, who had seen her share of bare breasts and nude bodies on the beaches of Europe, was no prude. But the explicitness of the evening's "entertainment," in an official workplace function, left her speechless.

By the time the X-rated show ended, Magdalena was fuming. Bare breasts were one thing. Degrading porn at dinner was another. She stood up and headed straight to where Jerry Sanders was sitting. He didn't pick the entertainment, but he was in charge. As she approached, she considered what to say and how to say it. She didn't want to come across as emotional. She needed to make her point in a way that he would understand.

Kneeling beside Sanders, Magdalena looked him in the eye and said, "You and I need to talk." Her heart was racing; this was her boss. "I am an engineer at your company. What just happened was unacceptable to me personally. This show of naked women made me feel like I'm not a respected employee. You *say* you want to make sure your employees are well treated, but is this how you treat your newly recruited engineer?" Her tone was even and strong. She forced a smile. She wanted him to know that *her* problem was *his* problem.

Sanders stared back, furrowing his brow as if she were telling him something in a language he didn't understand. It was clear to Magdalena that the meanest son of a bitch in Silicon Valley had no idea what to do with the young woman in front of him.

Finally Sanders said, "Why don't you sit at my table for dinner, where I'll be entertaining our top distributors? I heard you're a good engineer, and I know they'll enjoy the company of a good-looking young woman."

Magdalena let the last comment go. She had said enough for now, and she wanted to keep her job. In her work with computer designers at companies such as McDonnell Douglas and IBM, she was going to have to network with these men at bars, at parties, and over dinners. *Not networking* was not an option; these were her clients and potential clients. And they were all men.

Magdalena soon perfected the art of drinking without getting drunk, leaving the hotel bar or restaurant alone, and getting up early to give a data-laden morning presentation. She had been trained from her childhood in Turkey to be clear in the messages she sent to men. When she rode the ferry across the Bosporus, she knew not to make eye contact with men. She understood that the way she walked, talked, sat, dressed, tilted her head, aligned her body, and shook hands expressed her availability to men. For the first seventeen years of her life, she had been trained in how to avoid being raped—the worst possible fate for a woman in the Middle East. It was training that served her well in Silicon Valley.

After nearly three years at AMD, Magdalena left to join the very first Unix desktop company, Fortune Systems, which had fewer than fifty employees. Fortune had a wild ride, from its flashy IPO—the seventh biggest in history—to near bankruptcy. Despite its financial downfall, she loved the frenetic feel of the start-up. At Fortune, she had a huge job overseeing all the software systems that ran on the Fortune computer, the Unix operating system software, and all of the applications software including Oracle's database and Lotus's 1-2-3 spreadsheet.

After leaving Fortune, instead of staying in tech, she went to work for the management consulting firm Booz Allen, expecting to focus on the marketing of tech companies. It turned out to be one of those blind spots like she'd experienced while programming at Stanford. At Booz Allen, she found herself marketing cruise ships rather than computer chips. She was tasked with coming up with unbiased questionnaires and running focus groups with first-time customers on cruises to the Caribbean and through the Panama Canal. As she savored her Campari and orange drinks on deck and appreciated the view, she wondered what had happened to her career. She spent the next few years—her dark period—as a mirthless marketer. The time seemed to absorb its own light, like a black hole.

While her career faltered, her personal life flourished. She met attorney Jim Wickett, eight years her senior, who was as gentle and easy-going as she was driven and detail-oriented. Her first impression of him was that he talked a lot. He told her on their first dinner date that he intended to marry her. "You've just had too many espressos," she replied, rolling her eyes. They went on to have two sons, Justin and Troy, now five and three. But Magdalena, at thirty-four, felt empty without a directed and challenging career. She needed something besides her consulting jobs and her children to fulfill her.

And that's why Magdalena came back to technology, the world of circuits and logic that had always moored her, and reinvented herself as an expert in the Internet. Now all she had to do was convince some venture capitalists that she was right—that e-commerce was about to change the world.

THERESIA

"Are you kidding me? Joining a start-up is riskier than starting a restaurant!"

That was the reaction that Theresia got from her boss when she announced that she was leaving her corporate post at Bain consulting in San Francisco to work for Release Software, a new start-up in Silicon Valley. In the past, Theresia had always done everything by the book, but now she was sure she had seen the future—and it was digital.

At Release, with her meager start-up wages, Theresia had to make some adjustments, notably in where and how she lived. She soon joined the ranks of couch-surfing entrepreneurs. From a privacy standpoint, living night to night on someone else's sofa wasn't so different from living in a dorm at Brown. And she was thrilled to be entering the rough-and-tumble world of Internet entrepreneurs. Her parents and grandparents had taken huge risks in moving from China to Indonesia and later from Indonesia to the United States. Maybe her immigrant past had paved the way for her entrepreneurial future.

Release had been founded to enable companies to distribute software electronically, rather than as disks packaged in boxes and sold in retail chains. The start-up was the brainchild of Matthew Klein, a self-described "hacker and nincompoop" who at six foot seven was so consumed with his thoughts that he often ran smack into low branches and doorjambs. He had gone to Yale and Stanford, where he programmed a payment mechanism into Shareware, a proprietary software that was free but asked users to pay by the honor system. Klein, who didn't have faith in the honor system, had landed $1 million in funding for Release from venture capitalists Steve Jurvetson and Tim Draper.

Klein found Theresia through another Stanford business school classmate and Release employee, Mark Benning, a former star hockey player at Harvard. The company's fourth employee was Li An, a Chinese immigrant who spoke limited English but was fluent in engineering. An had responded to a flyer that Klein taped to a lamppost on the Stanford campus. The other founding member of the team was Chip Hall, who became vice president of marketing.

Of the five employees, Matthew Klein viewed Theresia as the blue-chip, most together member of the team: Brown engineering, Bain in Boston, Stanford business school, Bain in San Francisco. She knew technology and business strategy and was a fast learner in sales and marketing. She cold-called dozens of companies, e-mailed executives at all levels, and sped from meeting to meeting in her cherry-red Acura. And she had something the other awkward founders lacked: social skills. She knew how to present to a group and do basic things like get a good seat on a plane and rent a car. She taught Matthew that he shouldn't wear white gym socks with dark suits. She told him about the elaborate protocol when exchanging business cards with the Japanese. She told him how to do expense reports and get a good deal on business travel.

Theresia agreed to join Release because of Matthew's self-deprecating brilliance and because of the allure of an Internet start-up. She had been at Stanford when Jerry Yang and David Filo started Yahoo! as a graduate school project. The two had raised $3.3 million from Sequoia

Capital. When Yahoo! went public a year later, it had a market capitalization of $848 million. Theresia had been in the computer center at Stanford when she first downloaded Mosaic (a precursor to Netscape, the pioneering Internet browsing software). She interned one summer of business school at Silicon Graphics, founded by Netscape co-founder Jim Clark. (One of her jobs at a Silicon Graphics sales kickoff event was to sit inside a hollowed-out server the size of a refrigerator and respond as if she were a computer as people typed commands.) She had been at Bain—which had offered to reimburse her business school tuition if she worked there for two years—when Netscape went public in August 1995. The sixteen-month-old company, which had never posted a profit, was suddenly valued at more than $2 billion. That same year Elon Musk enrolled at Stanford to study applied physics. Two days after arriving, he applied for a deferment, convinced that the start-up zeitgeist wouldn't come around again anytime soon. He started Zip2 to help the media industry move from print models to an electronic model.

Two years earlier, at twenty-five, Theresia had married her former Bain colleague Tim Ranzetta, who now worked as a buy-side analyst at a mutual fund company in Boston. Theresia Gouw Ranzetta flew out to see her husband every chance she could. But the two were trying to save money, given that she was working for stock rather than salary. And she didn't mind the bicoastal arrangement. Not having a husband around to worry about gave her more time to work.

And that's exactly what she did in her new job at the start-up Release, which had office space on the second floor of an old building called Casa Mills in Menlo Park. The company's goal was to become the largest software distributor over the Internet. The building at 250 Middlefield Road frequently had brownouts, and a good Internet connection was as elusive as sleep. Theresia and the gang resorted to drilling a hole in the floor to siphon power for their servers from their neighbors below, who had the MacDaddy of high-speed Internet, T1 lines carrying digital data at 1.544 Mbps.

The guys working below, who had an Internet start-up called Four11, needed all the computing power they could get. They had online yellow pages, white pages, and a video phone directory, and they were preparing to go live with one of the first free Web-based e-mail services, called RocketMail.

One night as Theresia worked on a presentation and her co-founders took a break to play the video game *Doom,* the electricity blinked on and off like a flirtation—then went dark. Theresia peered out the window and down the street. Most of the buildings were dark, but the lights were still on at the U.S. Geographical Survey offices across the street, and lights were still on at Four11 below. Through the holes in the floor, she heard the familiar beeping of the gigantic UPS (uninterruptible power supply) backup batteries. As the hours passed and the batteries drained, Theresia heard Four11 founder Geoff Ralston and his crew—which included a handful of impressive women, Jessica Livingston, Katie Mitic, and Gloria Gavin—strategize over the next steps. She smiled when she heard their nutty plan to restore power.

At around two A.M., as she packed up by flashlight, Theresia spotted Ralston and his crew carrying armloads of extension cords. They trotted across Middlefield Road to the Geographical Survey offices, talked to a security guard on the main floor, and proceeded to lay orange extension cords all the way back across Middlefield Road, strapping them down as they went. They pulled the final cord into Casa Mills through a window, and computer power was restored.

Sitting in her car in the Casa Mills parking lot, Theresia couldn't help but smile at the extension cords spanning Middlefield Road. This was life at a start-up. She sat with the engine running, wondering where she could go to sleep.

MJ

The *click clack* of heels on the Spanish tile floor in her Palo Alto home got MJ's attention. The heels belonged to her daughter, Kate, who was ten years old. Kate had a pair of dress pumps and liked to pretend she was off to work, just like her mom. MJ's son, Will, who was seven and couldn't sit still, scampered after their cat, Heidi, so named because she was always hiding. MJ's three-year-old, Hanna, was clinging to her leg. MJ's husband, Bill Elmore, also a venture capitalist, was out the door early for meetings.

It was a Monday morning, the start of a new workweek, and MJ kept a close eye on the clock. She needed to be at IVP at eight-thirty for the weekly meeting. As she scrambled eggs, Will asked in a continuous loop for cocoa puffs instead. Meanwhile the family Labrador, Cindy, scratched at the door to be let out. MJ ignored her vibrating Motorola StarTAC phone.

After everyone was dressed and breakfast was on the table, MJ greeted their beloved nanny, Tina, kissed the kids goodbye, reveled one last moment in the happy chaos, and closed the garage door, like a seal to the outside world. She marveled at how the venture guys—her husband included—seemed to compete for who could hold the earliest meetings. *How am I supposed to make a meeting at six A.M.?* She would not miss mornings with her kids. Now, alone in her car and free of children bemoaning her choice of music, she slipped a Faith Hill CD into the player.

As she pulled out of the driveway, MJ wondered how her mother, Dorothy, had managed to raise five kids in that small house in Terre Haute. MJ remembered the ice on the inside of her bedroom window during the long winter months. Her mother had worked the night shift at JCPenney, yet had done all the cooking, cleaning, shopping, and sewing, with virtually no help. MJ's dad was gone all day teaching; he spent his weekends working on his car or sequestered in his photography darkroom.

Picking a piece of scrambled egg off her navy slacks, MJ headed toward Sand Hill Road. The Faith Hill CD had a way of making the commute shorter and more enjoyable. Among the songs was her favorite: "Take Me as I Am."

SONJA

Sonja was enjoying lunch in the heated ski lodge at Sun Valley, comfortably well away from the slopes, when investment banking star Thom Weisel approached her table.

"Sonja, I signed you up—you're in the race," Weisel enthused. He had flown bankers and venture capitalists, including Sonja, to the famed Idaho resort in a chartered jet. A decorated athlete in skiing, cycling, speed skating, and running, and past president of the U.S. Ski Team, Weisel was known for hiring Olympic athletes and Navy SEALs and turning them into bankers.

But Sonja, who had skied all morning, had not signed up for Weisel's weekend boondoggle to become the next Jean-Claude Killy; it was all she could do not to choke on her lunch. Surrounded by men, with all eyes on her, she was not about to show fear. The southern belle who had been cut from her high school sports teams and hadn't made the cheerleading squad because the dance moves were too fast, had skied maybe five times in her life—with her church group in Virginia. Her favorite part about skiing was après-ski.

Now she was being asked—more accurately, ordered—to participate in a timed downhill event with the hard-charging boys of banking, including some notable Olympic skiers. Yet Sonja couldn't say no. She needed to be a good sport. After all, this was Thom Weisel, who had sold his company, Montgomery Securities, to NationsBank for $1.3 billion, the same investor who had helped take public several seminal companies, including Amgen, Micron Technology, ROLM, Integrated Device Technology, Yahoo!, and Siebel Systems. It was no surprise to anyone that he wanted his firm's name on the *left side* of a company's initial public offering prospectus. The lead banker always got the coveted left side.

Like any venture capitalist, Sonja wanted to fit in with Weisel's alpha male bankers. Being liked in Silicon Valley was a currency. It's what made one VC invite another in on a deal. It was a tacit requirement in a complex game. For the few women in the game, being liked meant learning to be assertive without being aggressive, to be heard without being loud, and to like money without being seen as greedy. It meant when a partner wanted to take her to a shooting range to teach her to shoot, she readily obliged. It meant saying yes to a downhill race when she barely skied.

So Sonja fastened her boots, gathered her things, and braced for the freezing air. Her only coat of armor in this race was courtesy of Patagonia. She was one of only a handful of women VCs invited to this weekend getaway. She was younger than most in the group and more junior in her career. The other women at the lodge were wives or girlfriends.

Near the top of Bald Mountain, with what looked like a blizzard bearing down, Sonja surveyed the handful of teams, each of which had five skiers. Her teeth chattered as she listened to the race parameters. Skiers would race one at a time. Gates were formed by poles set twenty-six feet apart. Every skier had to pass through every gate, without missing one. The team with the fastest total score would win. Sonja, in her puffy black jacket and ski pants, spotted an Olympic skier on a competing team: Otto Tschudi, a Weisel executive who had skied for Norway in two Olympics, turned pro afterward, and was rated one of the top fifteen slalom skiers in the world. Sonja's skiing career consisted of bunny hills followed by green-for-beginner runs and a few blue-for-intermediate. As she waited her turn at the top of the run, her teammate launched down the hill as if competing for gold. Sonja was up next. Eyeing the chutelike run, she feared this was not going to end well. She felt like the Grinch's dog, Max, looking fearfully over the snowy precipice.

But Sonja understood that this three-day weekend was not about catching up on sleep, sitting by the fireplace, or hitting the spa. Even the top skiers signed up for intermediate races to ensure they would win. Behind the pretense of casual fun was cutthroat competition. Behind the merriment of the lavish dinners was jockeying for who sat where. Seating charts for meals were closely held and carefully constructed weeks before the event. Weisel studied the charts, barked orders to an assistant, and rearranged players like chess pieces—all while riding his stationary bike.

Atop the snowy slope, Sonja briefly closed her eyes and visualized making it down the hill safely. Her teammates could rip, shred, and tuck at the finish line. She would ski slowly to the bottom. *Obstacles are my allies.* She took off at a decent pace, focusing everything she had on slow and steady. She thought only of the next gate, not the whole course. One turn at a time, each building on the last. Another gate, another ally.

The snow beneath her was icy, and the wind had picked up. She focused on her breathing. *Plant your poles down the hill. Feel your shins against the tongue of your boots. Relax your toes. One wrong move, and you're out of the race, maybe the game.*

Finally, her legs shaking, Sonja made it to the bottom of the mountain without a wipeout. She crossed the finish line to cheers. She certainly wasn't the fastest; she was probably the slowest; but she had made it. At dinner that night, she was seated next to Weisel and she was stunned to learn that her team had won. She walked away with high fives and nods of approval, including from Weisel, and a Sun Valley picture frame.

In her time in venture capital so far, Sonja had shot guns, knocked back whiskey, cold-called countless companies, chased down competitive deals, babysat triplets—and now, performed some scary skiing maneuvers. She had not made it this far by backing down from challenges or sitting on the sidelines. That's why Menlo Ventures had elevated her to partner, four days before her thirtieth birthday. She was the youngest partner in the firm's twenty-year history.

MAGDALENA

Arriving at 3000 Sand Hill Road, Magdalena sank back into the warm seat of her car and closed her eyes, psyching herself up before making her big pitch to Menlo Ventures. Like all major venture capitalists, Menlo had the power to help transform a great idea into a company or even an industry—and Magdalena was firmly convinced that CyberCash was a great idea, because the future of commerce was on the Internet.

She was dressed in a colorful but conservatively tailored skirt suit with shoulder pads, a far cry from her days at the Stanford computer center, where she had entertained herself and fellow geeks with her memorable vintage costumes. She got out of her car and walked along the pathway framed by manicured grass and bright flowerbeds. There to greet her was her CyberCash co-founder, Dan Lynch, a gentle and lumbering soul with a mop of graying brown hair and oversize horn-rimmed glasses. He always wore the same thing: slacks and an ill-fitting golf shirt.

"Hey, girl," Lynch said fondly. He was preternaturally happy, telling her, "I make promises, you deliver on my promises." Lynch was a known entity in tech circles, having managed the computing laboratory at the Stanford Research Institute and helped build the Arpanet, the network that became the basis for the Internet. Earlier Magdalena and Lynch had started a company called Internet Access, to bring corporations online. But the two couldn't raise any VC money, and their company had been merged into UUNet, a similar commercial Internet access provider.

As Magdalena and Lynch walked into the conference room at Menlo Ventures, she was struck by something unusual and a bit out of place. But it wasn't the 1970s furniture or art. In any event, she had a presentation to give and began concentrating on projecting what one former boss called her "delicious *eff you* attitude." She shook hands, hugged one of the partners, John Jarve, who had invested in UUNet, and pulled her PowerBook Duo and docking station from her briefcase. Magdalena and Dan had sixty minutes to present, followed by time for questions. Where Magdalena was the pragmatic, get-it-done founder, Dan was the big-vision blue-sky guy.

Like most venture firms on Sand Hill Road, Menlo dedicated Mondays to hearing pitches from entrepreneurs, offering three ninety-minute slots, including one that went through lunch. Magdalena focused her presentation on three categories of merchandise perfect for this new world of e-commerce: wine, clothing, and books.

She presented a diagram showing how merchants, banks, and shoppers used CyberCash's "certified wallet" to do encrypted and secure transactions. But as she talked, her attention was pulled to the copper-and-wood conference table. The VCs were eating takeout from the Sundeck restaurant. The food looked so good. Magdalena always surprised people by how much she ate during the day. She scoffed at Americans' idea of a salad for lunch. She needed a *real meal,* she would say, salad, entrée, and dessert.

"Electronic commerce is where geography disappears and where the middleman disappears," Magdalena continued, walking the VCs through the mechanics of CyberCash. "The consumer deals directly with the merchant. As the middleman disappears, the merchant can pass on significantly more favorable pricing to the consumer." CyberCash encrypted credit card numbers; offered "micropayments" to buy, say, one news article at a time; and offered "cyber coins," for twenty-five-cents-a-pop video games. But the promise of e-commerce wasn't clear to many of those in the conference room. The VCs peppered Magdalena and Lynch with questions: Why would a consumer do this? Could a *digital bazaar* become a significant thing? Wouldn't shoppers want to flip through the pages of a book before buying it, or talk to an expert in a wine store, or try on a dress?

The baffled disconnect reminded Magdalena of July 1969, when she was ten years old, growing up in Turkey, and listening to the news that Apollo 11 had landed a man on the moon. She had gushed about the historic landing for days afterward and couldn't comprehend the shrugs or apathy. "What's wrong with you guys?" she implored her friends. "America spent the money! Came up with the technology! This is a new frontier!"

The incomprehension felt similar today, though the frontier this time was the nascent but boundless Internet. While Dan fielded more questions, Magdalena shifted her attention to the oddity she had been drawn to when she first walked in, the puzzle piece that didn't fit, the circle in the row of polygons. At the Menlo table, crowded with men, sat a *woman*. Nordic-looking and twenty-something, she had tidy, shoulder-length blond hair and blue eyes and wore a tailored navy suit and a white blouse. *Interesting,* Magdalena thought. *I wonder where they found her.*

Later she would learn the woman was Sonja Hoel. Sonja, for her part, paused in her copious note-taking to take Magdalena in. She appeared poised, smart, beautiful, and Mediterranean-looking. But neither woman held the other's attention for long. For Sonja, work was about merit, and gender was irrelevant. For Magdalena, singling out another woman in Silicon Valley would be like embracing a fellow Armenian on the beach in Istanbul just because she was Armenian. It was irrelevant.

As the pitch ended, Magdalena realized that reluctance hung in the air. The VCs had more questions than answers. But she knew that everything about CyberCash was unique, and that usage of the World Wide Web was exploding. She had talked recently with a man named Jeff Bezos, who months earlier had quit his job on Wall Street to launch an online bookstore called Amazon out of his garage, thanks to funding from his parents.

Magdalena made it clear to the Menlo group that she and Dan would be talking with other VCs, including Kleiner Perkins Caufield & Byers just up the road, and that they had interest from a number of companies, including Intel. Magdalena shook hands with everyone, including Sonja. But there would be no sisterhood bonding on this day. Magdalena understood Sonja's polished veneer and knew an outsider when she saw one.

As Magdalena headed back to the parking lot with Dan, she sensed that their pitch wasn't going anywhere at Menlo Ventures. They were not going to be offered a term sheet. But Magdalena was a survivor. If she could deal with transplanting herself to America and working two jobs while earning two degrees at Stanford, she could surely deal with today's rejection.

Just before she left Turkey to attend college in America, neighbors, friends, and family turned out to say goodbye to her. As was the tradition, they threw buckets of water behind her car for good luck. The luck wouldn't work if you looked back. And she never did.

THERESIA

As part of her couch-surfing routine, Theresia sometimes stayed with Greg and Sarah Sands, who had been her Stanford business school classmates. Greg had gone on to become the first product manager at Netscape. He'd written the initial business plan and even coined the company name. Other nights Theresia stayed with Angela Tucci, another business school friend. Competition for second bedrooms in Silicon Valley was fierce, given employees at start-ups were often paid in stock instead of cash. On the eve of an important meeting for her start-up Release, Theresia ended up at Tucci's place. After a few fitful hours of sleep, she gathered her things and hopped back in her car, where her belongings were all neatly packed. She was nothing if not organized. As a girl, she had kept her Barbie dolls in Ziploc bags, with clothes in one, accessories in another. She gunned her car onto Highway 101, heading toward the offices of the software giant Symantec, one of the places she would be giving a pitch to.

On the drive, Theresia listened to syndicated sports talk radio host Jim Rome, who had famously baited Rams quarterback Jim Everett into on-air fisticuffs by repeatedly calling him "Chris Evert," a reference to the female tennis legend. *Everett should have taken it as a compliment,* Theresia thought as she flipped stations. She looked at the clock on her dashboard and switched to AM radio for news.

The host was talking about the 1995 bombing of the Federal Building in Oklahoma City, which had killed 168 people, including 19 children, and injured more than 500 others. She turned up the volume.

No matter how many times she heard the bomber's name—Timothy McVeigh—she couldn't bring together what she heard with what she knew about McVeigh from high school.

Back home in western New York, Theresia and McVeigh had worked together at Burger King. They both had run track in high school, been huge Buffalo Bills fans, and graduated in 1986. McVeigh wore camouflage and loved guns. He had been raised by a dad who went to church, belonged to the autoworkers' union, and worked the night shift in the Harrison Radiator factory in Lockport, where Theresia interned one summer. What struck her whenever she thought about McVeigh was that there had been nothing unique about him growing up. He was indistinguishable from everyone else in town.

She turned off the radio when she heard a commentator ask whether the bombing—and its homegrown "all American" terrorist—represented the end of the American dream. She didn't want to hear about the end of any dreams today. She had plenty of her own to fulfill.

Theresia arrived at Symantec early. She spotted Release founder Matthew Klein, and the two headed inside. Klein was wearing white gym socks with his dark suit, but she decided not to say anything. She appreciated him for what he was—a geek's geek, guileless, smart, and exuding a sort of utopian optimism. She wasn't sure he even noticed that Theresia was a she. The only time gender came up was at outside meetings with venture capitalists, bankers, and corporate executives, where Theresia was often mistaken for an intern, a secretary, or a girlfriend. She was asked, "Where's the coffee?" and "Are you going to take notes?"

Only months before, while working for Bain in San Francisco, Theresia had a client in Los Angeles who apparently thought he could kiss the women who worked for him. He first made suggestive comments to a junior female colleague of Theresia's, then tried to kiss her. The woman told Theresia about his comments and behavior, and the two decided the client had been more inappropriate than threatening, that their work with him was wrapping up and he was too important to lose. When Theresia was in the client's office at the completion of their work, the man shook Theresia's hand, pulled her close, and tried to kiss her. She deflected by laughing it off and pretending he had been going for a European double kiss.

Release felt gender neutral and horizontal, not hierarchical. No one had power over anyone else. Every day was both fraught and full of potential. Every day it was about rolling up your sleeves and getting stuff done.

The meeting began on time, with an unsmiling Susanne Brey, a Symantec executive, running the show. Her efficiency intimidated Matthew. She was clearly not going to coax the pitch out of him.

Matthew, using the coaching that Theresia had given him, began, "We developed an ability to take any program, any executable program, and wrap it in our payment shell." Theresia nodded encouragingly. He continued, "Look, you don't have to bother your developers. You don't need to do any integration, or learn any API, or change even a single line of your source code. Just give us your final gold master .exe file—the same thing you send to the factory that manufactures your CD-ROMs. We can wrap it up for you and put it in an online store for people to download, and you collect the money."

Matthew couldn't tell whether Susanne Brey disliked him or the idea. He hoped Theresia would take over. She had mastered this kind of strategic corporate dance—the language, the pauses, the eye contact, and the pacing. It was Theresia who had landed the meeting in the first place, making the case to Symantec that its Norton antivirus software required regular updates that could be done electronically rather than in boxed software.

Matthew's heart sank when he saw Brey checking her watch. That was Theresia's cue to take over. She covered as much territory as she could, as efficiently and quickly as possible. Then Brey stood. Their time was up. The meeting was over. Walking out, Matthew was deflated, sure it had been a disaster. Theresia shook her head. "Nope, it went great," she said, steering him back to his car. And she was right. They got the deal with Symantec and were soon landing deals with other major companies, including Netscape and the bookseller Barnes & Noble.

Their next stop that day was San Francisco, where they would present their business plan to investors who, along with a general tech audience, moved from room to room to hear pitches from start-ups that interested them. Matthew was pleased when he walked into their room and saw a big crowd. He and Theresia had done a few of these speed-dating, dialing-for-dollars events, and this was their biggest audience by far. But as he and Theresia set up, the crowd suddenly vanished. Disappointed, Matthew was told that the crowd had been there to listen to a pitch from the bookseller Amazon. Matthew looked at Theresia: "An online bookseller? How stupid!" Theresia, for her part, thought it was a great idea and planned to try to land Amazon as a client.

Release had more wins than losses in its meetings with companies and investors—though the start-up was always desperate for cash. Eventually it prepared to go public, with Merrill Lynch as the underwriter. The investing world had changed since Netscape's IPO in 1995. The fervor over Netscape's dramatic upward valuation had ushered in new economy companies that were born, funded, acquired, or went public in record time. Suddenly, making money—actual revenue and profits—was far less important than capturing clicks and eyeballs. Tens of billions of dollars were pouring into venture capital funds, and almost any company with a "dot-com" after its title was attracting suitors. For every $100 invested in businesses across the United States during this period, more than $40 went to Internet-related companies. Never had so much money been created so quickly by so few people. Jokes were made about the virgins of the valley—those rare souls who had yet to take a company public. Porsche Boxters were as common as the iMac, offered in a slate of colors.

In 1998, Theresia and the Release team had almost finished their S-1 initial SEC registration form, required to take the start-up public. They had close to $15 million in subscription revenues. They brought in a new CFO, Carolyn Rogers, to help pre-IPO. But in a surprise move, Rogers won the support of the board and became CEO herself, replacing Matthew.

The board told Matthew that at this stage, the Silicon Valley game required "adult supervision"—someone with experience running a company. Alternating between sadness and anger, he couldn't help but admit to himself: *What do I know about running a company? Hell, what do I know about anything? I've been a student for most of my life. My business experience consists of writing computer code in my pajamas.*

In another surprise, Rogers decided that Release was too small to go public at this stage and told the board to put everything on hold. Theresia had a feeling Rogers wasn't going to stick around for long, and she felt the time to go public was now. As Theresia told Matthew and the board members, "I've really enjoyed this, but I've seen this movie before. I think I know how it ends. I hope I'm wrong. I'll stay for as long as you want me, but . . ."

To Theresia, this was the end of the Release she knew and believed in. It was time to start something new.

MJ

MJ parked in her usual spot in the back lot at the IVP offices and walked past the sprawling oak tree. It reminded her of a tai chi practitioner, its limbs long and purposeful in their reach. She had finally got rid of her Ford Pinto, selling it on Craigslist. On rare occasions when she spotted an old Pinto in the land of German sports cars, she was reminded of what it was like to first drive up Sand Hill Road, looking down through the rusted-out floorboards.

MJ headed into the lobby of Building 2, graced by a large artwork depicting a slightly torn and burned thousand-dollar bill, titled *Burn Rate*. MJ, one of the first women in history to make investing partner at a VC firm, had been at IVP for more than a decade now. She had come of age professionally in the 1980s, a boom time for venture capital. The growth began in earnest when IVP founder Reid Dennis—along with fellow VCs Pitch Johnson, Tom Perkins, and Bill Draper—successfully pushed Washington lawmakers to lower the taxation on profits from sales of investments. Some of the biggest companies to go public during this time were Genentech, Compaq, Apple, Oracle, and Microsoft.

When MJ was hired in 1982, one of the first deals she and Dennis landed was a start-up called Sequent Computers. MJ knew Sequent co-founder Scott Gibson from her Intel days. When she briefed Dennis on the deal and mentioned "there are a lot of venture guys after them," Dennis looked at his watch, made a few calls to rearrange his schedule, and said, "Let's pay them a visit." So they flew in his twin-engine Cessna to Beaverton, Oregon. Hours later MJ and Dennis left Oregon with a deal: IVP would invest $5.2 million, giving Sequent a pre-money valuation of $15 million. (Pre-money is the value of a company or asset prior to the investment.) They had nothing in writing, but Gibson trusted MJ from their days at Intel and knew Dennis's reputation. His handshake was considered golden. Now in 1996, Sequent had more than $800 million in annual revenues and partnerships with Oracle, Boeing, and Siemens AG, among others.

IVP now had more than $187 million under management in its seventh fund. The VC firm had helped finance, build, and take public eighty companies, collectively employing more than one hundred thousand people, generating $10 billion in annual revenue, with a market capitalization of more than $20 billion. MJ and Dennis hired all the new partners. They established three areas of investment expertise: early-stage info tech, late-stage info tech, and life sciences. MJ's focus was primarily on the fields of software, communications, and computer-aided engineering. She had invested IVP funds in Applied Digital Access, Aspect Communications, Bridge Communications, Frequency Software, Netrix, Red Pepper Software, SuperMac, SynOptics, Unify, and Weitek.

Entering the IVP offices, MJ greeted her secretary, Andi Heintz, grabbed coffee, and closed her door. Sipping coffee in silence was her tai chi, her Zen moment. Work was the only place where she could finish a cup of coffee. Here challenges came at her one at a time.

Finishing her coffee, MJ welcomed Heintz in for a quick debrief before the partners' eight-thirty pitch meeting. Heintz had started at IVP in 1984; MJ had been her first female boss. MJ was also the only partner who kept her own schedule and got her own coffee.

Silicon Valley was in the middle of another economic boom, this one whipped up by the potential of the Internet. And like a computer chip, MJ's mind would process the divergent pieces of her typical day, from pancakes to pitches to lights-out. Her former Intel boss, Gordon Moore, had famously predicted that computing power—the number of components that could be packed onto a Silicon chip—would double every year. (He later adjusted that to every two years.) His prediction became known as Moore's Law. The same exponential growth was taking place in Silicon Valley. The Valley had started with two guys, William Hewlett and David Packard, founding HP in a garage, and it was now the epicenter of start-ups with billions of dollars of venture capital.

"Just keep things moving," MJ said to Heintz before the partners' meeting began. The pitches would often run late, and the partners tended to get comfy. MJ was the only one in the room with a working spouse *and* children. With an endless stream of people and deals to consider, it was possible to work around the clock. When other partners wanted to spend more time considering a deal, MJ was often a quick no. When the men juggled six to eight start-up deals, MJ focused on a few propitious ones. Good judgment and time management became her secret weapons. When it came time to fire a CEO or the founder of a nascent company for persistent problems—when the problems had long been agonizingly obvious—she wasn't afraid to drop the ax. VCs had a reputation for being quick to fire, but MJ had found the opposite—they always waited too long. Venture capitalists wanted their entrepreneurs to succeed.

MJ had already waited too long when she met with one of her entrepreneurs. Only twenty-eight at the time, MJ had been named a partner at IVP and she was the lead investor in the company. She had summoned the founder to her office to discuss the company's problems, including certain, to put it delicately, *personnel issues*. There sat the founder, who was always impeccably dressed. His eyes had a habit of wandering south.

MJ wasted no time. He was dating a female application engineer who worked for him. She told him what she knew and touched on other problems at the company. Without further ado, she said, "You're fired."

The founder looked shocked, then indignant. "I'm not going to be fired *by a woman*," he said.

MJ almost laughed. He was fine being funded by a woman but wouldn't be fired by a woman. She glanced behind her and to the side. "Well, I don't see anyone else here, do you?" she said. *"You are fired."*

MJ eventually unloaded the company for $1.39 million, at a loss to IVP of more than $1.4 million. But no one was complaining.

Over the years, in fact, MJ's quick dispatching of the founder had become the stuff of legend, often recounted in get-togethers among Heintz and her fellow secretaries at other firms. They called themselves the VVCAs—the Vivacious Venture Capital Assistants. Every few weeks, they would gather after work for drinks and to dish out gossip. They talked about partners at their respective firms, about the affairs, the houses, the exotic trips, the picky eaters, and the ones who needed their laundry retrieved. They rolled their eyes at the story of a VC who called from vacation to ask his assistant to clean the dog poop in his backyard.

MJ looked at her watch—it was time for the partners' meeting to begin. She headed into the conference room, while Heintz returned to her perch in the hallway. Petite, blond, and outgoing, Heintz watched as everyone went in and took their seats. Reid Dennis wore his trademark suit and bow tie.

Heintz hadn't immediately taken to MJ, who came across as an iron maiden in her gray, navy, and black suits, white blouse, nylons, and practical pumps. The purpose of the uniform, Heintz gradually came to understand, was less to look masculine than to avoid looking feminine. Heintz, who had once worked for the chief psychologist at the Langley Porter Psychiatric Hospital and Clinics in San Francisco, was intrigued by MJ and by the gender dynamics that played out at work. She had seen that women's success and likability were often negatively correlated; as one factor went up, the other went down.

Heintz's perception of MJ had really changed when she became a mom. Heintz had assumed that MJ was too career-focused to have kids, so she was shocked the day MJ confided that she was pregnant. As the first woman partner at IVP, MJ had to establish a precedent of maternity leave, and she took three months off with each child. And through it all, her career continued to prosper.

By this time, Heintz knew MJ well enough to know that she was a sensitive woman wearing an impassive mask and a suit of armor. She had flourished in the Darwinian game of natural selection that played out every day on Sand Hill Road. As Heintz peeked into the conference room, she could feel herself rooting for her boss. She was a modern version of Melanie Griffith's character in *Working Girl,* minus the industrial-strength teased hair.

SONJA

Sonja was running a different kind of race. After the skiing weekend, she had happily shelved her Patagonia jacket for her own suit of armor: a tailored jacket, blouse, pants, and pearl necklace. The companies around her were soaring to new heights. The NASDAQ—home to virtually all the dot-com stocks—had risen nearly 400 percent in the few years since Netscape's IPO. The Internet was being lionized as the transformative technology of the twentieth century, on par with the advent of the automobile industry, electric power distribution systems, and nuclear energy. Entrepreneurs and VCs used words like *gold rush* and *land grab* to describe the once-in-a-lifetime opportunity to get rich. Turf battles escalated between banks vying for hot initial stock offerings and merger deals. VCs chased after fresh-faced, wide-eyed dot-com entrepreneurs. Companies such as At Home and Real Networks had impressive IPOs, as did Verisign, Exodus, CyberCash, UUNet, and Inktomi. Companies like Priceline, eToys, Pets.com, GoTo.com, and Webvan experienced dazzling growth—as measured by eyeballs, page use, and unique customers.

Sonja was at work when she got a call from her friend Kim Davis, a venture capitalist at IDG Ventures in San Francisco. Kim had earned her bachelor's degree at Stanford and had been a year behind Sonja at Harvard Business School. The two women now lived a block from each other in San Francisco. Kim told Sonja that she had found a promising new Internet company in Seattle and needed an investing partner. "This is going to be a big company," Kim said. IDG had an $80 million fund; its typical investment deal was between $1 million and $2 million. Menlo's Fund VII was $250 million.

The Seattle company, F5 Labs, had been started by former bond trader and investment banker Jeff Hussey, who believed he had found something that was fundamentally missing from the Internet. As online traffic increased—some said usage was doubling every ninety days—websites were being strained to the point of paralysis. Overloaded servers were returning messages like HTTP error 404 "not found," or HTTP error 503 "service unavailable." Hussey knew that, ultimately, the Internet would not work if a major pillar of the infrastructure was broken.

F5 built a system of "load balancing" software called BIG-IP, which functioned like the guard at the airport who directs passengers to whichever security line seems shortest and has the least delay. Hussey had seed investors—friends and family—and a new financing offer from the boutique San Francisco investment firm Hambrecht & Quist.

Sonja understood that the deal was in play. She hung up with Kim and quickly made some calls, learning that F5's lawyer and chief financial officer were attending a Cooley Godward conference at a hotel in Monterey, about ninety minutes south. She grabbed her keys, hustled out to her car, and was soon on her way to Monterey, the seaside town best known for its world-class aquarium and as the locale for many of John Steinbeck's stories. Sonja needed to convince the F5 team of the value of working with a venture firm rather than a bank. Menlo had financed major deals with Internet and communication equipment companies and had both the connections and the track record to be a strong ally for the nascent F5.

Sonja had come a long way from her days at TA Associates in Boston. Since arriving at Menlo in July 1994, she had led investments in several key deals, including in Vermeer Technologies in 1995, which provided tools for the growing market of Internet publishers. Vermeer had been acquired by Microsoft for $133 million in 1996, one month after Menlo invested. Sonja was the secondary investor—her partner Doug Carlisle was the primary—in Hotmail, the free Web-based e-mail service that Microsoft acquired in 1997 for an estimated $400 million, the largest all-cash Internet start-up purchase at the time. She had met Steve Jobs when Harvard Business School recognized Pixar Animation Studios as the entrepreneurial company of the year. Sonja had seated Jobs next to herself at dinner, hoping to have a conversation. Instead, Jobs spent most of the night leading Pixar employees outside to see his new silver Mercedes. He paid little attention to Sonja.

One of Sonja's favorite deals had been with Priority Call Management, a developer of computer systems (programmable digital switching platforms) to support enhanced telephone network services. PCM had been founded by the young Massachusetts-based entrepreneur Andy Ory. Ory and his father had spent countless nights at Kinko's writing and printing business plans. They cobbled together some cash—including Andy's father's retirement savings—and worked out of a small office above a truck stop. The younger Ory raised $4 million over four years, selling stock wherever he went, at weddings, at funerals, in elevators, at bar mitzvahs, in subways, and in airport hotels across thirty states. Ory and his father had been working for 107 days straight when Sonja came calling. By that point, PCM was running on fumes.

Sonja and Ory quietly joked that they didn't really know what they were doing. It was her first deal at Menlo, and his first start-up. But

Sonja trusted her instincts. She saw huge market potential both in PCM and in the tireless, bespectacled Ory. PCM targeted communication service providers (telephone companies wired and wireless) that had the foundational infrastructure of cell towers and equipment to connect one cell phone to another. PCM sold those carriers value-added features like voice mail, calling cards, call waiting, caller ID, and call forwarding—turnkey solutions that could give the carriers a package of premium features needed to stay competitive in the deregulated telecom market. Sonja lobbied her partners to invest $3 million in 1995. By 1998, PCM was a $50 million business and growing fast.

Sonja was grateful for her unofficial mentor at Menlo, Tom Bredt, who loved working with entrepreneurs to help them build great companies. Bredt had worked at Bell Labs in New Jersey, where William Shockley and his colleagues had sparked the semiconductor revolution with the fabrication of the first transistor. When Sonja put together the PCM deal, Bredt took the PCM board seat, given his experience. But he told Sonja, "Come with me and let's see if we can help this company become successful." He liked to ask entrepreneurs, "What's keeping you awake at night?" Sonja shadowed him at board meetings and in one-on-one meetings with entrepreneurs. He was a patient listener and had a succinct way of summarizing problems and solutions.

Sonja hoped her mentorship by Bredt would pay dividends at her meeting with the F5 folks. Good timing wouldn't hurt either.

MJ

Once again, the eight-thirty morning pitch meeting at IVP extended into the early evening. MJ had been largely unimpressed by the pitches she'd heard. The entrepreneurs had talked about the technology—not the market. Most entrepreneurs came in with new technology in search of a problem. MJ was attracted to entrepreneurs who identified a huge problem and created technology to solve it.

Now her younger partner, Geoff Yang, a hotshot in the new info tech space, was holding the floor. His investments in IVP Fund VI had done so well that the partners agreed to give him "super carry," a bigger share of future profits from investments made in Fund VII. After the limited partners—the investors—were paid off, Yang would be awarded a bigger slice of the financial pie than the other partners.

Yang had wanted to be a venture capitalist from the time he was in high school. He earned his economics and engineering degree from Princeton, then his MBA from Stanford. He'd worked at IBM and Goldman Sachs before joining IVP in 1987. Very high energy, he described his job in the dot-com days as similar to "drinking from a fire hose." Corporations came to him wanting to know about the Internet, asking how to navigate "clicks versus bricks," and proposing joint ventures with IVP so the big firms could reinvent themselves as incubators. He went to the trade shows and industry conferences, networked like crazy, and slept very little. Like MJ, Yang had three kids. Unlike MJ, he had a stay-at-home spouse and worked six days a week. He went to bed at eleven P.M. and awoke at three A.M., did e-mail, went back to sleep at 4:30 A.M., and got up to start the day at 6 A.M.

MJ found herself continually packing more into her life. Beyond a husband, a job, a house, three kids, a dog, and a cat, she had bought her parents a house nearby. This was the life she had engineered for herself, a continuum of her games of hide-and-seek in the tall cornfields of Indiana. She had always been strategic about finding her way around closed doors and over hurdles that appeared insurmountable.

During the last partners' meeting, Yang had talked about what he called a "passive deal," where IVP made a return of only twelve to fifteen times its investment. Weighing the pros and cons of a new potential investment, Yang said, "We can easily return ten times, but I don't know if that's worth it. Do we really need this when we're doing deals returning one hundred to one thousand times?" In normal, non-boom-time years, VCs tried to earn ten times their investment. If they did ten deals, their hope was that two or three of them would yield huge returns. Typically, about 80 percent of the wins came from 20 percent of the deals, something VCs labeled the "Babe Ruth effect." Ruth struck out a lot, but he also set all the slugging records. VCs had to hit those home runs to compensate for the strikeouts.

MJ agreed with Yang. In the frothy dot-com investing world they currently lived in, a return of ten times was "kind of a yawn." Everywhere MJ turned, she met another person claiming to be a VC. Her hairdresser was suddenly moonlighting as a VC. Her friend's landscaper was a VC. Everyone was talking about the hot dot-com deals they were investing in. In 1998, Amazon's stock returned 970 percent; AOL, 593 percent; and Yahoo!, 584 percent.

At six P.M., with the pitch meeting over, the guys made plans to meet for drinks. But there was only one place MJ wanted to be. She always made dinner for her family. She touched base with her husband, Bill; he said he'd be at work for at least another hour—which probably meant later. He had co-founded a venture firm, Foundation Capital, and was working start-up hours. MJ had met Bill at Purdue. He had sandy hair and the bluest eyes she had ever seen. He was both an engineering major and a Purdue cheerleader. In fact, he was everything her family was not: well traveled, adventuresome, athletic. He also seemed giving, which felt in some ways like the opposite of her father.

Nowadays Bill liked to boast that he had something few men had: a wife who was a partner at a venture capital firm. He was proud of her in public. Yet at home, it was MJ who made dinner, got the kids into baths, checked Kate's homework, and began the nightly reading of *Goodnight Moon* to Hanna, *Blueberries for Sal* to Will, and *The Trumpet of the Swan* with Kate. When Bill came home late, she heated his dinner. MJ, in effect, had multiple jobs—doing twice the amount of housework and three times the amount of childcare as Bill. To be fair, this was a choice she had made, in part because she remembered how she missed her own mother when she was working nights at JCPenney.

At around ten-thirty, after watching the news, she told Bill she was going to bed. He said the same. It was a joke she kept to herself. On her way to bed, she started a load of laundry, turned on the dishwasher, took the dog for a walk, and picked up the living room. By the time she crawled in, Bill had already been asleep for an hour.

SONJA

At the hotel in Monterey, Sonja found the CFO and attorney of F5 and made her case for why F5 should work with Menlo. The meeting went well and the timing turned out to be perfect. Within a week, F5 founder and CEO Jeff Hussey flew to Silicon Valley from Seattle to meet with Sonja and the Menlo partners. Hussey had never been to Sand Hill Road—and was all nerves. A fast talker normally, he forced himself to slow down. He had never run a company or written contracts, and he had no idea how to raise money for a start-up. Seattle was a great city to build a company in, but it didn't have the infrastructure of Silicon Valley: the venture community and the acquisitive companies that did research and development by way of mergers and acquisitions.

In the conference room at Menlo, Hussey ran a rudimentary Power-Point presentation for the Menlo partners, but he relied mostly on the whiteboard. He made the group laugh with appreciation when he shared a bit about the company's origin story: "I had this epiphany. I thought, 'Someone should build a load balancer! Someone should do for servers what was done for disk storage.'" He was referring to a technology called Redundant Array of Inexpensive Disks—RAID—that provided disk redundancy and speed optimization by distributing data across drives. "I thought, Wow, what if we could build this gizmo that is a redundant array of inexpensive servers?"

He scribbled diagrams and numbers and noted that revenues were increasing 30 percent a month. Pointing to the diagram of how the load balancer worked, he turned to the partners and said, "Look, everything on Earth is going to be connected to the Internet. Something must change as it pertains to server economics. My view is that every piece of Internet traffic will one day flow through a load balancer. Nobody will build a network without a load balancer."

The following Monday—July 6, 1998, Sonja's birthday—Sonja and Kim Davis flew to Seattle to make an offer. Sonja, blond and preppy, and Kim, tall, leggy, and African American, made quite a pair. Sonja had the term sheet, which explained the details of the investment offer. She had valued F5 at $55 million, based on revenues, projections, the market, various industry and comparable company multiples, other offers, and a sense of what Hussey would need to accept the deal. She had learned that one of the most important parts of her job was to figure out what the entrepreneur needed to make the deal happen. Menlo aimed for a minimum tenfold return on its investments, which would put F5's potential at $550 million.

"We want to invest," Sonja told Hussey. "What's your valuation?"

For some reason, the question took Hussey by surprise. He had been watching other Internet companies get wild and frothy valuations. He had more revenue and customers than all his direct competitors combined. F5 clients included Microsoft, Montgomery Securities, Alaska Airlines, Monsanto, and dozens of other notable corporate names. Still, he was perpetually running out of money. Every day as an entrepreneur felt like an emotional Bay of Fundy, with vertiginous highs and lows. The ride took him from a peak of euphoria to the pit of despair daily.

He went over the numbers in his head. "Well, okay, the valuation is sixty million pre," Hussey said, referring to the value of the company without the proposed investments from Menlo and IDG Ventures, the firm where Kim worked.

"I can do fifty-five million pre," Sonja said.

Hussey shook his head. "It's gotta be sixty."

After a long pause, Hussey said, "I suspect you two need to call the mother ship. I'm going to step out, so you can make that call. I'll come back when you're ready."

Sonja and Kim talked for a moment before Sonja dialed the Menlo headquarters. It was late in the day, and the only one there was Mike Laufer, a young partner who specialized in health care companies. Sonja told him, "Mike, we need to get this up to sixty." Laufer's response—"Sounds good"—was all she needed.

When Hussey came back into the room, Sonja thrust out her hand and said, "We have a deal." Hussey got his $60 million pre-money valuation. Menlo would invest $5.7 million, and IDG Ventures was in for $2 million.

Within a year, F5 Labs, which changed its name to F5 Networks, went from a bright idea to a public company—having raised a relatively paltry $12 million since inception. Jeff Hussey, not yet forty, soon found himself with six hundred employees and a company valued at $2 *billion*. Menlo's investment of $5.7 million returned more than $100 million.

THERESIA

With Release in her rearview mirror, Theresia was weighing her job prospects when she got an unexpected request to do some consulting. Release founder Matthew Klein had hatched another start-up, but his first few pitches to VCs had yielded nothing. So he turned to Theresia for direction. She offered her opinions about what he needed to say and change in his pitch for Tech Planet, a start-up that would provide home office tech setup and consultancy.

After incorporating Theresia's changes, Matthew's next three meetings with VCs were a different story. Almost before he finished his pitch, the VCs asked, "Where do I sign? I want to give you money now." Meanwhile Geoff Ralston of Four11, the entrepreneur who had frantically laid extension cords across Middlefield Road to keep the power on, had sold RocketMail to Yahoo! for $92 million. It became Yahoo! Mail.

Theresia's dealings with Matthew on Tech Planet reminded her of how much she loved the phase of a company when it was just getting started, when chaos and purpose collided daily. During her time at Release, she'd also seen the important role that venture capitalists played, providing everything from money to expertise. What she hadn't known before Release was how VCs secured later rounds of funding. The early-round Series A VCs—those investors who came in after "angels," or friends and family—would connect with VCs at other firms for subsequent funding rounds, such as Series B funding, Series C, D, and so on. Series A marked the first round of financing from a VC, and the first time a company offered stock to outside investors. Subsequent rounds reflected a company maturing and scaling. The calls by early investors to later-round VCs made all the difference.

Theresia had several friends who were VCs, including Greg Sands, who had left Netscape and joined Sutter Hill Ventures. A business school friend, Robin Richards Donohoe, had gone to work for the well-known VC Bill Draper, helping him launch the world's first venture fund in India. Donohoe was now a partner and loved her job. Jennifer Fonstad, who had been a year ahead of Theresia at Bain in Boston, had become a partner at Draper Fisher Jurvetson a year after joining. (Steve Jurvetson and Tim Draper had backed Release.) Fonstad had told Theresia stories of working on Mitt Romney's 1994 Senate campaign against incumbent Ted Kennedy. Fonstad had traveled with Romney, a founder of Bain Capital, and listened to his stories about building businesses from the ground up, including Staples, where he had been the first investor. Romney had stocked shelves in the first Staples store. Fonstad hadn't realized the hands-on role venture capitalists played. When the political campaign ended and Jennifer was headed to Harvard Business School, she decided she liked the idea of taking something that was fundamentally undefined and building definition around it.

As soon as Theresia began going on job interviews, she got multiple offers. Several came from start-ups, and several more from venture capital firms. Greg Sands, who had been an angel investor in Release, told her that Accel Partners was looking to hire a new associate who had engineering and Internet experience. Bruce Golden, a partner at Accel, called her references, including Matthew Klein. When asked what distinguished Theresia, Klein told Golden, "Let me begin by stating that I'm about to be effusive. Theresia is the most outstanding person I've met in my whole life." Accel partner Jim Breyer, a heavy hitter in the industry, was impressed that Theresia was multidisciplinary, understood technology, and had start-up experience. Breyer also found her "ethical and possessing an intellectual curiosity that was critical to success as a VC." Breyer, Golden, and the Accel partners concluded that Theresia was "wicked smart, driven, analytical, had a good work ethic, and could play well with others." The question remained, though, for the Accel partners: Could she parse through hundreds or thousands of investment opportunities and pick the ones that would be big moneymakers? That was the unknown.

In the end, Theresia joined Accel as a partner-track associate. She was eager to work with several start-ups rather than just one, and to learn from industry leaders Breyer and Peter Wagner and from Accel founders Arthur Patterson and Jim Swartz. Before her first day at Accel, she went shopping at Banana Republic for the VC uniform of the day: khaki pants and a light-blue button-down shirt. The look was terrible for women, but she had a secret source of solace—designer shoes. She loved combing through sales racks at Neiman Marcus for discounted designer heels. She would wear the uniform, but she wouldn't give up her shoes.

Theresia's job as an associate at Accel was to manage and create "deal flow." Every day partners forwarded dozens of e-mails to her, most without a single word of explanation. She had to read down the e-mail chain and figure out what was being proposed and whether it was worth a partner's time. It was a heady blend of triage—where she could not afford to miss something critical—and methodical analysis and research. At the same time that she was assessing which ideas had merit, she was encouraged to find her own deals and develop her own areas of specialty.

Shortly after starting, Theresia was told of a meeting coming up with two Stanford PhD students who had created a new algorithm for search. It was her job to meet the students, Sergey Brin and Larry Page, and visit with them before they pitched the partners on their new page-rank algorithm. It was called Google.

SONJA

Sonja treated Kim Davis, her partner in the F5 deal, to a trip to the Four Seasons on the Big Island to celebrate their lucrative triumph. It was Sonja's way of thanking her friend for showing her the deal. The women, both single, both in their early thirties, spent their days lounging by the pool, watching waves, and snorkeling in the nearby lagoon. They talked about work, men, family, and money, and why women had a hard time admitting they *liked* money. Men could be unapologetic in their pursuit of it, while women were steered away from the relentless drive for wealth. Men used philanthropy to advance themselves, while women used it to advance others. In other words, money was complex for women, one more thing to skillfully navigate.

"Women have to be careful about money," Sonja said. "If a woman marries a man who is wealthy, she is a gold digger. If a woman works to make a lot of money, that doesn't look good. I like money because it gives me options: to be single, to be married, to help my parents and others. My mother's stepfather wouldn't let her go to college. She didn't have options."

Sonja added with a smile, "I may only have the chance to get rich once. I'm not going to blow it."

Kim had similar discussions with other friends and role models, including the early VC Ann Winblad and entrepreneur-turned-VC Heidi Roizen, both well known and respected in the Valley. Heidi had shared advice on money and on dealing with oafish comments and bad be-havior by men in the industry. As co-founder of the software company T/Maker, Heidi had gone to dinner with the senior VP of a major PC manufacturer, to sign a deal critical to her start-up. Just as wine was served and toasts were made to their great future together, the man told Heidi he had also brought a present for her, but it was under the table. He took her hand and placed it on his unzipped pants. Heidi left the restaurant, the deal fell apart, and she went on to find other backers—notably Ann Winblad.

"The tables of power are always filled with white men, but I've latched on to amazing women," Kim said, raising her drink.

Sonja had been fortunate enough to have an important female role model, too. At TA Associates in Boston, she'd learned the trade from Jacqui Morby, one of the first women to make partner at a venture capital firm. Morby worked out of TA's Pittsburgh office and came to Boston every few weeks, wearing pastel-hued suits that reminded Sonja of Easter eggs. Morby and Sonja would hop on planes to visit interesting companies and meet executives and entrepreneurs. Morby taught her the importance of visiting good companies even if they weren't raising money. She believed the venture business was more about the people than the transaction. Morby had been the first at TA to find companies with potential by studying computer magazines, trade publications, and Dun & Bradstreet reports, cold-calling the companies, and refusing to take no for no. It was Morby, too, who had told Sonja to go after a deal "like a bird dog," the phrase that had echoed in Sonja's mind when she tracked down John McAfee in his car.

Sonja told Kim the bits and pieces she'd learned about Morby dur-ing their business trips together. Morby had been married to a success-ful banker and had two children when she decided she wanted more out of life. At forty, Morby enrolled in the all-women's Simmons Col-lege Management School, taking classes at night. A few months shy of graduation, she interviewed with an investment banker from Paine Webber in Boston for an unpaid internship. After a lengthy talk that seemed to be going well, the banker leaned in and told Morby, "We think you'd be great, but you have two small children." Before Morby could reply, he went on, "Your husband works at the Bank of Boston. He needs you at home." The banker added, "My wife couldn't do this."

Kim rolled her eyes at the story.

Morby had started at TA Associates as an unpaid intern in the late 1970s, when *The Mary Tyler Moore Show* had caused a stir with its touching depiction of a single, independent, and empowered working woman. Morby made partner in 1982, a year before MJ Elmore. She met with the young Bill Gates and Larry Ellison and landed deals with the earliest software companies, including Digital Research, McCormack & Dodge, Capex, and many more, at a time when investing in software was considered risky.

Sonja told Kim a story Morby had shared with her about meeting Microsoft co-founder Bill Gates. Arriving at Microsoft in Seattle for an early-morning meeting, Morby was told that Gates was on his way from the airport. She studied the office environment of the companies she visited—and Microsoft HQ was a mess. Computer boxes and empty Coke cans were scattered about. After an hour of waiting, she finally spotted a harried young man with large glasses. He was shaking his head and talking to himself, clearly furious about something. It was Gates, she realized.

He had just flown in from Texas, where his meeting "couldn't have been worse." He'd lost a deal he thought he'd won, got no sleep, and had been pulled over for speeding on his way to the office. He apparently was fuming that Tandy—one of the earliest personal computer manufacturers, marketed through Radio Shack—had made a deal with a company *other than Microsoft*. Tandy needed a software programming language called a COBOL (Common Business-Oriented Language) compiler for its TR-1000 computer. Gates had been working to convince Tandy to contract with Microsoft, even though he didn't yet have the compiler they needed.

Morby asked Gates about his operating system, MS-DOS, due to be released in August. Gates said he had a local guy, Tim Patterson, working on the programming. It would allow users to open, navigate, and manipulate files on their computer. The discussion continued for another hour, and the two agreed to meet again within two weeks.

Morby didn't get the Microsoft deal, but after her meeting with Gates, she met with computer scientist Gary Kildall, who had written the very first operating system, CP/M (for Control Program/Monitor), to connect computers. Kildall wrote the software from scratch, beating Microsoft to the market. His company was Digital Research, Inc.

Sonja continued, "Jacqui and Kildall actually sat in a restaurant called the Buckhorn Barbecue near the Nut Tree complex, and Kildall grabbed a bunch of napkins and began to draw a diagram." Kildall showed Morby how the operating system, which he had written and controlled, was the basis for everything. "Applications fit around that," he said as he added to his diagram. He kept drawing as he talked, explaining the three basic layers of any computer system: the hardware, the operating system, and the applications (which at this time were not yet bundled together). He told Morby, "He who controls the operating system controls the computer industry." Morby became an investor in Digital Research, Sonja said, and watched a battle escalate between Digital Research and Microsoft—which Microsoft won.

As Sonja admired the gorgeous Hawaiian sunset, she felt, more than ever, that she was following in Morby's footsteps. Kim was inspired by Morby's story and admired Sonja's work ethic and her hustle. For her part, Kim had called two other venture capitalists the day she called Sonja to tell her about F5. One had been Geoff Yang, the partner at IVP with Reid Dennis and MJ.

"You moved faster," Kim told Sonja. When Sonja and Kim returned to Silicon Valley, there would be two women on the board of the multibillion-dollar F5.

As their extended weekend getaway in Hawaii wound down, the women went shopping. They had a tradition of buying "deal baubles" to commemorate a great deal. As they surveyed the jewelry in the hotel shop, a saleslady looked at them dismissively and asked, "Do you work at the hotel?"

Big mistake, Kim thought of the woman's snub. Obviously, the saleslady wasn't aware of all the baubles the two women could have bought there. Sonja and Kim exited the shop, arm in arm.

PART
THREE

The Outsiders Inside

1997–2000

MAGDALENA

Wearing dark sunglasses and a Hermès head scarf, Magdalena eased her 1958 red convertible Corvette into the parking lot of US Venture Partners. The Corvette had been a gift from her husband when she finally became an American citizen. The Corvette was quintessentially American, and a reminder that dreams do come true, even for a Turkish girl who had been an outsider in her own homeland.

The late 1990s had been very good to Magdalena. CyberCash had gone public in 1996, and she had recently built and quickly sold another company, MarketPay, that offered embedded point-of-sale software. In just a few years, she had evolved from an online shopping evangelist—with more detractors than followers—to an e-commerce guru. In 1997 *Red Herring* magazine named her Entrepreneur of the Year.

Now, as one of the hottest new business figures in Silicon Valley, Magdalena was being courted by top venture capital firms, including USVP, to make the leap from serial entrepreneur to financier. It was a far cry from her days of struggling to raise funds on Sand Hill Road.

Magdalena was greeted inside by one of USVP's partners, Steve Krausz. USVP had wanted to invest in MarketPay when MarketPay was little more than a prototype, but the acquisition offers had come in quickly.

"Come join us," Krausz said to Magdalena. USVP had been founded in 1981 by venture pioneer Bill Bowes, a friend and contemporary of Reid Dennis, and the founding shareholder of Amgen.

Magdalena removed her glasses and scarf and took a seat. She wore a dark suit and a pink Gap T-shirt. "I know you invest money, but I don't really have any idea what a venture partner does," she said. She had

turned down VC funding for CyberCash, opting instead to forge part-
nerships with existing companies, including Intel and Cisco. (Her stock
in UUNet had also paid off when MFS Communications acquired the
company for more than $2 billion.)

Krausz, who like Magdalena had a degree in electrical engineering from Stanford, talked about the role of a venture capitalist as both
coach and mentor to CEOs; as someone who built great leadership out
of untested mettle; and who helped disrupt the status quo by using new
technologies to solve old problems. He talked about building companies
that could make the world a better place.

As an entrepreneur, Magdalena had seen how the scale of power was
tipped heavily to the VC side. She looked at the job of a VC as fairly
cushy, given that VCs invested other people's money. She wasn't sure she
was ready to shake her entrepreneurial fervor: "At some point, I'd like
to start another company."

Then in her typical no-nonsense manner, she said, "The job is really
all about making money, right? That's the goal. No one is paying you
to change the world. Your duty is to return more money to the limited
partners than they gave you."

Krausz smiled. Magdalena was right, he said, but so was he. Yes,
being a venture capitalist was about figuring out how to earn consistently superior returns from investments in inherently risky and ado-
lescent business ventures. But it was also about improving the world at
large, and that's what made it worthwhile.

After meeting with the rest of the USVP team, Magdalena returned
home to weigh the pros and cons. She considered other offers from
start-ups and venture firms, but in the end she decided to give USVP a
try. It felt like a good fit.

Once on the job, she sat in on meetings and talked about the business
with partners, assistants, and entrepreneurs. She quickly bonded with
USVP's general partner and guiding force, Irwin Federman, finding him
more Jewish rabbi than Silicon Valley VC. (Bill Bowes had stepped away
from day-to-day operations of USVP but remained a vital figurehead.)

Federman, tall, with a stentorian voice, was full of big-hearted emotions and the pursuit of eternal truths. He wore a suit and tie, was punctual to the second, opened doors for others, and always picked up the tab. Magdalena felt she could learn the business from this wonderful man.

Magdalena was immediately fascinated by the behind-the-scenes drama of partners' meetings. Though big-hearted, Federman could reduce a company's pitch or a partner's idea to rubble. There were six general partners, each with a distinct personality and way of presenting and arguing. *This is just like a dysfunctional family, only with a ton of money,* she said to herself, looking around the table. There was the heir apparent, the black sheep, the taciturn intellect, and the red-faced partner who had to have his way.

On the flip side, she was dazzled by the intellectual discourse. *This is a debate society!* she realized. The debates were a beautiful mix of art and science, emotion and intellect. As in electrical engineering, there was logic and there were blind spots. The partners had to do their homework, present ideas convincingly, defend every number and every bold statement, and win the rest of the group over. The VCs learned something new every week about fields as varied as retail, biotech, cybersecurity, and more.

One day early in her VC tenure, about halfway through an afternoon of meetings, Magdalena looked around the conference room in search of food. Popping out of her seat, she headed to the side buffet and filled a plate with cookies, then proceeded to go around the table, offering a cookie to each partner. She did the same thing with the coffee. The room went silent. Even the assistants took notice from the other side of the glass. Magdalena knew that many professional women avoided doing anything too "secretarial." But for Magdalena, pouring coffee and offering food was simply being polite; it was how she had been raised.

She knew she could be the girl from Istanbul with the frilly dresses and white gloves, and her father's daughter who loved hammers and nails more than any toy or any doll. No one was going to be confused by what she had to offer.

THERESIA

Theresia was back at a foosball table, ready to crush the competition. She was a bit rusty from her college days at Brown. But as she focused on the table, her competitive instincts kicked in. She still had it: *The spin shot! That surprise bank shot!* Just as she was going in for the kill, she stopped herself.

She looked across the foosball table at her dark-haired opponent and silently cursed herself: *What the f— am I doing?* Sergey Brin was no inebriated frat boy or blue-collar hustler. The Russian-born math whiz and Stanford computer science graduate had come to Accel Partners to talk about his start-up, Google. His co-founder, Larry Page, the more introverted of the two, watched from the sidelines. Theresia wondered if Larry wasn't talking to her because she was an associate, not a partner.

Theresia cooled it with the spin shot, and as much as it pained her, she curtailed her signature middle-rod pull shot. Her only job at the moment, as an associate, was to entertain the Google guys and develop a rapport with them. Everyone in the Valley wanted a piece of Google. In this case, playing to win meant making sure she lost.

It was the spring of 1999. Brin and Page, who had met as PhD students in the computer science department at Stanford a few years before, had reportedly come up with an improved way to search the Web. The field was crowded with search companies, including Excite, Yahoo!, WebCrawler, Lycos, Ask Jeeves, and Alta Vista. But what had caught the attention of Accel partners Mitch Kapor and Jim Breyer were the well-placed endorsements of Google search by its early adopters, the engineers and software developers. "This thing Google is better than anything else," Kapor and Breyer were told. "This is all we're using."

Google was growing fast—getting more than ten thousand searches a day. Brin and Page had moved the start-up from their Stanford dorm room to a garage rented to them by Susan Wojcicki, then to a small office above a bike shop here on University Avenue in Palo Alto. Theresia kept an eye on the time, aware that partners' meetings often went late.

Accel occupied floors two through four of the building at 428 University Avenue, about three miles from the VCs of Sand Hill Road. They were on the second floor, with the foosball and Ping-Pong tables, a kitchenette, and a small patio overlooking the parking lot, which they shared with Union Bank. (Accel administrative assistants liked to track the Ferraris and Porsches parked in their visitor spots five and six.) The second floor also served as Accel's "incubator," where a handful of promising entrepreneurs were given free office space to hatch or develop new business ideas. The third- and fourth-floor offices were for venture partners and general partners, including Jim Breyer, Peter Wagner, Bud Colligan, Bruce Golden, and Mitch Kapor. Co-founders Arthur Patterson and Jim Swartz had offices on the fourth floor, where all the major deals took place. There the carpets and walls were white, the wood was a whitish blond, doors were of glass, paintings were modernist washes of color, and the tables were white marble.

Theresia, thirty-one, did her best to engage Brin and Page, who were five years younger, by talking about Stanford, start-ups, and Accel, founded in 1983 by Patterson and Swartz. Brin and Page, in jeans and T-shirts, were friendly but restless, reminding her of the many socially awkward, burrito-eating, computer-loving grad students she'd met at Stanford.

She had done research on the duo. Sergey was known to have a wild sense of humor, an obsession with exercise, and a way with women. He used to Rollerblade around Stanford's computer science building, and now he played full-contact roller hockey with Google employees at lunch. Larry communicated more through gestures and body language, unsettling employees with a raised eyebrow, a lowered tone, or lack of eye contact. The two were known to fight like brothers, but they were more similar than dissimilar. Both were the sons of high-powered intellects steeped in computer science. Sergey was interested in data mining—analyzing large amounts of data to discover patterns—and Larry was interested in downloading the Web, which Sergey considered the most interesting data to be mined.

Theresia had also done her homework on Google. Brin and Page had originally called their company BackRub. The process of ranking Web pages based on how many other Web pages linked back to them was called PageRank. But neither name lasted long. They decided that a *googol,* the number one with a hundred zeroes after it, better reflected the amount of data they were trying to sift through. From googol, they landed on the more user-friendly Google.

Brin and Page, while working on their doctorates, had taken the Web crawler they developed and figured out how to calculate the tendency of Web-browsing people to congregate on specific pages, returning *the* most relevant page rather than *a* relevant page. Other search engines defined the concept of relevance as the relationship between a page and a query. The page would be relevant to the question if the terms of the query appeared more often than average on that page. PageRank, by contrast—named after Larry Page and with a patent pending—was a property of the page itself. PageRank didn't just crawl the web; it returned the most popular things first. Theresia loved the geeky aspect of it: that the measure of the importance of Web pages was computed by solving an equation of 500 million variables and two billion terms. She knew that most other search engines, like Yahoo!, were still using humans to help build the ontologies.

Before the Google guys began making the rounds looking for financing, they had followed a well-trodden path to the offices of attorney Larry Sonsini, who had helped incorporate, build, and take public just about every major tech company, from ROLM and Apple to Netscape, Pixar, and hundreds more. Brin and Page had visited Sonsini on a Saturday in 1998 to talk about incorporating Google and raising money. They told him their goal was to "make information ubiquitous," and they discussed how much money Google would need to grow. The three concluded that Google would need about $20 million. Sonsini made suggestions on which venture firms to visit.

Years earlier Brin and Page had considered selling their technology to a search company for less than $1 million. But with the exception of Excite, no one had been interested in their approach to search.

When the time came, Theresia led them to the fourth floor, where pitch meetings were held. Accel had had its share of hits, including RealNetworks, Macromedia, Portal Software, Polycom, and UUNet. Returns in 1999 were more than one hundred times investments. But Accel didn't have a superstar start-up in its portfolio—Apple, Netscape, Yahoo!, or Amazon, the logos to end all logos. Jim Breyer likened the unicorn hunt to the art world, where a curator at the San Francisco Museum of Modern Art said, "Of every ten artists I pick, nine of them will end up failing. But that one out of ten becomes the next Picasso." The Accel team hoped Google would be their Picasso.

After a few minutes of chitchat outside Accel's fourth-floor conference room, Theresia handed Brin and Page over to the partners. The door closed, and Theresia took a seat at the back of the room. She had been at Accel for less than six months and was sprinting to land a seat at that white marble table. It wasn't so different from her teenage days flipping burgers at the back of Burger King and setting her sights on working the cash register.

She was doing deal flow triage for the partners, meeting with entrepreneurs offline to learn more, and calling on her contacts at Stanford and from her days at Release Software to see who was doing something interesting. She had zeroed in on cybersecurity as an area of specialty, given what she'd already learned about encryption from her time at Release. She shadowed Arthur Patterson at board meetings for his cybersecurity companies Counterpane and Arcot Systems. She enrolled in security networking training certification classes, where she was always the only woman. She chased down her own hot deals, including Sameday, an online delivery service seed-funded by engineer-turned-entrepreneur Bill Gross of Idealab in Pasadena, and PeopleSupport, which provided outsourced Web-based customer management services to dot-coms via chat and e-mail. The company was growing fast, with more than one hundred clients and four hundred employees.

Later, after the Google meeting, Theresia had to laugh when she walked through Accel's reception area and heard a familiar request:

"Miss, can you check on our meeting time?" A decade out of college, four years at Bain, two years of graduate school, and three years at a start-up, and Theresia was still mistaken for an assistant or an intern, being asked for coffee, for directions to the bathroom, for the time of a meeting.

She had learned that being a woman could be both advantage and disadvantage. As an intern at General Motors' Harrison Radiator Division outside her hometown of Middleport, she had found that sometimes the novelty of being a woman in the all-male machine shop was a positive. Her job had been to test out a new air-conditioning compressor that didn't use Freon. Many of the men treated her like a daughter, letting her operate the simple machines and tools and moving her prototyping projects on alternative refrigerants to the front of the queue. By contrast, male interns who used the shop on their own—picking up so much as a wrench—would likely have been slapped with a grievance by the UAW labor union.

When she was a junior at Brown working as a research assistant in the scanning electron microscope lab, Theresia had encountered one of the more challenging sides of being a woman. Her research job had been to prepare silicon composite samples to be studied under a million-dollar-plus microscope. Older female students had warned her early on about a certain "handsy technician." The women of the whisper network told her, "Always wear pants, and always wear running shoes. If it gets bad, you gotta be able to bolt." They assured Theresia that the technician was otherwise harmless and backed off when rebuffed. So she wore pants and running shoes. As predicted, the technician made a move, placing his hand on her thigh. She stared him down, moved his hand away, and returned to her job. If he tried again, she would do the same thing. She wasn't going to lose her internship because of an opportunistic, middle-aged lab manager.

Theresia learned to take the good with the bad. Not long into her job at Accel, she was invited to join a panel of VCs to discuss the best parts of the Internet. She was seated onstage next to a male venture capitalist. The moderator asked him, "What are your favorite technology websites?" When he posed the question to Theresia, he said, "Tell me, Theresia, what's your favorite cooking website?" She weighed the question and told herself, *Don't be thin-skinned or bitchy.* Smiling, she answered, "You clearly don't know me, as I don't cook at all."

Theresia, surrounded all day, every day by type A guys, had adopted some of their habits. She interrupted often and spoke loudly to be heard. But she had also gleaned tips from successful women. One female executive had told her to speak up early in meetings: "If you wait too long to speak up in a meeting as a woman, you'll become invisible. It'll be too late." Bain executive Orit Gadiesh (who would go on to become chair of Bain & Co.) advised Theresia, "Don't take notes. Others will think you're there to take notes. Your memory will have to suffice." Gadiesh also shared her strategy for what to do when male clients directed questions only at other men, even those who were her junior. "I told my associates before meetings started that when that happens, they should look to me and ask what I think. Your male team can be your ally."

Theresia believed that women had to work twice as hard to convince men they were *quantitative.* If someone asked, "What's the CAC? What's the LTV? What are the margins?" she always knew the numbers on customer acquisition costs; lifetime value ratios; and profit figures as a percentage of the company's net revenues.

In the days that followed the meeting with Page and Brin, Accel put together a term sheet for Google. But Google soon announced that it had taken a $25 million round of equity funding from two firms, Kleiner Perkins Caufield & Byers and Sequoia Capital. VC stars Michael Moritz of Sequoia and John Doerr of Kleiner would join Google's board of directors. Sequoia, started by Don Valentine, had made early investments in Atari, Apple, Cisco Systems, LSI Logic, Oracle, Electronic Arts, and Yahoo! Doerr, who early in his career had made a name for himself as an engineer at Intel—working Operation Crush when MJ was there—had since coming to Kleiner backed Amazon, WebMD, Intuit, and Sun Microsystems.

Larry Page said in the funding announcement, "We are delighted to have venture capitalists of this caliber help us build the company." Brin added, "A perfect search engine will process and understand all the information in the world. That is where Google is headed." Moritz said, "Google should become the gold standard for search on the Internet. . . . The company has the power to turn Internet users everywhere into devoted and life-long Googlers."

Although no one at Accel liked to lose—and this was a biggie—the partners had too many deals in the works to mourn for long. The hunt for Picasso continued. Accel had finished raising $480 million for its Fund VII just after Theresia was hired. Remarkably, the entire fund was invested in less than ten months—a frenzied pace. In normal times, it would take two to three years to invest that much. Accel did thirty-nine new deals in eleven months, all driven by a handful of people, including Theresia.

Theresia would soon be named an investing partner, becoming the first woman with the title in the firm's seventeen-year history. Accel cofounder Arthur Patterson gave her a watch with the Accel logo, Breyer congratulated her, and she shared the news with her husband Tim, and family and friends. As usual, her mother worried she was working too hard, while her father worried she wasn't working hard enough. But Theresia knew her father was proud when she heard him tell his friends that she worked with all men.

MJ

IVP announced an in-house contest to see who at the venture capital firm could return $100 million or more on a single investment. The winner would get the car of his or her dreams, paid for by the other partners. MJ was determined to win.

Her competitive streak had been born in deprivation rather than sports. It had been nurtured in junior high, when she saw for the first time how the other half lived. When the middle school in the wealthy part of Terre Haute burned down, students who lived near the school were sent to MJ's junior high. MJ made friends with the new students and began to see their homes and way of life. She would never forget the day she was invited to drive all the way to Indianapolis just to go to lunch and see *Gone with the Wind*. MJ's family never went out to a restaurant for a single meal.

MJ was betting that the poker-playing entrepreneur Dave Stamm, founder of a company called Clarify, would get her to the IVP winner's circle. Clarify had been founded to bring customer service experiences around the world out of the Dark Ages.

Like MJ, Stamm had gone to Purdue and worked at Intel during Operation Crush. He once demonstrated a new chip he'd co-created, the 8048, to Intel honchos Andy Grove, Gordon Moore, and Les Vadász by using his own programmed game of blackjack and a lemon as a power source. The 8048 chip, which Stamm had lived and breathed for two years, became ubiquitous in appliances and keyboards.

After leaving Intel in 1980, Stamm co-founded Daisy Systems, a pioneering electronic design automation company. Vinod Khosla, who went on to co-found Sun Microsystems, was a founding team member. After Daisy merged with another company and was later acquired, Stamm began to look around for what to build next. Once he had that idea, he needed funding.

And that's how he'd first approached IVP several years earlier. Walking into the swank IVP offices, Stamm realized it had been a while since he had seen MJ. He still remembered their first encounter at Purdue, when he was a senior and she was a levelheaded freshman surrounded by goofy eighteen-year-old frat boys. At Intel, she had been a great team player, focused and smart. When Stamm entered the IVP offices, MJ was seated in the conference room with Norm Fogelsong, another IVP partner. She looked composed, as he had remembered her. Stamm, using acetate slides and a projector, explained the idea he'd landed on to help companies manage and automate interactions with current and potential customers. He said there was nothing like it on the market.

"You know when you call Maytag repair, or Microsoft, or FedEx, or any other company, and you have a problem with the product?" Stamm asked. "You get one person one day and another the next and there is no record of any prior conversation?" He looked at MJ and said, "I've solved that."

MJ thought about her own overworked washer and dryer and her own frustrating calls to customer support. Stamm was starting to get her attention. This sounded like a solution to a big and important problem. "Tell me more about your premise," she said.

Stamm explained that he had spent months in the public library, poring over company records and annual reports on microfiche (this was during the early days of Internet), looking for areas of growth within companies.

MJ thought, *Wow, he has even done market research!*

"I looked at how many people were in each department from year to year," Stamm continued. "I saw that customer service is *exploding*. Cisco, for example, is on a hiring trajectory where, if the trend continues, eighty percent of their employees will be working in customer service. That is obviously not sustainable." Stamm found similar hiring trends in customer service departments across industries.

"When you call for tech support now, you basically get nothing," Stamm said. He had seen firsthand the record keeping of customer service departments: yellow Post-its slapped on computer monitors. "Clarify software will allow a customer service agent to pull up a customer's historical sales and service information when a call comes through. It also allows a company to track when something's fixed, and to know how it was fixed. It's managing customer relations in a very efficient way."

As Stamm looked at trends within companies, he thought about the various business functions of a company: finance, engineering, marketing, sales, and customer service. He asked himself, *Do these divisions have software to help them do their job better?* The answer was yes for all except customer service, marketing, and sales.

MJ loved the idea but wanted to hear Stamm's take. "Why do *you* think this will sell?" she asked.

"Well, I have five people—five big companies—who say they will buy it," Stamm replied. "I went to five VPs of customer support who I knew from Daisy and said, 'Here's what I'm going to build. Here's what I plan to charge. If I build it, will you buy it?' The answer was universally yes."

MJ was impressed by Stamm's methodology. Entrepreneurs typically pitched the technology, not the market. Stamm had figured out the customers before writing a line of code. MJ got the names and phone numbers of the VPs of customer service.

Not long after Stamm's pitch, she invested nearly $3 million in Clarify. The start-up grew throughout the 1990s, winning a range of clients from Microsoft and Cisco to the biggest telecommunications companies. It revolutionized how companies operated. Early competitors included Vantive and Scopus. Siebel Systems had entered the domain in 1993 but with a focus on just sales. When Clarify went public in November 1995, the new category of software was given the name CRM, for Customer Relationship Management. And Clarify became the first public CRM company.

When Clarify missed a quarter and the stock plummeted overnight from around $20 to $7 a share, IVP swooped in and bought about $3 million more of Clarify shares on the public market—stabilizing the company at a critical time. In late 1997, as Clarify was being threatened by Siebel Systems, MJ helped install Tony Zingale, who had worked at Intel and Daisy Systems, as Clarify's CEO, to overhaul operations, from its products and mission statement to the executive team. MJ told Stamm, "We all want this to work. We need the strongest team possible."

She also ran interference between Zingale, a fiery Sicilian, and Stamm, who was soft-spoken and analytical. After one heated exchange, Zingale told MJ, "Dave is a brilliant engineer, but you hired me for a reason. It's my way or no way. I'm fighting Tom Siebel every day" for market share; "I'm not fighting Dave Stamm every day." Stamm eventually acknowledged that he was the idea, engineering, and start-up guy. As his company grew to more than five hundred employees, he realized he was out of his element as a manager. MJ found it refreshing to have a founder who was aware of his limitations.

Under Zingale, Clarify evolved from doing one thing—call center automation—to offering various products for customer service, including marketing, analytics, sales, and support. It became a platform of services, allowing companies to modify the interface by adding fields, tables, screens, and other tools.

By the late 1990s, Zingale and Stamm had learned to work well together, and Clarify had become a hot property. The industry was consolidating fast: PeopleSoft bought Clarify rival Vantive for $422 million; Siebel acquired Scopus for $460 million. And both PeopleSoft and Siebel tried to acquire Clarify. At one point, PeopleSoft was only days away from signing a term sheet, with a deal valued at about $1 billion.

It was only a matter of time before Clarify would cash in. And as MJ saw it, what better way to win the IVP in-house contest than to bring in a huge deal for Clarify. But there was a catch: She would have to make one of the biggest gambles of her career.

SONJA

Like just about every other VC in the Valley, Sonja was inundated with e-commerce pitches on everything from dog food delivery to furniture sales. She studied the logistics and costs of warehouses and shipping and found that few people had figured out a cost-effective approach to inventory and distribution. She invested in one e-commerce company, Bravanta, which focused on corporate gift giving, but the sales to date were underwhelming. Sonja kept asking herself, *Gosh, what's a good category?*

So when Varsha Rao and Mariam Naficy walked into the conference room of Menlo Ventures in 1999 and began their pitch for the
very first online beauty and cosmetics store, to be called Eve.com, Sonja
was intrigued. Eve had $250,000 in seed funding from investor Bill
Gross, one of the dot-com era's greatest visionaries. Rao and Naficy
had spent several months living out of suitcases while they incubated
Eve at Gross's company, Idealab, in Pasadena. Gross was convinced
that busy women would not only buy cosmetics, fragrances, and skin
care products online—they were small enough purchases—but would
also replenish their beauty products online out of brand loyalty and
expediency.

Sonja liked the small packaging and relatively inexpensive prices in
cosmetics, coupled with the high markup. She especially loved the re-
plenishment model, versus a onetime-purchase model. The company's
initial target customers were women ages twenty-five to thirty-four;
the potential market was huge. The dominant e-commerce markets of
the moment were books and electronics. Sonja saw Eve as a new category leader. She had attended the road show for Amazon's IPO, held
in 1997 at the Stanford Barn. She didn't buy into the IPO but thought
books were a good market, given that consumers didn't need to handle
a book before buying it. She watched another online store, eBay, raise
$5 million from Benchmark Capital that same year. When eBay went
public in 1998, Benchmark's shares were worth $417 million.

Sonja was also impressed with the credentials of Rao and Naficy.
Rao had matriculated through public schools outside Boston, earned
undergraduate degrees in math and economics from the University of
Pennsylvania, worked for two years at Wasserstein Perella, an investment bank in New York, and gone to work for McKinsey & Co. after
graduating from Harvard Business School. Naficy, who grew up in
the Middle East and Africa, had been an investment banker at Goldman Sachs and earned her MBA at Stanford, graduating in 1998. The
women had entered the start-up world after seeing that women faced
a slow slog up the corporate ladder. They wanted to build a business

where they would be in charge. They looked at the consumer market as gender neutral: Your product was good or it was not.

Naficy caught the start-up bug while at Stanford; Rao became interested in the Internet at McKinsey, where she worked with clients on new digital marketing. The two women were roommates after college, bonding over the Sunday *New York Times,* Bagel Bites, and similar immigrant backstories. Rao's parents had immigrated to the United States from southern India—her father from Madras and her mother from Bangalore. Her mother had a master's degree in physics and her father was an accomplished chemist. Naficy's parents were Iranian and Chinese and had fled Iran for America in 1979, when the shah was toppled from power, when Mariam was nine.

Naficy's first idea for a start-up was a marketing automation software company. Rao wasn't impressed. "That sounds interesting but kinda boring," she said. "I've heard that something like ninety percent of start-ups fail. We should do something where *we* are the target audience, where it's fun and interesting, and where our unique point of view can help us."

Which is how Eve came into being—and how Rao and Naficy found themselves in the Menlo conference room, with Sonja and her fellow VCs awaiting their pitch. The two women told the group that they had secured online distribution agreements with a range of high-end brands, from Versace, Bvlgari, Calvin Klein, and Elizabeth Arden to Urban Decay, Club Monaco, and Hard Candy. They had hired industry leaders, including former *Glamour* beauty director Charla Krupp, to provide an editorial point of view on must-have products for women. They had also picked up the do's and don'ts of deal making: When visiting executives at Chanel, for instance, they made sure to wear only Chanel makeup and nail polish. They changed products with each company meeting.

As Naficy spoke about the $7 billion U.S. market for prestige makeup and high-end brands, Rao observed Sonja and her fellow partners. Naficy knew from earlier pitches that most men didn't understand why women would buy and replenish cosmetics and skin care online. The concept had no intuitive connection. Bankers and VCs told them, "Women don't shop online."

When it was Rao's turn to speak, Naficy had her own chance to survey the room. She had learned two things in the start-up world: She was going to be told no every day, and cognitive biases shaped how decisions were made. Ninety-four percent of VC investing partners were men, and 98 percent of the start-ups that got funded were founded by men. Similarity bias—the heuristic tendency to be comfortable with those like oneself—was implicit. Naficy, who had studied heuristics and animal behavior in college, was certain of one thing: People who look like you are more likely to protect you from being eaten.

When their pitch was over, and it was time for questions, the men of Menlo turned in unison to look at Sonja: *What does Sonja think?*

Sonja, although she still needed to do her due diligence, smiled and said, "I love it." Menlo made its first investment of $1.5 million in Eve, with Charter Ventures also investing $1.5 million. With this cash, Eve was valued at $9.5 million.

A few months after Sonja made her investment and took a board seat on Eve, her belief in the company was validated—though in a strange way. It started while she and a girlfriend were sipping wine and watching television. Barbara Walters was grilling Monica Lewinsky in her trademark caring-castigating way.

A few weeks earlier President Bill Clinton had been acquitted of perjury and obstruction of justice charges for lying about his Oval Office tryst with Lewinsky when she was a twenty-two-year-old White House intern. "Monica, you have been described as a bimbo, a stalker, a seductress," Walters began her interview.

Sonja cringed throughout the two-hour *20-20* special. "Monica was left to twist in the wind," Sonja told her friend. "It's an abuse of power, a he-said she-said, and the he-said typically wins."

But the interview, hyped as the biggest TV event since the "Who Shot J.R.?" episode of the popular 1980s series *Dallas,* had unexpected consequences. Suddenly, women who had largely lambasted Lewinsky for her behavior wanted the *lipstick* that Lewinsky wore in the TV interview. Stores across the United States sold out of the lipstick—Glaze by Club Monaco. Women clamored to be put on long wait-lists to buy the berry-hued product.

Only one online site had the rights to sell Glaze: Eve. In short order, Eve became one of the top ten e-commerce sites.

As Naficy and Rao saw it, lipstick was more than lipstick. Red lipstick was what suffragettes had worn when they took to the streets to fight for the vote; it was what female workers wore during World War II, when red hues were given labels such as "Fighting Red," "Patriot Red!" and "Grenadier Red!" It was what Rosie the Riveter wore along with her red bandanna, overalls, and bulging biceps. It was beauty and defiance in a tube.

More venture funding flowed to Eve. Naficy and Rao staffed up and took out full-page ads in newspapers and magazines. They were invited by *Vogue* magazine to a party for the release of photographer Annie Leibovitz's book *Women,* which featured portraits of famous women, including Hillary Clinton, and anonymous women, from coal miners to engineers. Leibovitz's exhibit at the Corcoran Gallery in Washington would be followed by a small party at the White House, with President Clinton and the first lady in attendance.

At the White House, Naficy and Rao listened to President Clinton give an eloquent speech on the power of women, with Hillary at his side. It was as if "Monicagate"—as some called the impeachment scandal and presidential misconduct—had never happened. Needless to say, no one said a word about Lewinsky or her plum-hued lips.

Sonja believed that Monica Lewinsky had been largely mistreated by the press and in the public eye. But regardless, the wildly successful ride of Eve had reinforced Sonja's belief that beauty had a place among bits and bytes.

MAGDALENA

As Magdalena became more familiar with her job as a venture capitalist, she came to expect certain things. Men would far outnumber women in meetings. Some of her ideas would get shredded by the Rabbi of USVP. Competition for deals was fierce, and elbows were sharp. Her friends asked her, "How did a nice girl from Turkey end up in venture capital?"

When she first started as a VC, Magdalena had made the mistake of thinking like an entrepreneur. In those early meetings, she acted like one entrepreneur helping another, trying to solve problems from the inside rather than present ideas and solutions from the outside. With time, she realized her role was really adviser and coach, as Steve Krausz had described. She wasn't the cowboy anymore; she was his trusted sidekick.

Even in this time of a surging NASDAQ and Internet mania, Magdalena focused on nuts-and-bolts companies rather than dot-com start-ups. She invested in what she knew: Internet infrastructure and security. One of her first investments was made in a company that provided security services in e-commerce, business, and government applications.

Magdalena regularly met with the founders and engineers, including a cryptographer and computer scientist. The company's leaders included an Arab from the Middle East and an American Jew. The men appeared to get along beautifully, prompting Magdalena to call the start-up the "Middle East Peace Company." But one day, as the men talked in Magdalena's office about seemingly routine business matters, voices rose, and the two founders suddenly stood chest to chest. Magdalena moved instinctively toward them. Out of the blue, the Jewish engineer threw a punch at the Arab. He missed—and hit Magdalena smack in the eye.

No one moved. Magdalena forced a weak smile and shook her head. She was seeing stars but remained preternaturally calm.

"I'm okay, really," she said, slowly sitting down. She did enough scolding of her boys, ages ten and eight, at home; she didn't expect to have to reprimand grown men at work. The men stood awkwardly and somewhat defiantly until Magdalena made them shake hands. "Look each other in the eye when you do it," she said, sounding very much like a mom. Finally, with the appearance of calm, Magdalena declared the peace company reopened for business—albeit with a shaky accord.

After the men left, Magdalena sat at her desk and checked her eye in her compact mirror. She was going to have a shiner. While she loved men generally, she really had to wonder about them at times.

When she traveled with her partners on business, she packed few clothes but several Hermès scarves. When she changed her scarf for dinner, her partners were sure she had changed her whole outfit. One day she returned to the office after getting a haircut and blow dry, and a partner didn't recognize her. Maybe now, she told herself, the men wouldn't notice that she had a black eye.

Magdalena put the fisticuffs incident behind her and focused, as always, on what came next. She soon headed to her first off-site event with the men of USVP. They traveled to beautiful coastal Monterey, only to spend long days in air-conditioned conference rooms with the shutters closed, as they brainstormed over which market segments to concentrate on next, how to be a better venture firm, and how to spot trends before competitors.

After another long day, the group left the hotel to head to dinner. As they walked together, Magdalena tuned in to the men's chatter.

"I bet Irwin got an erection watching the show!" one young partner said about USVP honcho Federman, who had recently seen a musical with sexy tango-style dancing.

The ribbing continued until it dawned on the men that Magdalena was walking beside them.

"Oh, jeez, I can't say that anymore," the partner said sheepishly. "We have a woman here now!"

All eyes settled on Magdalena.

"Listen," she began, "you should say whatever you feel like saying. Humans are mammals. Erection is part of our biology. That's the reality of humankind and I'm not offended by it."

She was genuinely unfazed. Talk about sex and human anatomy

didn't bother her. She knew few American idioms and deciphered language literally, like Spock from *Star Trek*. When she was punched in the eye that day in her office, she wanted to reply just as Spock had done when the *Enterprise* hit turbulence and tossed crew members around the cabin. Asked what had happened to him, Spock replied, "The occipital area of my head seems to have impacted with the arm of my chair."

At the same time, though, she drew the line on the topic of equal pay for equal work. Not long after the off-site meeting in Monterey, Magdalena, who had been working under the title of "venture partner," was invited to become a "general partner," which gave her more authority, responsibility, and "carry," or "incentive allocation" based on profits. General partners shared in the upside of profits on investments. The limited partners got their share, and what was left would be allocated to the partners based on a combination of track record, current performance, seniority, and potential. The serving size of each slice of pie was a closely guarded industry secret, often even within a firm.

Irwin Federman offered Magdalena 6 percent of the carry. She did the math based on the number of partners at USVP and figured equal carry would be roughly 15 percent. She didn't expect to have the same profit percentage as the Rabbi or veteran partner Steve Krausz, who had joined USVP in 1985, but 6 percent was insultingly small, and not reflective of the value she was adding.

"I'm honored by the offer," she told Federman, "but the numbers don't work for me." She smiled and walked out. She was perfectly fine being a venture partner. She had been in enough negotiations to know that Federman could tell she wasn't bluffing.

Later that afternoon, Federman came into her office and closed the door. The firm was willing to up the offer. She would start at 8 percent carry. She smiled at the Rabbi and said she would love to join the ranks of the general partners.

Magdalena hadn't objected to the 6 percent out of greed. As she often said, "I made my money in Silicon Valley, and I'm willing to lose it in Silicon Valley." But she wanted what was fair.

The following Friday, Magdalena walked into the all-glass conference room as a general partner for the first time. She hadn't expected any recognition or fanfare, but she was touched by the outpouring of support from the all-female administrative staff.

Magdalena had startled the assistants when she served coffee and cookies to the partners. She had impressed them by hiring smart young women as assistants, telling them, "This job is a stepping-stone. I don't want you to do this as your career." She had changed the rules by bringing her assistants into meetings with her. When she was told that that wasn't done, she replied, "They're my assistants. I can do anything I want. That includes bringing them to meetings. And by the way, you should do the same." And when she learned that only partners were being invited to a birthday party being thrown for USVP founder Bill Bowes, she protested, saying the assistants worked harder than most and had to be included. No one seemed to be listening to her, so she said, "I'm not going unless they're included." In the end, everyone was invited.

So when Magdalena took a seat at her first meeting of the general partners, the assistants silently cheered. Her win was their win.

THERESIA

Shortly after Theresia made partner at Accel, the firm hosted its quarterly off-site "team building" event. Accel co-founder Arthur Patterson had adopted the Louis Pasteur quote "Chance favors the prepared mind"; he liked to gather the team to talk trends coming down the pipeline. Partners from Accel's other offices flew in for the off-site, held in the Napa Valley north of San Francisco. Patterson told one and all, "The more you engage socially together, the more it helps you work together in business. You have that much more knowledge and respect for one another. Personal interaction has to underlie professional cooperation." An important part of the bonding involved a "fun and friendly" competition.

So on a gorgeous early-spring day, Theresia gathered her things and headed out onto the field near Yountville for a game of football. She tucked her shirt into her shorts and wrapped the three-flag belt around her waist. Her assistant, Angela Azem, watched from the sidelines. She forced a smile and gave a thumbs-up. Angela had seen "fun and friendly" before at Accel. She feared Theresia had no idea what was coming.

Theresia was on a team with all guys, including the silver-haired Patterson and Jim Goetz, an engineer and entrepreneur who had recently joined Accel as a partner. There were six players on each team, with five allowed on the field at a time. Patterson came from a successful New York family; his father, Ellmore Patterson, had been chairman and chief executive of J.P. Morgan & Company. Arthur had attended Harvard, where he played on the varsity football team. So had Jim Swartz, two years ahead of him. Swartz now headed up the other team.

It took about two plays for Theresia to realize that fun and friendly were not part of the equation. The flags, which suggested fun and games, were a bait and switch for contact and blocking. Theresia alternated between playing running back and receiver on offense, and cornerback and free safety on defense. But when Jim Goetz saw the way she could throw the ball, he gave her a turn as quarterback, telling her, "You throw and catch better than half the guys out here!" Theresia had learned how to throw a spiral in high school, practicing with a player who became a starter for West Point.

Team Patterson took the early lead. When Theresia threw a pass to Patterson, Goetz ran to block, and somehow the men collided head to head. In the heat of another play, Theresia was elbowed hard in the stomach. Angela cringed from the sidelines. When Theresia brushed it off, Angela whispered, "Badass."

A few minutes later Theresia called a timeout. Bruce Golden, on Swartz's team, had pulled a hamstring, and Patterson was bleeding from his ear. Theresia told Patterson, "This isn't fine." She spotted a girls' team playing soccer nearby and ran over to see if they had a first aid kit. She insisted on patching Patterson up.

As the game continued, Team Patterson was ahead by a touchdown.

Team Swartz had the ball, with time running out on the clock. In the closing seconds, the Swartz team quarterback threw a Hail Mary pass that was caught for a touchdown. His team cheered as if they'd won the Super Bowl.

Patterson, his ear bandaged, jumped around on the field yelling, "Trick play! Swartz came in off the bench! They had an extra player!" Team Swartz had had too many players on the field. A penalty was called, and Team Patterson walked away battered and bleeding but victorious.

Other companies used cook-offs, scavenger hunts, or board games to bond. But in the world of venture, testosterone ruled.

Back in San Carlos, Theresia, feeling a little bruised and battered, stepped into a role as a different kind of team player. Her husband, Tim Ranzetta, had left his job in Boston and returned to Silicon Valley in 1999. They lived for a year in a small cottage behind a house in San Carlos, then bought their own home. Tim now co-owned a paper shredding company in Salt Lake City and commuted every week. He picked up paper for shredding from corporate clients and then resold the shredded paper. Theresia lovingly called him her "white-collar trash collector."

As Theresia landed bigger deals and started making more serious money, the dynamics of their marriage shifted. She had far surpassed her college dream of moving to Silicon Valley and earning six figures. Tensions surfaced between Theresia and Tim without either of them discussing why. Tim was now managing his money *and* Theresia's money. It was the only arrangement Theresia knew. It was what married couples did.

But Theresia got tired of Tim criticizing her for her "retail therapy"— those occasional shopping trips to Neiman Marcus to find a gorgeous pair of shoes on the sales rack. So she negotiated with him: In the future, she would manage 10 percent of her bonus, putting the money into her own account, to be used as she wanted. To avoid arguments, she took to waiting until he was out of the house to spirit bags of new shoes from the trunk of her car into her closet.

MJ

MJ, who shepherded Clarify through its ups and downs, had seen the company revolutionize the customer service industry, just as Dave Stamm had predicted. Then she heard news that was both exhilarating and unnerving.

The networking equipment giant Nortel, which built the optical networks for the Internet, had made an astounding offer to buy Clarify: an exchange ratio of 1.3 Nortel shares for every Clarify share, a lucrative arrangement that put the Nortel offer at about $1.5 billion. As Nortel executives said, "We own the pipes, and we want to own what runs through the pipes."

But in a move that rattled MJ, the Clarify board, and CEO Tony Zingale, founder Dave Stamm insisted that the deal must be based on what Nortel's stock was worth *when the deal closed,* which could take six months.

MJ said, "What if it drops by half?"

"What if it doubles?" Stamm replied.

MJ and the board suggested that they put a collar on the deal to hedge against possible losses. The board wanted a 10 percent collar up or down: If Nortel's stock rose by 10 percent, the deal would be worth $1.6 billion. If it lost 10 percent, it would be worth $1.4 billion.

"No way to a collar," Stamm insisted. "The tech market is on fire. I don't want to put a collar on this. Whatever the stock is trading at the time the deal closes is what we get. Let's roll the dice and see what the stock does. If it doubles, we get double. If it goes to half, we get half."

Stamm noted that Nortel had a diversified international customer base. "Our volatility is greater than theirs," he argued. He also insisted on structuring the deal so that there was no lock-up period for selling shares. "Every shareholder is free to sell the stock on day one," Stamm said.

MJ was not accustomed to playing high-stakes poker in such situations, but she appreciated Stamm's passion. He was chairman of the board, and even more important, Clarify was his baby. He had built a billion-dollar business from an idea hatched through microfiche at the public library. Waiting it out with Nortel was a huge gamble and could potentially cost Clarify hundreds of millions of dollars. But MJ had made her mark by siding with the entrepreneur. "We need to trust Dave," she told the board.

So the deal was completed. And when it closed six months later, Stamm—and the Clarify board—were dealt a royal flush. Since the start of negotiations, Nortel's stock had risen more than 50 percent. The $1.5 billion offer for Clarify was now worth $2.1 billion.

MJ's $6 million investment in Clarify returned well over $100 million to IVP. She won the vaunted in-house contest. But when it came time to claim the prize—the car of her choice—she opted to donate the money to the new Center for Entrepreneurial Studies at Stanford's Graduate School of Business. MJ didn't care much about cars, apart from her beloved Pinto, but she had to admit she liked the idea of beating the boys at their own game—especially as a part-time partner. In lieu of cash, the IVP partners collectively donated $128,000 to the center.

MAGDALENA

Magdalena was having lunch at the Peninsula Golf and Country Club in San Mateo with a young star at Oracle Corp., Marc Benioff. The two had become friends when the database giant became CyberCash's partner, selling its server software to banks. Benioff, a senior vice president at Oracle and trusted friend of the company's hard-charging billionaire cofounder Larry Ellison, often sought out Magdalena's counsel. He trusted her advice completely.

Speaking softly—the country club terrace was a techie hangout, and he didn't want to be overheard—Benioff said, "Tom [Siebel] and I have been discussing the fact that small- and medium-size companies cannot afford Siebel's software and that a subset of Siebel Systems functionality would serve them well. The small- to medium-size enterprises can't spend a million dollars to sign and another million to implement, so it has to be a hosted offering. But I think Tom is worried about cannibalizing his business."

Benioff added, "I think the idea—delivering business applications as a service over the Internet—is great and even large companies would prefer it if it did not require millions of dollars and a year to implement." After a pause, he asked, "What do you think?"

"I think it's a great idea," Magdalena said without hesitation. "I think enterprise software with its multimillion-dollar price tags for license and implementation will go away over time." She had long been convinced that "big and clunky" networked software companies would soon be replaced by nimbler pay-as-you-go software-as-a-service, where a business could buy only the software it needed, as it needed it. "We need software that is 'pay by the drink,'" she said.

Benioff asked, "So should I do this?" And "Can I do this on my own?"

Magdalena smiled seeing the start-up sparkle in his eyes. "Yes, and yes," she said. "And I'm going to help you in every way I can. I will invest, raise money from VCs, help you hire, and help you sell."

Benioff had recently taken a six-month sabbatical from Oracle to practice meditation in Hawaii and travel to India to visit ashrams and learn from spiritual masters. A highlight of his time in India was meeting Mata Amritanandamayi, known as the "hugging saint" because she had embraced an estimated 25 million people. Benioff returned to the States and to his job at Oracle wanting to build something of his own. He believed the Internet was the way of the future, and he intended to integrate his love of technology with his newfound belief in service.

Magdalena knew that the spirit of entrepreneurship had always been a part of Marc's life. When he was a teenager, he and a few friends started a company called Liberty Software to make adventure games for the Atari 800. He earned extra money going to people's homes to repair antennas and CB radios, and he worked for Apple Computer the summer before his junior year at the University of Southern California. Largely unsupervised, Marc started writing software for a game about raiding IBM's headquarters. His manager at Apple said the game wasn't appropriate and later suggested Marc consider a job at Oracle. They had the best salespeople in the world, he was told. In his first year at Oracle, Benioff was named rookie of the year.

After lunch at the country club, Magdalena jumped on a call with Benioff and Parker Harris, who was running a software programming and consulting company called Left Coast Software with two engineers. Benioff wanted to recruit him, but Harris was worried about getting buy-in from his partners. Harris's team thought the software would be too easy to write, given their years of experience in the CRM field (including recently at Clarify, Dave Stamm's company).

Harris asked Magdalena, "Why do you think this company will win? What are the barriers to entry?"

"There are no barriers," Magdalena said. "You have to run faster than everyone else. And execute better. That is your only defense— better execution than everyone else."

Soon a small team—including Parker Harris, Frank Dominguez, and Dave Moellenhoff—began working out of a one-bedroom apartment Marc rented next to his own flat on the top of Telegraph Hill, a stone's throw from Coit Tower. They used card tables and folding chairs for desks, and kept a lifetime supply of Red Vines licorice on hand. A picture of the Dalai Lama hung above the fireplace. Benioff, who signed all of his correspondence with "aloha," was still employed by Oracle, but turned his energies to building his start-up. Magdalena did the same, working her day job at USVP while throwing herself back into start-up fever in the evenings.

At home, she juggled her mother, her husband, Jim—who was busy with his own career as an attorney—and her boys, Justin, eleven, and Troy, nine. Her older sister and her niece and nephew cycled in and out of her responsibilities. She hired a "manny"—a male nanny—once it became clear that her boys were overpowering their female babysitters, like Gulliver overtaken by the Lilliputians in *Gulliver's Travels*.

Jim played easy-going California dad to Magdalena's European disciplinarian mom. Jim and the boys did the fun things together, hanging out at Jim's ranch, where they took care of animals, drove ATVs, operated heavy machinery, and got dirty and dusty. Magdalena was the one who checked homework and pushed the boys to do better. The couple rarely argued, but still their styles were markedly different.

She attended PTA meetings and ran school auctions and fund-raising events. She took collecting fifteen dollars for a gift for a coach as seriously as she did handling a million-dollar investment. Everything that got budgeted and scheduled got done. When the other parents began debating school decorations—orange, purple, or sparkly—Magdalena walked out, leaving such details to others.

The boys had a vague sense of their mom's professional life. One weekend afternoon in Palo Alto, Magdalena took Justin and Troy and Justin's friend to a café. As Magdalena waited at the counter to order, a woman at the table next to her kids leaned over and asked, "Is that Magdalena Yeşil?" The woman had seen Magdalena on TV talking about e-commerce. Justin's friend was the first to reply, saying, "No, that's Justin's mom."

After the kids were in bed, Magdalena made a beeline to her office or to the kitchen table to get in a few more hours of work. One night a fax came in that Jim brought her, sent by Marc Benioff. At the top of the fax were Larry Ellison's and Magdalena's names.

"What are you doing with *these* guys?" Jim asked, studying the fax.

"I'm building a company," Magdalena replied. "To be called Salesforce .com."

SONJA

By early 2000, Eve, the online cosmetics giant, had surpassed even Sonja's expectations, becoming nearly twice the size of Sephora online. The Internet darling was beginning to attract some high-caliber suitors.

One of Eve's biggest fans was seed investor Bill Gross at Idealab. Idealab was comprised of more than forty dot-com companies, including eToys, GoTo.com, Pets.com, Friendster, NetZero, and CarsDirect. EToys was worth $7.8 billion when it went public, making Idealab's original $200,000 stake worth $1.5 billion. GoTo.com was worth $5 billion when it went public, and Idealab owned 20 percent of it.

But Bill Gross wasn't the only one paying attention to Eve. The world's top luxury brand company, LVMH—Moët Hennessy Louis Vuitton—based in Paris, had purchased the perfume and cosmetics company Sephora in 1997 and opened its first U.S. store in New York in 1998. LVMH had previously made a bid for Eve, inviting co-founders Varsha Rao and Mariam Naficy to a breakfast meeting in San Francisco. They had given the women fancy pens as gifts. "Why don't you join us? We will all do this together." Rao and Naficy found the LVMH people lovely, but they wanted to establish their own online cosmetics business.

Yet as Sonja surveyed the business landscape, she knew that the calculus had changed—dramatically. Eve now carried more than two hundred brands and had raised twenty-six million in venture funding. Naficy and Rao were soon invited to another meeting with the execs from LVMH. This time LVMH wanted to buy Eve for *one hundred million dollars*. Naficy and Rao were thrilled. They respected LVMH and the executives they'd met, and they thought Eve would now become part of the international conglomerate. They had achieved what they set out to do, to build the top beauty e-commerce site. The financial terms were beyond anything the founders had imagined. The money was game-changing. Rao's father had told stories of going without shoes as a child because the family couldn't afford them. Naficy's family had fled Iran during the revolution with two suitcases to their name.

The offer also felt well timed. Some economists were predicting a market downturn, and investors were turning skittish. Sonja thought the offer was exceptional and a huge win for Idealab as well.

But Bill Gross thought differently. He had just raised more than $1 billion from institutional investors and was planning to take Idealab public. He was not about to lose his crown jewel. He said as much during a hastily called board meeting to discuss the LVMH offer. After some back-and-forth, he agreed to consider the deal if he could keep his stake. He was Eve's biggest shareholder, with 22 percent of the company. A call was arranged between Gross and LVMH to see whether the two could work together. But in the end, LVMH was not willing to buy only a portion of Eve.

Sonja grew increasingly concerned over the impasse. Naficy and Rao weren't sure of their next step. Gross had provided critical early support and vision, but they didn't want to lose a $100 million deal. Sonja considered both sides before stepping in. She told Naficy and Rao that she would talk with Gross.

She got Bill on the phone the next day. After some casual back-and-forth, Sonja didn't mince words. "Bill, I would like to remind you that as a board member you represent *all* the shareholders and not just yourself," Sonja began. "The offer from the LVMH group is fantastic, and all of the other shareholders, including Mariam and Varsha, want to take it. It will be a big burden on you if you veto the deal and later Eve fails."

Gross listened but said little. Sonja couldn't read his reaction.

A day later Gross made his move. Idealab would buy 80 percent of Eve for $110 million. Not only that, he guaranteed that the stock options held by Eve employees would be worth a minimum of $50 million within eighteen months. As the largest option holders, Naficy and Rao would each get $17.5 million within a year and a half, no matter what happened to Eve.

Not surprisingly, they accepted Gross's offer. Rao told Naficy, "Sonja pushed, and Bill stepped up." Naficy put it another way: Sonja had protected them from being eaten. And she had helped make Rao and Naficy very wealthy women.

Sonja did quite well, too. She took her venture capital earnings and bought a "dot-com house" overlooking the San Francisco Bay, located near the area of Pacific Heights known as the Gold Coast. The 3,400-square-foot home, originally built in the 1940s, had been on the market for months and was something of a white elephant. The electrical circuits overloaded if Sonja ran her hair dryer and the television set at the same time. She closed off several rooms, had little furniture to fill the big space, and invited a friend who was going through a divorce to come and live with her. They loved those rare warm San Francisco nights when the water turned into a flawless purple slate and the sky was streaked with pink. It reminded Sonja of the line by journalist H. L. Mencken, who wrote upon arriving in San Francisco, "I am thrilled by the subtle but unmistakable sense of escape from the United States."

Sonja was now thirty-three years old. She was dating a writer, and the two were getting serious. But the southern belle continued to love her Silicon Valley job, telling her friends, "I get to talk on the phone all day *and* spend money!"

A group of high-society ladies soon invited her to lunch to welcome her to the tony neighborhood. She was amused when the questions began, a reminder that San Francisco, for all its progressiveness, was still a place where old money looked down at the new economy. First, the Chanel-clad inquisitors wanted to know what her *father's* line of work was; surely *he* had bought the mansion.

"My dad is a professor of civil engineering," she said. So they asked what her *husband* did for work. "I'm not married," she said. This was met with dead silence. There had to be a *trust fund,* they figured. Sonja smiled; she told them she had a job and had purchased the house herself.

Leaving lunch to walk back home, Sonja paused to behold the breathtaking view of San Francisco Bay. She had begun to feel like nothing bad could possibly happen to her.

PART
FOUR

Survival of the Fittest

1999–2002

MJ

MJ, in a somber-looking suit, arrived at the IVP offices and quickly disappeared behind closed doors with partners Reid Dennis and Norm Fogelsong. IVP was losing its way. The vaunted venture capital firm was slowly but surely breaking up.

Andi Heintz, leader of the VVCAs—the Vivacious Venture Capital Assistants—could sense the concern: the whispers, the closed doors, the hours away from the office, *off calendar*. She knew a company divorce was coming. What she didn't know was that the divorce wouldn't involve just one of the partners; it would involve them all.

The crisis had started quietly months back, when VC whiz Geoff Yang, hired by MJ and Reid Dennis twelve years earlier, had come to see an inverse relationship between the "fun factor" and efficiency at work and the number of people in the room. The more people at the conference table, the less fun and less efficient. And for him, IVP was no longer fun.

In Yang's view, the IVP family had grown up and grown apart. There were no knockdown fights and no slammed doors. But IVP now had three divisions: tech start-ups, led by Yang; late-stage tech, led by Dennis, MJ, and Fogelsong; and life sciences, led by Sam Colella and Beckie Robertson. A multitude of partners with different specialties, objectives, skills, interests, and returns—and all needed to agree on deals.

Yang had come to dread Monday partners' meetings, where he had to reduce his explanation of tech companies to the lowest common denominator because the life sciences folks didn't understand the nuances of information technology. The life sciences people had to do the same with the tech team. And there was a disparity in returns: Late-stage tech had an internal rate of return of 68 percent between 1994 and 1999, while life sciences was returning 12 percent. Yang was consistently hitting home runs with investments in tech start-ups.

"Life sciences is not my basis of knowledge," he told MJ. "I can understand medical devices, but when it comes to biotech, that's very specialized. They're talking down to me. I'm talking down to them. There is no added value. I can't add partners to my team of new tech because the next thing you know, we're in a general partners' meeting, and we may as well rent out an arena."

Yang had decided it was time to start a new firm, to be called Redpoint Ventures. He recruited three partners from Brentwood Venture Capital—all guys, all around the same age. Yang said that they were continuing the legacies forged at IVP and Brentwood rather than starting a firm from scratch. The tech start-up space was on fire, and investors were throwing money at him. Yang talked up Redpoint as a *merger* of two old-line gold standard firms, IVP and Brentwood.

Similarly, the life sciences people could form their own specialized firm. "Each specialized team can have its own firm," Yang said. "No one has to carry the other."

MJ and the other partners went along with Yang's idea at first and even invested in Redpoint. But it eventually became apparent that veterans MJ, Dennis, and Fogelsong—leaders of the late-stage tech investments—were the odd people out. Soon Yang was joined at Redpoint by former IVP partners Tom Dyal, Allen Beasley, and Tim Haley and by former Brentwood partners Jeff Brody, Brad Jones, and John Walecka. Late-stage investing—in companies that had at least $10 million in revenue but still needed growth capital—was out of favor, even if it was showing strong returns for IVP.

Yang, a TV and movie buff, loved quoting from the film *Top Gun:* "You're not going to be happy unless you're going Mach 2 with your hair on fire." But MJ and her allies were now becoming increasingly unhappy; they felt as if they were on the outside looking in.

As MJ's administrative assistant watched MJ, Dennis, and Fogelsong enter yet another closed-door session, she wondered if this marriage had run its course. *It's time for everyone to be honest with where they're at,* she thought. The dot-com boom had been good to Silicon Valley, including the venture capital admins. When Heintz started at IVP in 1984, entrepreneurs arrived in suits and ties, handed out copies of thick presentations, and returned for multiple meetings over a period of weeks. In more recent years, IVP practically wrote checks to entrepreneurs as they walked out the door. It was exciting. She and other VVCAs had cocktails while talking about the IPOs they'd got in on and the stock they'd been able to buy before the company went public. They'd gush to one another, "I paid fifteen dollars a share and now it's two hundred a share!" And at the next get-together someone would say, "Now the stock is splitting!"

But now IVP was splitting up, and her boss Yang, whom she liked and respected, was taking charge. Yang and his other partners quickly raised hundreds of millions of dollars, while reiterating that Redpoint was a *continuation* of the best of IVP and Brentwood. Yang's action in forming Redpoint prompted Beckie Robertson and Sam Colella on the life sciences side to start their own health care firm, Versant Ventures.

IVP had rapidly become the child no one wanted. After months of everyone tiptoeing around the issue, it was becoming clear that once IVP's current Fund VIII was invested, Dennis would pretty much be out of the game, along with Fogelsong and MJ.

That did not sit well with MJ. Though she had cut down on her IVP hours in recent years to spend more time with her family, this was not the way she wanted to end her career.

THERESIA

In early 2000 Theresia was in the basement of the Four Seasons Hotel in New York for all-day meetings with Accel team members. They were raising money for their next fund, Accel VIII. Lunch was brought in; there was no Wi-Fi. At the end of the day, as the team headed upstairs, phones buzzed with messages. Wives, assistants, entrepreneurs, executives, colleagues, and investors had been trying to reach them.

"The market has gone crazy!" one of Theresia's partners exclaimed.

In March 2000 the stock market, which in recent years had only gone up, plummeted. In February, Alan Greenspan announced plans to aggressively raise interest rates, leading to some instability. *Barron's* followed with an ominous cover story: "Burning Up: Internet companies are running out of cash—fast." Although some market analysts brushed off the downturn as a blip, nearly a trillion dollars' worth of stock value evaporated in a month. As spring turned to summer, the darlings of the Internet boom—the dot-com companies—became pariahs. Fortunes were devastated, or lost entirely. Even stalwart companies like Intel and Cisco were the walking wounded, their valuations reduced by 90 percent; Amazon faced possible bankruptcy.

Theresia and her partners triaged in emergency meetings around the conference table at Accel. She was no longer fielding calls and researching companies. Instead, she was picking which of her investments would live, and which would die. She had two things in mind: *Keep your moneymakers* and *Cut the burn*—meaning, "cut the companies that are rapidly burning through their available cash." A company needed to get to profitability with what it had, or be sold for its asset value, or it would quietly be closed.

Theresia studied the financials on an investment she'd made in Sameday, the Bill Gross–incubated company that did same-day delivery of e-commerce packages. She had invested in 1999, but now, as e-commerce companies closed their doors, Sameday was in trouble. It would need to be sold.

Theresia dragged herself home every night, telling her husband, Tim, "It's Armageddon out there." She felt stuck in the lowest point of a J-curve, where losses dipped below the initial value. A year and a half into her venture career, she still couldn't shake her fear of failure. She wasn't afraid of missing a mortgage payment or being out of a job; she could always find another job. Rather, she was afraid she wouldn't prove to be smart enough, agile enough, for this job. She'd heard of other VCs being ominously "disappeared"—parked in a firm's portfolio company. A VC who was not going to make it to the next level would just be nudged out of venture and into doing marketing for a faltering start-up.

Theresia had another dot-com company, PeopleSupport, that could go either way: fall into the rubble or rise from the ashes. Co-founded in 1998 by Lance Rosenzweig, PeopleSupport was the first company to provide outsourced Web-based customer service by way of online chat and e-mail. It had caught on immediately, growing from thirty employees to more than four hundred in its first six months. Theresia invested in 1999, along with Bob Kagle at Benchmark. By early 2000, PeopleSupport had more than one hundred dot-com companies as clients. Revenues soared from $500,000 in 1999 to $6 million in 2000.

Rosenzweig had a great sense of humor and was a strong communicator—he was a debate champion in college. Before co-founding PeopleSupport, he owned a company that sold plastic checkout bags to chain stores, including Wal-Mart and Kmart. In the mid-1990s, just as he was losing customers to Chinese companies that could sell bags to U.S. retailers for a fraction of his price, Rosenzweig watched the rise of online shopping. He studied how e-commerce worked and found a breakdown between retailers and shoppers that ended with what the retailers called "shopping cart abandonment." In those days people accessed the Internet via home phones using dial-up modems. Most Americans had only one home phone. A customer with a question about a product—delivery time, the color, shipping, a return—had to disconnect from the Internet to use the phone to call customer service.

Rosenzweig and PeopleSupport co-founder David Nash created the first outsourced chat service for online retailers. They opened a call center in Los Angeles and ran offbeat recruitment ads, such as "I dare you to send us your résumé. Hell, we're only the hottest dot-com start-up in town," and "Stock options are better than a knee to the shorts." The call center was located in Westwood, Los Angeles, and most of their employees were UCLA students or graduates. Dot-com companies signed up in droves to outsource their customer support, sending their own employees to Westwood to train the PeopleSupport team.

But suddenly PeopleSupport was losing clients in droves. The darlings of the dot-com boom were going under. Pets.com, begun in February 1999, closed after buying a $1.2 million Super Bowl ad and burning through $300 million in investment capital. Webvan, a grocery home-delivery service that attracted funding from Sequoia Capital, Goldman Sachs, Benchmark, and others, filed for bankruptcy after burning through hundreds of millions of dollars.

Theresia got an e-mail from Rosenzweig titled, "What to do now," prompting a meeting. "Everything is crashing, and all our clients are going out of business," he said to Theresia. He'd had a similar come-to-Jesus talk with Benchmark VC Bob Kagle, who told him, "The people who are saying that this is just a blip are wrong. This is not a blip. This is a permanent shift. Just assume you can never raise more money."

Theresia and Rosenzweig strategized over how to keep People-Support alive. It helped that she was a board observer, not a board member. A board member had the authority to hire and fire, while a board observer was more ally than boss. In Theresia's experience, entrepreneurs were often more candid with board observers.

Fortuitously, in the weeks before the downturn began, Theresia and Rosenzweig had been working on securing a new round of funding with Paul Madera, of the late-stage VC firm Meritech. As markets declined, Rosenzweig worked frantically to close quickly. The deal was signed on April 14. The next day brought another savage drop in the markets, with the Dow down 616 points and the NASDAQ down 10 percent. The NASDAQ lost a quarter of its value in a week. Rosenzweig was convinced that had the deal been delayed by a day, People-Support would have teetered into bankruptcy.

At the "what to do now" meeting, Theresia told Rosenzweig, "First, we need to start by winning some non-dot-com companies. You need big companies that aren't going away and can pay their bills."

He nodded. He had an idea as well—to add phone support to chat and e-mail services. "However our customer wants to interact, we want to interact," he said.

Theresia liked the idea of adding phone support but was concerned about rising costs amid plummeting revenue.

But Rosenzweig was one step ahead. He wanted to move customer support from Westwood to a low-cost international location. "I learned an important lesson in the shopping bag industry," he said. "If you get a cost advantage in Asia, you can defeat anyone. Once we add phone support, we'll become a full CRM outsourcer."

PeopleSupport became the first outsourcer to set up shop in the Philippines to support American clients. Rosenzweig chose the Philippines because the culture was like America's, the Filipinos' English was excellent, and an infrastructure was in place to handle calls cheaply. The telecommunications company Global Crossing had spent billions of dollars laying undersea fiber-optic cables, which—with a compressing technology developed by Lucent—enabled calls to be routed cost-effectively to the Philippines. The savings were immediate and compelling. PeopleSupport could offer its services at much lower costs than any of its competitors.

Theresia knew that PeopleSupport still faced giant struggles, yet it felt like one of the few dot-com companies that at least had a chance. Moving forward, her survival strategy would be to eke out a combination of "saves" and new deals. But in this economic drought, water would remain hard to come by.

SONJA

With the dot-com bubble bursting around her, Sonja held on to her optimism. She believed the deal Bill Gross had made to buy the beauty start-up Eve would go through. The offer had come together before the bubble burst, and the deal hadn't yet closed. She refused to listen to colleagues and pessimists who said all bets were now effectively off.

Sonja reassured her entrepreneurs, Mariam Naficy and Varsha Rao, that Gross's offer for Eve would move ahead. "We have an offer, and we're proceeding," she said. "If you think it's going to fail, it's going to fail. If you believe it won't fail, it won't."

Bill Gross was also an optimist. Months earlier, in January 2000, he had raised $1 billion in private financing. In April, Idealab filed a registration statement with the SEC, announcing its intention to go public. General Electric chairman John Welch Jr. joined the Idealab board. Gross believed that e-companies could go in only one direction: up. The downturn was but an annoying anomaly.

As the economic decline deepened, though, Gross, the energetic run-don't-walk start-up king, was forced to deal with this unwelcome reality. He needed to start selling, closing, and restructuring his companies. Even as he did this, though, he kept the faith that he could move Eve toward profitability.

As Sonja predicted, Gross closed the deal with Naficy and Rao. He bought Eve for more than $100 million. Menlo Ventures made millions on the deal, and Naficy and Rao each walked away with their promised $17.5 million.

Around the same time, the beauty giant Estée Lauder announced it was buying an Eve competitor for a reported $20 million. Beautyjungle, another online cosmetics retailer, laid off 60 percent of its staff. Another competitor, Beauty.com, was sold to Drugstore.com.

Gross brought in retail specialists who suggested turning Eve into a giant e-commerce portal. He later tried folding two of his smaller e-commerce companies that sold jewelry and furniture into Eve to create one big department store, when he realized that the company would not reach "acceptable levels of profitable growth in cosmetics alone."

By October 2000, the NASDAQ had plunged to another low. Gross's crown jewel was no longer worth anywhere near what Idealab had paid for it. Eve was losing money on every customer purchase, because of the high costs of acquiring customers. Not only that, in the heady dot-com days, Gross had *guaranteed* that the stock options held by Eve employees would be worth a minimum of $50 million within eighteen months.

Meanwhile Naficy and Rao did what they could to keep Eve alive. In mid-October, Rao arrived at Eve's San Francisco headquarters for another day of brainstorming. But instead, she was met by a steady stream of employees who had been let go and were carrying boxes out of their seventh-floor office overlooking Market Street. Workers carted off equipment. Rao and Naficy were among the 164 employees told they were being let go that day. Bill Gross had sold Eve to rival Sephora, owned by LVMH, the company that had twice tried to buy Eve. LVMH had offered $100 million only months earlier. Today, for an undisclosed sum, Sephora would get Eve's customer database, its name, and its URL.

Stunned and saddened, Rao took one last look around the office. A large monitor on the wall featured Eve's familiar homepage with all the latest makeup, tips, perfumes, fashion shots, and stories. She posted a message saying, "We hope that shopping with us has been a beautiful experience." Visitors to Eve.com were redirected to Sephora.com.

Sonja looked at the positives of the deal. She admired Bill Gross for keeping his word. "It could've gone the other way," she told Naficy and Rao. "For me, it's nice to know Eve will live on in Sephora."

MJ

MJ couldn't stop thinking about the Redpoint and IVP split, even as she left IVP on Sand Hill Road late one afternoon to make it to her son Will's baseball game. She then headed to her daughter Kate's science competition. At home, she comforted her youngest daughter, Hanna. Their golden lab, Cindy, had a heart tumor and wasn't going to live much longer. Then her dad called. MJ had moved her parents out from Terre Haute years earlier, buying them a home in nearby Santa Clara. Her dad was calling to say he wanted to go to the store to return the soap he didn't like. He wanted his $1.50 back. A few minutes later she received a call from the mommy network, as MJ called it, asking MJ to co-chair the harvest carnival. Finally her husband, Bill, walked in; he needed to do some work from home, he said.

Heading to the bedroom to change into more comfortable clothes, MJ caught her reflection in the mirror. She barely recognized herself. She now had short hair and wore a dark suit with a white blouse tucked into her pants and belt, and sensible heels. When she'd started at IVP, she had been told she looked like a young Jaclyn Smith, one of the stars of the hit TV show *Charlie's Angels*. She'd had long brown hair, a beautiful figure, and a smile as sweet as her demeanor. When she'd driven west in her Pinto to California, her CB radio handle had been Too Hot to Handle.

But she'd realized quickly that her looks generated the wrong kind of attention. The "you look pretty" or "nice dress" remarks that came when she walked into a conference room full of men made her increasingly uncomfortable. No one complimented a man on what he was wearing. So MJ changed her look. She cut her hair, stopped smiling in work photos, and adopted the boxy suit. She did all this with one goal: to be able to walk into a meeting as an equal, without a single man commenting on her appearance. And she succeeded. As her partner Norm Fogelsong said fondly, "MJ is one of the guys."

She had reduced her hours at IVP to spend more time with her kids: Kate, who was thirteen, Will, ten, and Hanna, six. But she also wanted to improve her marriage. The Bill she had known at Purdue was an optimist and adventurer, a competitive swimmer with a lean body and the deep tan of a California lifeguard. The Bill of today seemed more negative than positive, at least when it came to their marriage. He still boasted about her job in public but lamented in private that she didn't have time or energy for him. While he wanted to spend some weekends away, just the two of them, she wanted to stay home, to do things with the kids as a family, and to get the house in order. When she was finally at home, she found herself compensating for being away so much because of her job.

That night, with everyone off to bed, MJ sat on the sofa in the living room and reached for her cinnamon Gummi Bears. Some people turned to alcohol; MJ turned to sugar.

She was more harried working part-time than full-time, trying to cram a week's worth of work into three days. When she started volunteering at her kids' schools, she was stunned by the amount of volunteer work done by the mommy network. She signed up to be a room mother and now, apparently, was co-chair of the school harvest carnival. She always felt like she was coming up short. She wondered why men did not experience the same familial pressures, even when both spouses worked. Bill never offered to help run the household. But MJ never asked for his help, either. She was an overachiever who enabled underachievement. *That's exactly what my mom did,* she thought, eating more Gummi Bears. On the wall hung a framed caricature done for her recent forty-fifth birthday. It was titled "MJ Multitasks!" and showed her in a suit and pearls juggling five balls, each with a name: Kate, Will, Hanna, Bill, IVP. The thought bubble read, "It maximizes my dexterity." *Maybe that's true,* she told herself. Clarify, after all, had been a home run, bigger than any investment by the full-time VCs.

MJ pondered the Redpoint-IVP divorce. She wasn't angry at Geoff Yang for creating Redpoint. She liked him and considered him a VC rock star. He'd had a strong idea, and he was running with it. What irritated her about Yang was how he insisted on introducing her: "This is my *older* partner, MJ." For a smart guy, it was an insensitive way to introduce a woman.

In the past when MJ hit a wall, she found a way around it. She was in the business of solving problems, and she'd learned that the best solutions often came from the simplest ideas. With the house now quiet, an idea came to her. The answer was obvious. She felt like she had landed on a simple solution to the problem of IVP and Redpoint.

MJ stashed her Gummi Bears where no one could find them and headed to bed.

THERESIA

Looking for water in the desert that was the U.S. economy, Theresia started to nose around in cybersecurity, calling the contacts she'd made through Arthur Patterson and her colleague and friend Jim Goetz. She reached out to her previous contacts and made a point to attend industry conferences. She found that being the only woman in the room was a plus. If she could establish credibility, she could successfully stand out. She handed over business cards knowing that the name Theresia was an exception. At Accel, which had more Jims (Breyer, Goetz, and Swartz) than women investors, she grabbed any advantage she could. Cybersecurity was hardly a hot market, but Theresia saw potential in this relative backwater.

Since starting in venture capital, Theresia had heard all the sports metaphors applied to the VC world: being "down for the count," swinging for the fences, making a slam dunk. There were the constant analogies between batting averages and investment returns. But to her, the more nuanced question was: Are you a home run hitter who also strikes out a lot? Or are you a Cal Ripkin, who consistently gets on base, hitting singles and doubles? The best hitters knew how to adjust to the pitches they were thrown. In 1999 and early 2000, everyone was swinging hard for the fences and hitting a lot of home runs. Now was a time to ease up and be more conservative. It was a time to hit singles and doubles.

She hoped that one of those base hits would include a group of Israeli former military guys and academics who had a new idea for protecting computers against hackers. Their first investor was Israeli. When they put out feelers for a top investor in Silicon Valley, they were told about Accel. Theresia's partners Jim Goetz and Peter Fenton suggested she take a look at the company, called ForeScout.

In a meeting at the Accel offices, ForeScout co-founder Hezy Yeshurun said, "Our basic idea is deception." He likened their strategy to the Israeli Defense Forces' approach, exploiting weaknesses and using surprise to gain tactical advantages. "We are different in that we assume that a determined hacker will always succeed in penetrating a network. So we will specialize in deceiving attackers and creating a smokescreen of data."

ForeScout had software that could see the number of endpoint devices on an organization's network. The sensors listened to raw information to discover every connected device.

"We can do all this without installing anything on the device," Yeshurun said. "Because of this, we can be more deceptive, as we are harder to find."

Theresia understood the potential of "agentless" security, which didn't require a company or an employee to put software on all the tech being protected. First-generation antivirus software, by contrast, had worked by identifying a digital footprint left in malware. Once the signature was found, the cybersecurity company could then send details of that signature in software updates. The problem with that model was that something bad had to happen before a fix could be generated. And the software had to be updated on every connected device.

After several weeks of due diligence and research, Theresia decided to invest in ForeScout. She figured that if all went according to plan, ForeScout would be bought in a few years. The big guys of cybersecurity were highly acquisitive. Yeshurun soon introduced Theresia to another Israeli, Shlomo Kramer, considered by most to be the godfather of cybersecurity. In the early 1990s, Kramer had co-founded Check Point Software Technologies in his grandmother's Tel Aviv apartment. Check Point became the market's first commercial firewall and grew into a billion-dollar company. Kramer was now an adviser to ForeScout.

As Theresia saw it, Kramer was still young. Eventually, he would get bored with investing and want to start another company. And she intended to be there when he was ready.

Yeshurun, a serial entrepreneur and professor of computer science at Tel Aviv University, was dismayed by how few women he met in finance and cybersecurity. It made him all the more delighted with his ForeScout investors. His first Israeli investor was a woman, Sharon Gelbaum-Shpan of Pitango Ventures, and now his first U.S. investment had been made by a woman.

Yeshurun and the all-male founders of ForeScout proudly came up with a nickname for themselves: The Babes Security Co. It was said with reverence. Theresia couldn't help but smile.

MJ

In her meeting with fellow IVP partner Norm Fogelsong, MJ quickly got to the point. "We should not let IVP die," she said. "This is not right. We should raise our own funds and keep IVP going."

The polite, buttoned-down Fogelsong, who loved venture capital for its equal parts engineering and market analysis, felt like cheering. He too had been pained by the idea that IVP could come to an end. The two talked it over a bit more before heading to Reid Dennis's office.

Dennis had been in the industry from the beginning, with the likes of Tommy Davis, Arthur Rock, Bill Draper, Tom Perkins, Eugene Kleiner, Bill Bowes, Dick Kramlich, Don Lucas, and Pitch Johnson. He had started out putting $15,000 of his own money into a little company called Ampex, which invented a magnetic tape for storing computer data. The tape would become a consumer product called a videotape. Dennis turned his $15,000 investment into $1 million.

MJ didn't need to be reminded that Dennis had been hurt before by shifting alliances. He had started IVP as Institutional Venture Associates in 1974 with Burt McMurtry and Burgess Jamieson. The three raised $19 million. One of their first home runs was an investment in ROLM, an early entrant in the digital telephone business. Then McMurtry decided he wanted to start his own fund; Jamieson wanted to do his own thing as well. The two men didn't want Dennis to continue to use the International Venture Associates name, so Dennis said, "Fine, I'll change it. We'll call it IVP," for Institutional Venture Partners.

In recent weeks, Geoff Yang had solidified his dream of creating his own venture capital firm. IVP's offices on Sand Hill Road had become Redpoint's offices. Dennis, who had originally thought he would continue at Redpoint, could see that it wasn't going to work out. He, MJ, and Fogelsong were being phased out. He told his wife, Peggy, "I don't want to get out of the business. And I don't want IVP submerged in Redpoint."

So when MJ and Fogelsong entered his office and presented their idea to keep IVP going, his eyes grew watery. "I'm thrilled," he said softly.

MJ knew at that moment that she would have to make personal sacrifices as well as let go of her school volunteer duties. She would have to focus her complete attention on rescuing IVP.

Dennis had given her a chance when others said women didn't belong in venture capital. He trusted her. She often wondered if it was because he had been raised by two strong women: his mother, after his father died when he was seven, and their Irish cook, Mary O'Brien. He had met and married Peggy when he was a sophomore at Stanford and she was a student at the College of Marin. They had had three boys and a daughter together. IVP was his family's legacy, too.

But MJ, Fogelsong, and Dennis would be challenged in raising money for a new fund. The economy was one of the bleakest in U.S. history. And they needed to hire a new team and find new offices.

MJ was up for the challenge. She recited her own favorite *Top Gun* quote: "Too close for missiles, I'm switching to guns."

MAGDALENA

It was lunch hour at Ken Preminger's Fitness Power gym on Sand Hill Road. Magdalena was dreading the ten minutes of abdominal exercises that would follow her twenty minutes of cardio. Her trainer, an Olympic rower, was a slave driver. She looked around the small gym, wondering who she would run into today.

She spotted a familiar face, an exceedingly fit man with blond hair and blue eyes. She struggled to remember his name. Was he an entrepreneur who had come to USVP to make a pitch?

"I know this guy," Magdalena said to her trainer, nodding at the man. For some reason he was allowed to work out without a trainer, one of the stipulations of membership. "Isn't he an entrepreneur?"

"You think he *pitched you*?" her trainer said, dumbfounded.

Magdalena nodded uncertainly.

"That's *Joe Montana*. The Forty-Niners quarterback? The guy who led the team to four Super Bowl championships?" Montana was also a VC at the time, at Champion Ventures.

Magdalena laughed at her mistake.

Abs and core work completed, Magdalena and her trainer headed to the next station—thirty minutes of weights. Her mind was consumed with her afternoon schedule: meetings with her USVP partners, preparation for a board meeting, and most important, a scheduled call with Marc Benioff to talk about a situation that had surfaced with their start-up, Salesforce.

As she thought about the call, Larry Ellison, the CEO of Oracle, approached, followed by his trainer, gym owner Ken Preminger.

Magdalena and Ellison, the first and second outside investors in Salesforce, were normally on good terms, tending to chat about camping, hiking, and Yosemite. She found him easy to talk to, though she also knew that he could go from charming to demanding in a nanosecond. Ellison, who had co-founded Oracle in 1977 and built it into the world's second-largest software company, was now the world's second-wealthiest individual, after Microsoft's Bill Gates.

But on this day, there would be no comparing notes on the great outdoors.

Magdalena looked Ellison straight in the eye and said, "You need to leave the board and stop copying us." Ellison had become a board member of Salesforce after investing $2 million.

As their trainers fidgeted in awkward silence, Magdalena went on, "This is a clear example of conflict of interest, of learning what we are doing at Salesforce and then copying us." The database giant Oracle had launched a CRM service that directly competed with Salesforce. Not only that, Magdalena noted in exasperation—the guy Ellison had sent to the Salesforce board meeting *in his place* was now running the new group at Oracle.

Magdalena had no problem speaking up about something she felt strongly about. Her father had taught her to stand on her own two feet as a child.

The friction between Salesforce and Oracle, a sort of David versus Goliath scenario, had generated a media frenzy. Ellison accused Benioff, a skilled salesman, of using the controversy to generate media attention for his company. As Ellison noted, dismissing any notion of copying Salesforce, Oracle was evolving from a database company to an online provider of software services. But the situation was also deeply personal. Ellison had been Benioff's mentor and friend. At six foot five, Benioff was sometimes called an Ellison "Mini Me." Ellison had supported Benioff when he took his sabbatical and launched Salesforce; he had invested millions and given Benioff flex time to get the company started. When Benioff announced he was leaving, Ellison told him not to poach more than three employees from Oracle. Ellison had gone out of his way to support his friend.

Benioff had already asked Ellison to resign from the board. Now Magdalena reiterated the message. Ellison, who had a way of sizing others up by narrowing his eyes, like a predatory bird, said, "No."

THERESIA

Theresia was in the all-glass conference room at Accel when the smell of food hit her. Her sense of smell was in overdrive. She could feel herself start to sweat as her stomach turned over. She eyed the corner wastebasket, the white carpet, and the white furniture. Throwing up was never a good option in an all-glass office. She hit mute on the phone and ran like the track star she had once been to the bathroom.

She was in the first trimester of her pregnancy and was not ready to announce the news. It had been nearly ten years since she and Tim were married. She'd held off on having children for as long as she could, wanting to be at a secure place in her career. She was still in the early stages of her VC career and was determined to become general partner, managing partner, and ultimately, equal partner.

Accel had never had a woman investor before, so she had no road map to follow. Her two peers in the venture business who had children were Jennifer Fonstad, her colleague from Bain who was a general partner at Draper Fisher Jurvetson and a mother, and Robin Richards Donohoe, a partner with Bill Draper. But Donohoe was already firmly established in her career; she had arrived, fortunate to work with a dream partner who was an advocate for women. Fonstad, like Theresia, was still climbing the ladder. She intended to have a talk with Fonstad about being pregnant while working in a firm made up almost entirely of men.

Theresia had been asked in early job interviews whether she planned on having children. What she was really being asked was whether she would invest the necessary time to be successful. Answering yes or no about children was perilous. If she said she preferred not to discuss her private life, she might be seen as combative. The Americans with Disabilities Act, which had become law in 1990, protected women against such questions, as well as others related to nationality, gender, race, and religion. But the questions were still slipped into interviews. She had been advised by older women to sidestep the question, if possible, with an answer such as "I have a strong work ethic no matter what is going on in my personal life."

Her pregnancy was welcome news to Theresia herself, but she was a worrier. She wondered how she would be a great mother and still be a great partner. She wondered how she would create the perfect environment for her family. Growing up, her worries had centered on getting perfect grades. At Bain and Accel, her worries had been about winning deals, while establishing a name for herself. So it was natural that she worried about the timing of her pregnancy. First the stock market had collapsed, wiping out $5 trillion in market value for tech companies. Then the country had been hit by the terrorist attacks of September 11, 2001. Fear and malaise filled the air.

On top of that, Theresia had to figure out what to do about maternity leave. She'd heard stories about women in other industries taking time off after having a baby and then returning to find their best clients taken away. What would happen when she was eight months pregnant and wanted to be the lead on a deal? Could she still do it, knowing she was about to have a baby? Bias against pregnant women and mothers was real and systemic. She had read the stories and research reports and talked to friends. Working moms were perceived as less competent and committed, even though the research proved otherwise. Women who had children in prime child-bearing years reportedly never recovered earnings relative to their husbands. No such bias existed for working dads, who in fact earned more than their childless male peers.

Robin Richards Donohoe shared a cautionary tale with her of the remarks of a certain well-known VC at the annual Kleiner Perkins Christmas party. Donohoe had just had her second child but was determined nonetheless to show up to the party. As she stood with a group of male peers, the jocular, well-known VC approached and said, "You all know Robin, right? She used to be a major deal maker. Now she's a mom."

It was a kick to the gut. But Robin had realized after her first child was born—she had been thirty-five at the time—that she couldn't have it all. She cut back to working four and a half days a week instead of five. With her second child, she planned to work four days a week. She made another difficult decision. With a big deal coming their way and Bill Draper traveling extensively, Robin told Bill, "I can no longer pull the Saturdays and Sundays and late-night due diligence. We need a third partner." She figured it would be better to give up some of her carry and some of her ego of being Bill Draper's sole deal maker to stay in the game. She was grateful she had become a partner before she had kids, had done a ton of travel to India to establish the fund, and had a supportive husband who was a singer and songwriter with flexible hours. Even with all this, though, work was a risky juggling act.

Robin's story kept Theresia tossing and turning at night.

MAGDALENA

Magdalena and Marc Benioff were confident they could raise venture funding for Salesforce. Magdalena, of course, had USVP, and Benioff knew VCs in the Valley, including former Oracle president Ray Lane, who had just joined Kleiner Perkins Caufield & Byers. Magdalena organized meetings so that various groupings of USVP venture partners could meet Benioff, chairman and founder, one day and Salesforce execs John Dillon, the CEO, and Jim Cavalieri, the systems engineering head, another day.

The meetings advanced up the food chain until it was time for Benioff to present to the full USVP partnership. Benioff could be mesmerizing when he was on, but he came across as aloof when he wasn't. He loved talking about how Salesforce's software for salespeople could be sold in an entirely new way: online and by service rather than as a massive package that was expensive to buy, complicated to install, and generally far more than what most clients needed. Salesforce had what it called "multi-tenant architecture," where the same software served different customers and made resource distribution more efficient. The CRM software would be accessed over the Internet with no hefty up-front licensing fees.

Parker Harris, Dave Moellenhoff, Frank Dominguez, Paul Nakada, and the programming and tech development team had built a prototype within a month of joining Salesforce in March 1999. (Dominguez flew down from Portland during the week and slept on a futon under his desk.) That July Magdalena had been the one to convince Benioff to leave Oracle to work on Salesforce full-time. She told him, "It's time for you to be a full-time entrepreneur." Salesforce had ten employees and a two-page website, with a recruiting page that requested that résumés be sent to cooljobs@salesforce.com.

Salesforce had gained traction by offering free trials to small companies, mostly start-ups. A few months later, with its staff doubled, it moved out of Benioff's adjacent apartment on San Francisco's Telegraph Hill and into a new space downtown at Rincon Center, where employees hit golf balls down the length of the office, flew remote-control helium blimps, and set up their own desks with materials from Home Depot. They ran brilliant marketing campaigns conceived by Benioff, hosted parties with the rock band the B-52's performing, and staged rallies and mock protests to disrupt competitors' events. They generated the kind of press coverage that most companies could only dream of. Benioff adopted the motto "If the press loves it, so do I."

Benioff told the USVP partners that Salesforce marked the "end of software" and that the company's Web-based service would be "as easy to use as Amazon." Salesforce had a Ghostbusters-like logo with the word SOFTWARE inside a red circle with a slash through it. The company phone number was 1-800-NO-SOFTWARE, and Benioff and the team wore NO SOFTWARE buttons.

USVP's Irwin Federman listened to the pitch and thought, *Okay, so you don't have to buy the whole salami. You can buy it by the slice.* The Brooklyn native and self-described "bean counter"—he started his career as an accountant—thought there was a market for it, but Benioff had valued Salesforce at *$100 million.* He wanted to sell 10 percent for $10 million. Federman looked at Benioff and thought, *He's got holes in his head. He's crazy.*

He knew Benioff through Tom Siebel, who had begun his career at Oracle as well before starting his own company, Siebel Systems. Federman was an early Siebel investor, as was Benioff. Both men had made a lot of money from their Siebel investments.

When it was Magdalena's turn to make the case for Salesforce, she told the USVP partners, "We are going to take on Siebel Systems. We are basically going to take the ten to fifteen percent functionality, the pieces of Siebel that people actually use, and offer that for a very small portion of the price you would pay for Siebel." Siebel charged a million dollars plus for the licensing, she said, which typically required an outside company such as Arthur Anderson or Accenture to come in and handle the implementation, which could take up to a year and cost another million dollars.

Federman listened closely to Magdalena. She had been investing in enterprise software companies and knew what she was talking about. But he still wasn't convinced. "I can't gag this down," he told his partners afterward. "It's all about valuation."

Magdalena, who had committed $500,000 of her own money to Salesforce over her lunch with Benioff in San Mateo, was shocked when USVP passed. But after making pitches to multiple firms—including Accel, where she met Theresia Gouw Ranzetta—and Kleiner Perkins, she realized there were two primary problems. Venture capitalists had a hard time believing that companies were going to put their most sensitive data—proprietary customer lists—on servers that were not their own. On top of that, Benioff himself did not always inspire confidence in investors—he could come across as a take-it-or-leave-it figure. He'd had a charmed career, thanks to Ellison. The two worked and played together, meditating in Japan and sailing the Mediterranean on Ellison's yacht. But Benioff on his own was unproven: a salesman, yes, a founder, not yet.

Not long after Federman turned Magdalena and Benioff down, he got a call from Tom Siebel, who told him, "Look, I've got the Internet domain name Sales.com, and I've decided to do what Salesforce is doing, only better."

Siebel reminded Federman that he'd had the idea early on to sell software on demand to small- and medium-size businesses. Siebel had offered Benioff, then at Oracle, the job of running the division. When Siebel changed his mind, Benioff, who had also been mulling over an idea for an Internet-based start-up for sales teams, had launched Salesforce.

Federman liked the concept a lot more coming from Tom Siebel. Siebel had a reasonable valuation for Sales.com and was a tech superstar. He didn't have any slogans, buttons, or B-52's, but he had already built a behemoth and had a great business partner in Patricia House, who co-founded Siebel Systems. Federman thought of Tom as the duck gliding effortlessly across the pond, and Pat as the little legs going a hundred miles a minute under the surface.

Federman told Siebel that USVP would invest in Sales.com. Sequoia Capital founder Don Valentine also became an investor in the new company.

Magdalena was incredulous when she heard the news. "You turn me down and you invest in a competitor?" Magdalena asked. "I've really got mud on my face."

Magdalena didn't always agree with Federman, but she admired him. He too had come to California with little money and knowing no one. He had taken the CPA exam and earned the highest score in California, and began to rise through the ranks, from bean counter to chief accountant to CFO to CEO; he'd led an extraordinary turnaround of a company called Monolithic Memories. Along the way, he'd met Tom Perkins, who became a friend and a leading venture capitalist. Federman saw venture capital neither as good nor bad. "As the Bible says, judge not lest ye be judged," Federman would say. "Everything doesn't need a report card. VC does what it does. Some things it produces are qualitative, some things are no good."

Federman then threw another wild card at Magdalena. He wanted her to work with the guy Siebel had chosen to run the new division of Sales.com.

"You want me to *counsel the competition*?" Magdalena asked.

"We have Sales.com as a portfolio company," Federman said. "You have Salesforce.com as your private investment. I trust you won't make us privy to Salesforce, and you won't make Salesforce privy to us."

As a board member of Salesforce—not to mention its first outside investor—she was, in effect, Marc Benioff's boss. She was helping to build Salesforce. On the other hand, she worked for USVP. It had a multibillion-dollar fund invested across industries but concentrated in several telecommunications companies at very high valuations. Those valuations were now tanking, as the economy went from bad to worse. She had her own money tied up in the fund. She was a significant bread-winner in her family, and the pressure to succeed was constant. More-over, each partner had committed his or her personal money through the firm to a real estate lease on Sand Hill with more footage than they now needed. They were locked into the lease at the same time that they were laying off staff. And Salesforce, which had come out swinging with some early successes, was now struggling like every other start-up. Magdalena was constantly worried that Salesforce might run out of money. Comfort was nowhere to be found.

Federman appreciated Magdalena's deal flow and her judgment. She was not an ideologue who always had to prevail. She was fact-based, data-driven, and practical. Federman felt confident that she would see the pragmatic, who-is-buttering-your-bread side of the Siebel deal.

Magdalena soon realized she would have to compartmentalize her brain. She likened it to people who had a ton of affairs yet managed to keep their spouses and their lovers separate and happy. She would just have to be respectful of her husband—USVP—and her lover—Salesforce—at the same time.

Mary Jane Hanna (right), age four, with her sister Shirley, seven, and father, Michael Hanna, 1958. *Photo courtesy of MJ Elmore*

Magdalena Yeşil with her father, Kevork Yeşil, in Moda, Istanbul, 1959. *Photo courtesy of Magdalena Yeşil*

Magdalena Yeşil in Moda, Istanbul, around 1961. *Photo courtesy of Magdalena Yeşil*

From left: Sonja Hoel, her father, Lester Hoel, her twin sister, Lisa, and her older sister, Julie, 1968. *Photo courtesy of Sonja Perkins*

Theresia Gouw with her grandparents, Jakarta, Indonesia, 1969. *Photo courtesy of Theresia Gouw*

Theresia on her high school volleyball team, 1985. *Photo courtesy of Theresia Gouw*

Theresia and her best friend Sangeeta Bhatia on graduation day from Brown University, 1990. *Photo courtesy of Sangeeta Bhatia*

MJ at Purdue, sorority photo, 1975. *Photo courtesy of MJ Elmore*

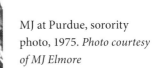

MJ at Stanford business school, graduation photo, 1982. *Photo courtesy of MJ Elmore*

MJ (front row, fourth from left) at an IVP retreat, 1987. IVP founder Reid Dennis is to her left. *Photo courtesy of MJ Elmore*

MJ in an IVP partner photo, 1994. *Photo courtesy of MJ Elmore*

The Elmore family, Christmas 1996. From left: MJ's son, Will, husband, Bill, daughter Hanna, MJ, and daughter Kate. *Photo courtesy of MJ Elmore*

Sonja (center) with father, Lester Hoel, and sister, Lisa Hoel, graduates from the University of Virginia, 1988. *Photo courtesy of Sonja Perkins*

Magdalena was named Entrepreneur of the Year by *Red Herring* magazine, 1997. *Photo courtesy of Red Herring*

Magdalena joins US Venture Partners on Sand Hill Road, 1998. Founder Bill Bowes is at front center. *Photo courtesy of Magdalena Yeşil*

Magdalena at a Salesforce Christmas party, Roy's Restaurant in San Francisco, ca. 2001. *Photo courtesy of Magdalena Yeşil*

Magdalena with husband, Jim, and their sons Troy (left), sixteen, and Justin, eighteen, 2006. *Photo by Joe Murray*

Theresia as a partner at Accel, with *Washington Post* CEO Don Graham and Facebook COO Sheryl Sandberg, at an Accel CEO event at Stanford, 2011. *Photo courtesy of Theresia Gouw*

Women of venture capital on a getaway in Hawaii, organized by Silvia Fernandez of Silicon Valley Bank. Silvia is in the black bathing suit and sun hat (far left), Magdalena is in sunglasses (front row, third from left), Jennifer Fonstad is seated next to Magdalena, and Sonja (front row right). *Photo courtesy of Silvia Fernandez*

Sonja and husband, Jon Perkins, in front of his restaurant Ferry Plaza Seafood, San Francisco, 2004. *Photo courtesy of Sonja Perkins*

Theresia with son, Luke, and daughter, Sarah, Lanai, Hawaii, 2012. *Photo courtesy of Theresia Gouw*

Theresia (front row, second from left) on the dais of the NYSE with Trulia founders Pete Flint (holding gavel) and Sami Inkinen, 2012. *Photo courtesy of Theresia Gouw*

Sonja featured at the *Forbes* Women's Summit in New York, June 2016. *Photo courtesy of Sonja Perkins*

Sonja and Jennifer Fonstad at Google in Mountain View, 2015. *Photo courtesy of Sonja Perkins*

Broadway Angels on *The Easy Way* boat in San Francisco, 2014. Sitting in the front row, Magdalena is at far left; Sonja is fifth from left, and MJ is sixth, followed by Jennifer Fonstad and Karen Boezi. *Photo courtesy of MJ Elmore*

Sonja founded the nonprofit Project Glimmer to inspire teenage girls and women to believe in themselves. *Photo courtesy of Sonja Perkins*

LATE FALL 2002

Magdalena normally avoided all-women's industry events, likening them to "bitch sessions." But she liked the woman who organized this annual women-of-venture-capital getaway to Hawaii, and she did a lot of business with the sponsor, Silicon Valley Bank. Plus, she looked forward to time away from the gloomy news from the markets, including business scandals involving Enron and WorldCom. She looked out the plane window at the shimmery, slate-gray Pacific Ocean, and hoped for relaxing days ahead.

Her expectations for the weekend were low. First, she never understood how women could call themselves "minorities." She grew up Armenian and Christian in Muslim-dominated Istanbul. Armenian Christians comprised less than 1 percent of the population in Turkey. That was her idea of a *minority*. Second, she felt that women were often more competitive with other women than they were with men. She'd read studies showing that women (and men) preferred to invest in companies run by men, especially by handsome men, and that two-thirds of female investors thought a project was better when pitched by a man than by a woman, even when it was the same project.

She saw it as a disservice to join all-women's groups or to speak on all-women's panels, arguing that no one promoted "all-male panels." A woman she knew in Turkey had once told her, "My mother was a great seamstress because she had a lot of 'stitch and bitch' sessions with her girlfriends. It was her 'stitch and bitch club.'" But in Magdalena's mind, gender was not just a woman's issue. Gender equality was an issue for both genders. Still, who could knock an all-expenses-paid weekend for twenty female venture capitalists in a swank oceanfront home on Oahu?

Silvia Fernandez, a senior vice president at Silicon Valley Bank, had come up with the idea for the annual gathering, after hearing her boss talk about all the off-sites that he hosted for the men of Silicon Valley. Realizing there were too few networking events for women, Silvia hosted the first getaway in 1999 with Sonja Hoel, Robin Richards Donahoe, and Kim Davis, who had done the F5 Networks load-balancing deal with Sonja.

Silvia wanted the weekends to be intentionally *antiguy:* Instead of whiskey, golf, and cigars, she planned mani-pedis, massages, and cooking classes. She understood the power of girl connections from her years in the Girl Scouts, when she learned to host events, dreamed up elaborate scavenger hunts and games, made connections for life, and realized the power of many.

After catching up on work during the five-hour flight, Magdalena was met at the airport and whisked to the beautiful private home of Silicon Valley Bank CEO John Dean, two doors down from the estate where the television show *Magnum P.I.* was filmed. There to greet her was Sonja Hoel, who embraced her like a long-lost friend. The women had first met in 1996, six years earlier, when Magdalena pitched CyberCash to Menlo Ventures. Since then their paths had crossed at occasional National Venture Capital Association events. Sonja began making introductions.

Kate Mitchell, a partner with Scale Ventures, said half-jokingly that she came to Hawaii out of curiosity "to meet the other nineteen women in venture capital!"

To Robin Richards Donohoe, the phrase *women venture capitalists* was almost an oxymoron, given how few of them there were.

By early evening, everyone attending had arrived. Magdalena, with a mai tai in hand, looked around and thought, *This isn't so bad.*

Silvia gave the women time to settle in. One joked that it felt like returning an animal to its natural habitat after years in captivity. After drinks and dinner, Silvia announced she had a few "ice breaker" games for everyone. The women refilled their wineglasses, and Silvia handed out sheets with the women's names in the left column and fun facts on the right. The object of the game: Try to guess which facts went with which names. Silvia and her SVB team had culled personal and professional tidbits for each woman by calling their administrative assistants and scouring Google.

"'Avid fly fisherperson and duck hunter, has two hunting dogs, taught an undergraduate economics course at MIT which was always oversubscribed (with mostly male students),'" Kate Mitchell called out. The answer: Maha Ibrahim, a partner at Canaan. "'Speaks two dialects of Chinese fluently, teaches spin classes three times a week, has run the Boston Marathon, has three children under the age of ten.'" It was a profile of Sarah Reed of Charles River Ventures.

Sonja had got to know Silvia through the annual getaways, but she was still impressed by her résumé: "Climbed a 20,000-foot peak in Northern Pakistan in the middle of a snowstorm, spent a vacation in the village of a tribe of former headhunters (not the Silicon Valley kind), had an 'Uncle Joe' who was a mafia crime boss in the 1950s, and had a youth soccer career that included taking the ball down the field and scoring for the opposing team."

As the evening progressed, the women changed into their pajamas and continued their conversations. As there were a limited number of rooms with beds, air mattresses were brought out and inflated. It was after midnight when the women finally retreated to their rooms and beds.

The next morning the women set about making breakfast for the group. A morning hike would be followed by snorkeling and spa time, culminating in the early evening with a private cooking class back at the house. Sonja, going over the itinerary, couldn't have been happier: no fist bumping, no black diamond runs, no gates to slalom through.

Saturday night Silvia introduced another round of games that mixed the personal and professional. First, she asked about some of the most memorable pitches they had received as venture capitalists.

Robin, a southerner like Sonja—Sonja attended UVA and Robin the University of North Carolina at Chapel Hill—recounted the time several entrepreneurs came in to pitch a new type of condom.

"My partner Bill [Draper] played right into it," Robin said. "He urged me to pursue the deal and to enlist my husband for product testing and product recap." Everyone knew of Bill Draper, who began his career in venture capital in 1959. (His father had started the first VC firm on the West Coast, Draper Gaither & Anderson.) But he also had a mischievous streak. "There was no way to talk about the condoms at meetings without getting into trouble," Robin said. "I tried to say this deal was out of our realm, that we were more *soft*ware based. Even that drew laughter."

"I once got a pitch from a prisoner at San Quentin," Kate Mitchell said. "The guy had an idea for a new type of toilet seat and toilet seat cover. He sent me a letter, written in this beautiful cursive and with perfect grammar. He clearly knew a lot about toilets and had been in business before landing at San Quentin. He drew this design of the new toilet seat, showing how it rotated, providing a new seat cover with every turn. We didn't fund it, but I was so impressed by the effort he made that I wrote back to him."

Magdalena remembered a pitch shortly after she'd joined USVP. "It was in this field that I knew nothing about—urinary incontinence for women," she said. "The pitch was for an RF [radio frequency] remote control, basically. The RF device would be inserted into the opening of your bladder, and you would have a remote control—like a garage door opener—that would open the bladder when ready, the pee would come out, and then you would close it.

"Anyway, I was sitting there listening to the pitch and thinking about due diligence," Magdalena said, drawing laughter. "I've had garage door openers that would open garage doors that were not my own. I know how much interference there can be. So I asked the inventors, 'What if you are in a public bathroom—let's say an airport with twenty adjacent stalls—and you've got several of these devices implanted, and you open someone else's bladder by mistake?'"

The women buckled over in laughter. Sonja looked at Magdalena with a straight face and said, "I think we financed that company!"

. . .

Theresia and MJ had been invited to the weekend but couldn't attend. Theresia was about to have a baby, and MJ was overcommitted at work and home.

Kate Mitchell, in subsequent years, loved telling the story of the first time she had attended one of Silvia's off-sites. She boarded the plane in San Jose, and even before it took off, Maha Ibrahim, who was sitting toward the front, pulled an electric breast pump out of her bag and waved it at her friend and fellow VC Amanda Reed, who was a dozen rows back. Reed then pulled out *her* breast pump and held it high. The women burst into laughter.

Over the years, Kate had met many remarkable women at the annual weekend getaway, including Jennifer Fonstad, Karen Boezi, Patricia Nakache, Carla Newell, Catharine Merigold, Cindy Padnos, and many more. They told each other stories of female entrepreneurs like Katie Rodan, a Stanford-trained dermatologist who self-funded two start-ups after being turned down by male VCs. Both of her start-ups—Proactiv, which revolutionized acne treatment, and the skin care line Rodan + Fields—grew into hugely successful companies. Katie's dad had told her early on, "Katie, be your own boss. Make your own money so you don't have to rely on anyone to take care of you."

As the night wore on that weekend, the women's stories became more personal. They talked about their favorite songs, and the craziest places they'd ever "done it." Silvia suggested they share their most embarrassing moments.

For Silvia, it was her wedding day. She was having the time of her life, drinking and dancing and wearing a vintage wedding dress that looked beautiful but fit imperfectly. In the midst of her reverie, there on the dance floor, she looked down and realized her strapless dress had fallen, and her breasts were fully exposed.

"What did I do?" Silvia asked the other women. "I pulled up my dress and kept dancing!"

The women also shared stories of some of the boorish behavior of the men they worked with. Heidi Roizen told about making a pitch to VCs for her early software company T/Maker, founded by her brother. As she made the pitch in the glass conference room, she noticed men in an adjacent room making sexually explicit gestures at her. Heidi finished her presentation and took her pitch elsewhere.

But there was often a point to the stories the women told each other. "I was in my twenties and working in the pretty much all-male corporate banking group at First Interstate in San Francisco," Silvia began. "I somehow got promoted at age twenty-four to a vice president position that I was not qualified for. I was calling on CFOs of Fortune 500 companies, including Bechtel and Transamerica Corp., and putting together lines of credit. One day we learned that the president of our bank was coming in—this was in the eighties—and I was to go out on client calls with him that day. I look down and see I've got a huge run in my pantyhose. This was the era of Nordstrom pantyhose. I was like, 'Crap!' So I pulled my colleague and confidante Mary into the bathroom and said, 'I need your pantyhose.' And she immediately stripped down and gave them to me." Silvia paused. "I realize we are no longer in the era of pantyhose. But my point is, you need your network. *You need that woman who will share her pantyhose.*" It was, in many ways, the central message of the annual Hawaii get-together.

Before heading off to bed, Silvia asked the women to share any advice or tricks of the trade that they had learned in the trenches. Kate Mitchell said that when she traveled to board meetings, she always made a point of listening to the morning news or reading above the fold of *USA Today* for at least one important sports story.

"I want to walk into a board meeting and say, 'What do you think about the Rodriguez trade?' Of course, I have no idea what this means, but that doesn't matter. The guys of course always know more than I do in this category and are always in a race to share what they know."

Early on in her career, Robin realized a lot of business gets done on the golf course. "I thought, 'Do I invest the time to become a good golfer?' I thought, 'No, I'm a good tennis player. I'll set up matches with the guys I want to network with.' Network with what you are good at." She offered the group a few additional tips from her years on the front lines: Work really hard your first ten years; save money; get your work travel in; and if possible, become a partner before you have children. Don't take one-on-one meetings with men at night but do attend association events and get-togethers. And most important, know that the person you marry will influence your career more than anything else.

On their last day in Hawaii, the women enjoyed a ride on a chartered sailboat, where they swam and snorkeled and shared news of recent deals in enterprise software, cybersecurity, and the nascent field of social networking. After a few hours, they reluctantly headed back to shore. On their way in, a crew member who had been intrigued by the women's conversation, asked whether they were in Oahu for the big banking conference. The women said no. Were their husbands with the bank? he asked. No again.

Finally he asked, "Who are you?"

Robin replied, "We're a women's think tank."

The weekend had been a welcome respite for those who, between work and family, had little time to seek out new friendships or attend networking events. The gathering felt like a trip home, a place they didn't know they'd even missed.

On the return flight, Magdalena wondered about the studies showing that women investors were more inclined to back men than women. Maybe they didn't have a precedent, she thought. Maybe they didn't know women like the ones she'd met in Hawaii. She thought of her friend's story about stitching and bitching. If her time in Hawaii was the sun-and-sea variation of "stitch and bitch," Magdalena was up for a lifetime membership.

PART SIX

Marriage, Motherhood, and Moneymaking

2002–2004

Marriage, Motherhood

MJ

MJ, determined not to let IVP die, decided that she, Reid Dennis, and Norm Fogelsong would raise the money for the next fund themselves. They brought in $225 million for IVP X, each putting in a chunk of their own money.

To be sure, IVP was on life support, having suffered the defections of Geoff Yang and others to Redpoint and Versant Ventures. As MJ's fund-raising plan went into high gear, she and her partners hired a new team that included Todd Chaffee, Dennis Phelps, and Steve Harrick. Their investing focus would be on successful late-stage companies that could make three to five times their money in three to five years, with an average investment of around $7 million. And as a continuation of Reid Dennis's lifelong enthusiasm for the stock market, the IVP partners would continue with public market investing in companies they knew well.

Even during the darkest days of the dot-com crash, when the small team hunkered down and pondered whether the world as they knew it was ending, Reid Dennis remained positive. One of his favorite sayings was "I don't know many rich pessimists."

Some of their early investments from IVP X in private companies included the cybersecurity enterprise ArcSite; the search engine Business.com; and Danger, founded by Apple alumni, including Andy Rubin, who made the first always-on, Internet-connected smartphone, the Sidekick. A few of IVP X's public market investments included the semiconductor company Artisan Components; @Road, a provider of software to manage a mobile workforce over the Internet; and Concur Technologies, a travel management and expense software maker.

It took time, but IVP got back on its feet, and when it did, MJ was able to return to her part-time schedule, now with no nanny. Her daughter Kate was busy with soccer, water polo, and tennis and was a bookworm who excelled at school. Will, now fourteen, played on Palo Alto High's football team and seemed to grow bigger and taller by the day, already dwarfing the petite MJ. On Friday nights, the football team descended on the Elmore household for MJ's home cooking. Will excelled at sports but was bored by school, and MJ fretted over his college placement options. Her daughter Hanna, ten, was dealing with normal middle school angst. They had a new rescue dog named Cruz who was part black Lab, part German shepherd.

The disconnect in MJ's marriage had not gone away; if anything, it was worse. Years earlier Bill had surprised her with a new car, a white Porsche convertible with manual transmission. Everyone—including MJ—was wowed by the lavish gift. But MJ was not a car person. Looking at the fancy sports car, she wondered how she would transport the kids. The car's engine was loud, making it hard to talk on the phone, and the kids struggled to get in and out of the backseat. She was grateful for the gift but left to wonder: Did Bill see her as a hard-charging, Porsche-driving exec? Actually, she would have been happier with a new minivan.

THERESIA

When Theresia went into labor with the birth of her daughter, Sarah, she felt good enough to send BlackBerry messages to the Accel office en route to the hospital and from her room. But just as she started to push—at which point she finally relinquished her BlackBerry—Sarah's heart rate tacked up and down, and Theresia's temperature spiked. At nine forty-five P.M., after a long and slow labor, the doctor ordered an emergency C-section and spinal block. Theresia, who had never had anesthesia, was given too much of it. The injection that was supposed to deliver pain relief to her lower body rendered her immobile from the neck down. She couldn't feel her limbs or so much as turn her head.

Sarah was born with only a minor infection but was nonetheless put in the neonatal intensive care unit. Tim followed his newborn daughter there, while Theresia's mom stayed in the room to take care of Theresia, who was still immobile.

Theresia knew from the beginning that Tim would be a wonderful dad. In addition to having five siblings, he grew up with a gaggle of nieces and nephews. Still, when the couple attended classes in baby care and it came time to practice dressing and undressing a doll in a onesie, Tim removed the onesie with a triathlete's flourish (he was in training)—causing the doll's head to pop off and fly across the room. They decided Theresia should probably be the one to dress their baby.

In Israel, Hezy Yeshurun and the team from the two-year-old cybersecurity company ForeScout had bets going on how long it would take Theresia after delivery to resume sending messages on her Black-Berry. Sure enough, as soon as the anesthesia wore off and she could move her head again, she was back in action, her thumbs flying across the small keyboard.

Accel had given Theresia six months of paid maternity leave, but she was called back to the office after only three weeks. Things at work had become challenging for the once-storied Accel, and she felt a responsibility to her partners, investors, companies, and the team. She had received word that partner Jim Goetz would be leaving the firm. Goetz, a friend and an ally, had joined Accel in 2000 and had become a managing partner in 2001 during one of the most tumultuous times in the tech industry's history. She was disappointed that he would be leaving later in the year.

Accel needed to get its mojo back. When the market correction began in March 2000, followed a year and a half later by the September 11 terrorist attacks, Accel was forced to reduce its $1.2 billion fund to $680 million, returning cash to the limited partners. In addition, founders Arthur Patterson and Jim Swartz had been stepping away from day-to-day operations, handing the reins of succession largely to Jim Breyer, Peter Wagner, and Goetz.

The limited partners were not happy with Accel's returns, and important longtime institutional investors—Princeton, Harvard, and MIT chief among them—were considering pulling out of the next fund.

Only three weeks after Sarah's birth, Theresia was back at her desk talking to entrepreneurs on a conference call.

"What is that weird noise?" one of the entrepreneurs asked. "Is someone inflating a bicycle tire?"

Theresia thought the sound was more like the churning of an old dot-matrix printer. "Sorry, guys," she said, "we've got construction going on here."

She realized that her once-chic all-glass office was not the best place to operate a lactation pump during a call. She and her assistant taped butcher paper over the glass for privacy and ordered blinds.

MAGDALENA

Magdalena was distracted as she worked with her sons on their math homework. Her other child, Salesforce, was in greater trouble. As Friday—payday—approached, Salesforce was in danger of not making payroll, again. The company was losing more than a million dollars a month. Investors were spooked, and the potential for bankruptcy was real. A 10 percent staff reduction had been ordered across departments.

Since its infancy, Salesforce had relied on small payments from small companies. It offered its software free for up to five users for the first month, and customers could add or subtract users and services at any time. All this was done on a contract-free "pay as you go" model. Small businesses, typically more open to adopting new technologies, were Salesforce's most important evangelists. All this had worked beautifully until the economy collapsed and most of those small Internet companies went bankrupt, decimating the evangelist ranks.

Magdalena pondered Salesforce's fate. There were parallels between raising kids, she realized, and building a company. Get them to crawl before they walk. Nurture, lead, and let go. When they're ready, push them out of the nest. Along the way, expect the bad and hope for the good.

Magdalena looked at her watch: It was 9:40 P.M. The family rule—her bad cop rule—was no Internet after 9:40 P.M. No amount of pleading, bartering, or protesting would weaken her resolve. If the boys' online homework wasn't finished, "too bad," she would say. The boys could stay up until 10:00 or 10:30 P.M., but they had to be offline. She loved being a mother to boys, to these fierce yet sweet spirits who got into knockdown fights, wrestled and punched, but were fine with each other ten minutes later. There was no pettiness, no drama, just old-fashioned resolution.

They were growing into independent young men. One day when Magdalena told the two of them that she was thinking about cutting back her hours at work to spend more time with them, Troy remained silent, but Justin said, "Mom, you're very good at what you do. I think it's a very bad idea for you to reduce your workload." She understood him to mean, *Mom, I don't want you hovering over me.*

After the boys went off to their rooms, Magdalena set up her computer and files on the kitchen table. Her husband had his own reading materials and assumed his spot on the sofa. Magdalena had night duty with the boys, and Jim had mornings. She made sure she was out the door to work before anyone woke up. She had no desire to be pulled into the morning chaos of missing socks, homework, breakfast, and backpacks.

Magdalena turned her attention to the cash flow crisis at Salesforce. Its business model—Marc Benioff's genius in attracting attention and defining the company—was intentionally anti–Siebel Systems: no licensing of products, no discounts, no implementation challenges with seven figures of added expense. It was one price for all, pay for what you need when you need it. It had been great for customers but crippling for Salesforce. Adding to its current problems, the company couldn't expand without hiring more salespeople, generating more expenses.

As Magdalena opened an Excel spreadsheet, she asked herself, *If investors won't give us more money, where can we get it?* They had raised just under $60 million since 1999 but were burning through $1 million to $1.5 million every month. They had maybe four months left before running out of cash.

They had two possible sources of money: equity from investors and payments from customers. Customers accessed Salesforce software entirely online, a novelty at the time. They could access it every day, all day, through an account on its website. Magdalena thought the website had a terrible user interface, with Amazon-like tabs across the top. Payments were made by credit card.

Siebel Systems, by contrast, licensed its software. Customers bought the license, took it to their offices, paid for it to be installed, and owned it outright, like moving furniture into a home. Salesforce operated more like an electric company, charging the customer by the amount of usage.

Studying sales revenue, expenses, and the commission structure, Magdalena zeroed in on one of the biggest problems. They were paying their salespeople commissions for a twelve-month deal, while collecting payments from customers one month at a time. As a result, money was going out much faster than it was coming in. Magdalena thought, *What if we offered a discount for up-front commitments and payments of one year? Or two years? Or even three? What if we collected all payments up front?*

The approach would bring new challenges, of course, beginning with setting up a contracts department. She made notes: *How much longer would the sales cycle be? What would the discounts look like? How would sales commissions be reset? Would this create a net win?*

Next, Magdalena looked at possible conversion rates: What if 20 percent of their customers committed to two years? What if *30* percent made the same commitment? She extrapolated out to three years. Standing up to stretch, she exclaimed, "Our cash intake would make it so we wouldn't even need cash from VCs! We'd be fine!"

Jim, still on the sofa, had learned to disregard such exclamations. It was just Magdalena working through a problem.

Well after midnight, Magdalena closed her computer and put away her papers. Now she just needed to sell Marc "No Contracts" Benioff on her idea. He continued to wear his NO SOFTWARE button to work every day and to tout no contracts, no licenses, no discounts. It was as much a part of him as his Hawaiian shirts and his golden retriever sidekick, Koa.

For Magdalena, saving Salesforce had nothing to do with protecting her $500,000 personal investment. It was about saving the team, the idea, the product, and the potential. If they didn't do something soon, Salesforce would go the way of so many other dot-coms, into the abyss of what venture capitalists euphemistically called "orderly shutdowns."

SONJA

At her office at Menlo Ventures, Sonja met with one of her favorite entrepreneurs, Andy Ory. Sonja had invested $3 million in his phone services company, Priority Call Management, in 1995. In 1999, PCM was acquired for $162 million.

When Sonja and Ory had first met as twenty-somethings, he was struggling. He couldn't land venture funding, hadn't slept in months, and was drinking endless amounts of coffee. His father had cashed out his retirement fund to support Priority Call Management, and the Orys had maybe $80,000 left in the bank.

Sonja felt as if she and Andy had grown up together professionally. They shared similar philosophies, including a strong belief that building a company came with social responsibility. Andy was known to tell his employees, "Do the right thing. In every instance, do the right thing." He believed that creating a company was about creating good for all the stakeholders. He felt a responsibility to raise people's standard of living; to pay taxes; to engage in social philanthropy; and to help people create wealth and build value.

Now Ory and his co-founder, Patrick MeLampy, had started a new company, Primary Networks, to enable voice and video calls over the Internet, a revolution that was just beginning.

The two had hatched the idea when MeLampy called Ory excitedly to tell him that wireless carriers had just standardized something called SIP—Session Initiation Protocol—enabling people to make calls over the Internet. "This is really transformational," MeLampy said.

Ory and MeLampy knew there would be huge obstacles to building a telephone network over the Internet. There would be firewall issues, security issues, and issues in getting a provider such as AT&T to connect over the Internet with another provider like Verizon.

Within a few months, Ory went to visit Sonja on Sand Hill Road. While the working name for their new company was Primary Networks, Ory used the code name Acme Packet in his presentations to VCs. It was something of an inside joke. Acme was the fictional company that supplied Wile E. Coyote with the artillery and gear he used to pursue the Road Runner. The "packet" represented the packets into which data is divided before it can cross the Internet.

"The point at which service provider networks come together to pass services between each other," Ory told Sonja and the Menlo partners, "is the weak link in the service delivery process. We believe that by developing a technology to enable service providers to handle those *border issues,* we will create a company with real and sustainable value over the long term." He called those way stations "session border controllers"—a category of product that didn't yet exist.

Ory acknowledged that creating a new category was far more difficult than innovating within an existing market. "The good news," he said, "is that if you create a category, you create a lot of value. We are creating something entirely new. I am convinced that every single carrier will one day have our SBCs on the edges of their networks."

As he talked, Sonja was reminded of Jeff Hussey, the entrepreneur who had founded F5 Networks after seeing something fundamentally missing in the development of the Internet. As online traffic increased, so did overloaded networks. Hussey's load-balancing software had solved that problem, and F5 grew into an industry leader.

Sonja knew Ory to be a phenomenal entrepreneur and visionary, although his Harvard degree had been in visual and environmental studies with a concentration in film. Communications were moving away from the network architecture called TDM—Time-Division Multiplexing—to IP, or Internet Protocol. Her investment strategy was to look for the next big market that would make tomorrow's big companies. Ory had the same approach, asking, *What will the companies trying to move communications online need? What core infrastructure is missing?*

The Menlo partners were taken by Ory's idea for Acme Packet and asked Ory what sort of funding he was seeking.

Ory hadn't thought that far ahead. He suggested, "How 'bout if Sonja flies to Boston in a week or so and we put together a business plan?" The partners agreed, and Sonja flew to Boston to work with him on a detailed plan. He soon returned to Sand Hill with a PowerPoint presentation, and talk turned again to financials.

Referring to ownership percentages in the company, Ory said, "I know you want to be in the twenties, and I want to be in the forties. I'd say the company is a $28 million pre-money valuation. You put $12 million in, and it's a $40 million post valuation."

The Menlo partners agreed. The $12 million investment would be Menlo's first commitment from its new $1.2 billion fund Menlo IX.

Back in Boston, Ory received a check from Menlo for $12 million, which he and his father took to the bank. The clerk said, "I'm sorry, we can't deposit this into your account. Your business name is Primary Networks."

Andy replied, "Okay, today we change our name to Acme Packet." As the paperwork commenced, Andy thought about the $12 million check he was holding. It represented people's livelihoods, mortgages, and health insurance. It was money that Menlo's limited partners had worked hard to make. And Menlo, he knew, would get paid only if his company became a success. The check represented the long road ahead.

With the economic downturn, a credit crunch, 9/11, and the Bush administration's war on terror, the wind was not at the backs of the economy or the Acme team. One of their investors even took Acme off the website following the telecom sector meltdown. But over time Acme landed one deal after the other. Soon it was routing all of Verizon's wireless calls.

Acme's session border controllers, or SBCs, were becoming a staple of the industry. Whenever a telephone call or video call needed to be routed from one network to another, they needed Acme Packet. Small companies, including Skype and Vonage, used SBCs when they needed higher-quality and more secure solutions.

Sonja, who had a seat on Acme Packet's board, never wavered in her support for the company. As she told Ory in their struggling early years: "Some of the greatest companies are way behind plan in the beginning, but then they just start beating the plan consistently." Whenever Acme needed more money, Sonja came through with it, something that wasn't true of Ory's other investors.

Gary Bowen, also an Acme Packet board member, knew the challenges that went into building the company and securing later rounds of capital. And he came to admire Sonja's business acumen. He told Ory, "Sonja represents the venture in venture capital. She is willing to believe and engage."

There was something else that Sonja did that impressed Ory. He attributed it to her being a woman. After every board meeting, she called him to ask how he *felt*. No one else on any board had ever called to ask him how he felt. She asked because she cared about him; they were friends. But she also wanted to better understand his thinking on business decisions. She was that rare individual who went beyond the numbers and strategies on a whiteboard. She was interested in his emotional state and how it related to the future of the business.

THERESIA

While Theresia loved being a mother, she was happy to be back at Accel full-time. She was fortunate to have an amazing support group. Tim enjoyed toting Sarah around; she was on a good sleep schedule; and Theresia's mom and dad lived nearby and loved spending time with their granddaughter. Her parents also helped find an experienced nanny who was a part of the Gouw's extended family. Theresia realized it was unrealistic for her to expect to be home for both breakfast and dinner each day, so she decided to try to be home for dinner and bedtime.

A female CEO whom Theresia had met late in her pregnancy advised her that the time to keep working long hours is when your child is young and won't remember her mother being away. "When they're older, preteen or teen, when they don't ask you to be around, that's when you need to be around," the CEO told Theresia. Then she added, "When they start carpooling to get around, sign up for carpool. That's when you learn everything that's going on."

Theresia was soon back to flying cross-country for meetings. The travel posed a challenge for her, since she was breastfeeding, sending her into cramped airplane bathrooms to pump. But she made it work. Sitting on the runway on a delayed flight to New York, she reviewed her notes for her upcoming ForeScout board meeting. She also had a meeting with Israeli cybersecurity star Shlomo Kramer, the ForeScout adviser who co-founded Check Point Technologies. He was the entrepreneurial security genius she'd made a point of befriending in 2001, knowing the day would come when he'd stop angel investing to start another company. He'd kicked around several concepts for a new approach to online security and had landed on an idea that felt big enough and important enough to pursue. The name for his new company was WebCohort.

Theresia had arranged to take Shlomo around to a handful of Wall Street banks while she was in New York, to meet with chief information security officers to gauge their interest and solicit feedback on his idea. The bank security officers were happy to meet with Shlomo, given that he had already built Check Point into a multibillion-dollar public company.

After the board meeting, Theresia and Shlomo headed to their first stop, Goldman Sachs. Where Check Point's firewall security protected networks, WebCohort would be the first-of-its-kind Web application and database firewall. Shlomo had landed on the idea after reading a report on the growth of Web application servers, which host a combination of files and programs to implement applications accessed remotely. Shlomo realized that security would be needed to protect the server and keep the Web applications secure.

Theresia told the information security officers, "Your crown jewels—your database—are only one, two clicks away from hackers." Hackers could easily create fake log-in credentials, she said, that would take them straight to the bank's Web server and data server and into customer accounts and records.

Shlomo added, "That's where everything personal is, including all your credit card info. The hackers who penetrate applications are interested in the data and the database, and they get in using sequel queries," or sequel injection attacks. "The Web applications are the front door to this data."

After Goldman Sachs, Theresia and Shlomo went to see executives at several other banks, including J.P. Morgan and Citibank. As they asked the information security chiefs about their systems and needs, their interest in what Shlomo was proposing ranged from enthusiastic to tepid. But most of the responses were favorable, no mean feat given the tough economic times, when budgets were tight.

"We had enough good hits that I feel encouraged," Shlomo said after the meetings. He thanked Theresia for suggesting they visit the banks.

Shlomo had co-founded his original company, Check Point, in his grandmother's sweltering Tel Aviv apartment. He liked to say that Check Point was the "Jewish grandmother version of the Silicon Valley garage start-up." He and his partners tested the software for Check Point on two borrowed Sun workstations that they named Monk and Dylan (for Thelonious and Bob). Check Point wasn't the first firewall security company, but it was embraced as the first firewall security company that was easy to use. Shlomo had had no idea when he co-founded Check Point that it would grow into an industry leader. With a gentle disposition and a genuine love of building things, Shlomo was hooked on seeing an idea take root, struggle, grow, and begin to flourish.

In his work as an investor and an entrepreneur, Shlomo was proud of his ability to identify talent. And that was what he saw in Theresia. He knew of only one other woman VC, the Israeli Sharon Gelbaum-Shpan, who was doing cybersecurity investing, including in ForeScout. But at the end of the day, Theresia's gender was irrelevant to him. What he liked about her was that she was smart and ambitious.

It wasn't long before news spread that Shlomo Kramer was launching a new cybersecurity company. News stories reported that his first and only VC investor—he was investing his own money—was Theresia Gouw Ranzetta, who was investing $5 million for Accel and would take a seat on the company's board of directors.

News of the deal upset some denizens of the Valley. Irwin Federman at USVP unleashed a flurry of un-rabbi-like expletives. Similar responses echoed at Venrock, which like USVP had backed Check Point and had expected to be involved in whatever Shlomo Kramer did next. Federman was a board member of Check Point. Shlomo's decision to go with Theresia on the WebCohort deal—to the exclusion of other Sand Hill investors—caught insiders by surprise. Suddenly everyone was asking, "Who is Theresia Gouw Ranzetta?"

But Theresia had spent years ramping up her knowledge of cybersecurity, first at Release Software, where she negotiated the company's encryption technology licensing deal; then in the network security and intrusion detection courses and seminars she took; and now working in lockstep with the industry-leading ForeScout team. She understood the various methods of analyzing network traffic for a range of risks, from signatures to behavioral techniques. And she had great respect for Shlomo. She had no doubt that WebCohort—soon to be renamed Imperva—would be a success.

Not long after landing her deal with Shlomo, Theresia was working in her office in Palo Alto when Jim Goetz walked in and closed the door. Jim had always been a straight shooter as well as a trusted friend.

There was a serious look on his face this morning. He wasn't here to shoot the breeze. He got right to the point and told her that some of the guys in the Valley were suggesting Theresia was flirting or sleeping her way to important deals.

Theresia closed her eyes. She couldn't say she was surprised by what Jim was telling her. She'd heard rumors like this before, mostly snippets passed along by her assistant. She was surrounded by ambitious, high-energy guys—an occupational hazard—so there was always talk, she knew. She went out to dinner with entrepreneurs all the time, and there was talk. She went to conferences, and sometimes, again, she heard talk. That was one of many reasons she appreciated Goetz so much: He'd tell her what the other guys in the locker room were saying. Theresia felt every woman in business needed a Jim Goetz in her life, particularly in a high-testosterone environment like Silicon Valley.

She had to network with the guys, or she'd miss out on some of the biggest, most important deals and opportunities. Yet when she did network, she inevitably stirred up rumors. Even when she was nearing the end of her pregnancy, "waddling and pregnant," as she put it, there was still, unbelievably, talk.

She had a term for these kinds of rumors: *manslaying.* Some of the men, she felt, were actively trying to cut her accomplishments down to size. She knew some women complained of being undermined by other women in the race to get ahead. But in Theresia's world, the jabs came from men—specifically, men who were less successful.

She'd spent enough time in the tech industry to know that successful women disturbed the natural male hierarchy. In the male-dominated world of video games, men were rattled by winning girl gamers. And those with the most to lose were not the most successful male gamers. The ones who attacked the females on the leader's board were the male players who were struggling to make the cut, who thought they could raise themselves up by taking the women ahead of them down. These poorer performers were not threatened by losing to successful male gamers; that was the natural order. But losing to a woman was embarrassing in some way. It made them feel socially inferior.

At the end of the day, Theresia realized manslaying was a problem in the minds of men; it was their problem, not hers. She was not going to let some insecure VC rumormongers stop her from landing big deals.

MAGDALENA

Magdalena was ready to take her idea—improving the cash flow of Salesforce—to Marc Benioff. She had crunched the numbers repeatedly, as well as sought feedback from the sales team leader, Frank van Veenendaal. Veenendaal had done his own analysis and had come to the same conclusion as Magdalena—her plan was the right way forward.

When she was confident her proposal was thoroughly vetted and cogent, she drove to San Francisco to meet Marc. They usually met at Salesforce's office at One Market Street or a restaurant nearby. Occasionally they'd sit in Magdalena's car, when she found a rare downtown parking spot where they could sit and talk without getting ticketed or towed.

Arriving early, Magdalena found a parking spot. She thought about how her life had always centered on solving problems. Even her name had once been a problem to solve. When she was born, her father had gone to the town center to register her birth. In Turkey, only the father could do this, and only the father's name appeared on the registry.

As her father filled out the paperwork and wrote "Magdalena Yeşil," the scribe at the registry stopped him. "Too long," he said. "The name doesn't fit. You need to come up with a different name."

Her father knew the real reason the clerk insisted on a new name— Magdalena was too Christian, and Turkey was a Muslim country. "I can't come up with another name," her father protested. "This is the name my wife wants. She will take my head off."

"Sir, you have to come up with something else," the scribe insisted.

"Mag-da-le-na. No one will even be able to say it." Her father had to think fast, and decided: "Lena. It will be Lena."

Her father begrudgingly signed the form and returned home. His wife listened to the story of what had happened, and set her face in a determined scowl. Forever after, she would tell Magdalena, "Your name is not Lena. It is Magdalena."

When Magdalena was old enough, she figured out how to apply for college in the United States. So many good things seemed to originate from America—the Apollo space program, Levi's, Coca-Cola. When she learned she needed to take the SAT, she found it was offered early in the morning in only one location across the Bosporus. So she talked a fisherman into taking her across in the dead of night, to make sure she got there on time.

Magdalena had an intuitive grasp at figuring out what people wanted from her, without their asking. She had learned from childhood that no one was going to solve her problems for her.

Parked just off Market Street in San Francisco, Magdalena watched Marc approach her car. They'd had their laughs over the years, but they'd also faced many difficult moments together. Building a company was stressful during the best of times. And Marc was a first-time entrepreneur with everything to prove. He would show the tech world that he could be his own boss, forever banishing the "Larry Ellison Mini Me" moniker he'd picked up at Oracle, or else he would join the ranks of failed founders. She rolled her eyes as Marc stepped into the car holding a water bottle filled with an oddly colored liquid. One day a little while back, as the two were about to go into a conference room to pitch Salesforce to an investor, Marc had grabbed Magdalena's bottle of water and poured some yellow powder into it. She thought the powdered vitamin mixture looked gross and protested, "It looks like we're drinking pee!"

Marc, dressed in his Hawaiian shirt, was not a spreadsheet type of guy. So Magdalena wasted no time in telling him she had a solution to Salesforce's cash flow problem.

"This may be our best—maybe our only—solution," Magdalena said.

She shared her findings on the need for up-front commitments, contracts, discounts for long-term deals, and a reorganized sales commission structure. Finally, she said, "Marc, I believe this is a great solution. It will solve your cash flow problem. It's what we need to do to save the company."

Marc stared at Magdalena as if she'd suggested euthanizing his dog. "We can't do this!" he exclaimed. "This is against everything we stand for."

To Marc, the "End of Software" mission statement and the NO SOFT-WARE logo were how the company differentiated itself. Salesforce was committed to providing every company—small, medium, and large—with the same affordable and easy-to-access software, with no contracts or up-front commitment.

"I've been putting my neck out there saying no contracts, no discounts since we started the company," he said. "This goes against our whole marketing campaign."

Magdalena had anticipated the conversation wasn't going to be easy. Salesforce ran ads showing an F-16 fighter jet shooting down a World War I biplane: The jet represented Salesforce with the most advanced technology, and the biplane was a symbol of the antiquated and slow-performance software too many companies used. They hired actors to parade in front of competitors' conferences with antisoftware signs. They placed antisoftware posters in their office windows, figuring it was free advertising. Marc ventured outside several times a week to check the positioning of the posters.

Magdalena, though, was not about to give up. "Salesforce's no-risk, no-commitment environment for our customers is threatening our very livelihood," she said. "We have got to the stage where we've proved our product's value. We know customers love it. We've earned the right to ask for a contract and up-front payment. I believe our customers already know that they will use us for many years, so why not collect up front and solve our cash flow problem?"

She told Marc she had talked with Frank van Veenendaal about it, and he believed most of their customers would stick with them.

"We're not changing the software or how it is delivered," Magdalena went on. "We're just creating a new payment model." Customers, she said, would move from pay-as-you-go to annual or even multiyear contracts, with discounts given to longer contracts.

But Marc shook his head determinedly. When the economy tanked, VCs and others had urged him to drop the dot-com in Salesforce.com, saying "Don't you know dot-coms are dead?" Dot-coms were now "dot-bombs" and "dot-cons." But Marc believed in the transformative power of the Internet.

Benioff was a lover of nature, technology, animals, and yoga, which he was known to practice with his dog, Koa, Salesforce's "chief love officer." But most of all, at heart, he was a salesman—and a pragmatist. He thrived on people buying what he was selling. Running out of money would leave him with nothing to sell. And so a week later, he agreed to move forward with Magdalena's plan.

The changes that Magdalena outlined took several weeks to get up and running. To Marc's surprise, half their customers had no problem with contracts. They were already sold on the software and welcomed the discounts. A handful of customers were angry and chose not to continue. The rest grumbled but were mollified by offers to be grandfathered in with the old model and price for a year before contracts would be required. The sales team had new motivations, too. They could earn double the commissions by landing long-term deals. And having contracts enabled Salesforce to start selling to larger customers. Soon, just as Magdalena predicted, cash started streaming in. In early 2003 Salesforce posted its first cash-flow-positive quarter.

As things stabilized—for now—Magdalena continued her habit of stopping by Salesforce to talk with the team. She liked visiting with Courtney Broadus, an engineer who had joined Salesforce from Oracle. Courtney told Magdalena a funny story about arriving at Salesforce for her nine o'clock job interview the morning after the B-52's concert sales event. Benioff had been walking around the office with a boombox blasting music. Not much of a drinker himself, Marc handed Courtney a glass of champagne. She said yes to the job offer from Salesforce because she believed that the delivery of software desperately needed to change. At this point, she had little faith in Marc as a leader and was not even sure of his ability to pay people. Nor was CRM especially sexy to her. But she wanted to be a part of a potentially revolutionary change in the way people worked. She wanted to be part of an Internet start-up.

Still, at the end of her first week at Salesforce, when she saw everyone sitting down for a beer at midday, she cried. "This was a terrible mistake," she told a friend. But the company grew and matured, and Courtney helped build the technology architecture behind various departments. She had been excited to meet Magdalena, as she thought boards were comprised only of "old white guys." She confided to Magdalena when Marc was not being Mr. Nice Guy and when she was impressed. Courtney thought one of his greatest strengths was "hiring into his blind spot." Marc also won fans with his random acts of kindness. He regularly picked up medical bills for staffers in need and had established a culture of philanthropy. She told Magdalena that the employees' biggest fear was being acquired by Microsoft. The Salesforce team had begun to realize they had a great product, and they wanted to stay independent.

Magdalena also got to know former Oracle employee Tien Tzuo, hired as Salesforce's employee number eleven in 1999. Tien was responsible for building Salesforce's first billing system. In 2003 Marc suggested he become the company's first global chief marketing officer. Tien told Marc, "I've never done marketing." Marc replied, "You'll be fine." Tien quickly figured out that his job was to execute Marc's ideas. Marc had a fondness for sending chocolate to journalists and making elaborate, themed posters for events and product launches, so Tien made the vision a reality. The posters were hits until Marc landed on the idea of a poster featuring his friend the Dalai Lama meditating under the slogan "There is no software on the path to enlightenment." Salesforce printed 650 of the posters and sent them to journalists and clients as invitations to a benefit for the Himalayan Foundation. The idea backfired, and the press weighed in with scathing stories and headlines: "On the path to enlightenment, Salesforce.com has taken a detour." Marc issued a public apology, and Tien fielded calls from the Dalai Lama's people warning legal action. But through it all, as controversies arose and faded, Tien appreciated Marc's willingness to take risks.

Meanwhile Tom Siebel realized that Sales.com wasn't going to work as a division within his behemoth company Siebel Systems, and he returned investors' money. Larry Ellison eventually resigned from the Salesforce board, although he held on to his Salesforce shares. He and Magdalena were back on friendly terms, talking about the great outdoors while working out at the gym on Sand Hill Road.

As the market finally began to pick up, the once-moribund Salesforce was soon in a race to go public with another enterprise born in the dot-com heyday—Google. Magdalena, juggling USVP, Salesforce, husband, and kids, didn't expect any thank-you from Marc for rescuing the company; she didn't need anyone telling her she'd done a good job. As she saw it, Salesforce was as much her baby as anyone else's.

SONJA

On her third date with the otherwise charming and funny Jon Perkins, Sonja suspected something was amiss. As they were enjoying their entrees, Jon checked his watch, said he would be right back, and disappeared, only to return twenty minutes later.

The next dinner date unfolded the same way. He told story after story that had Sonja laughing and holding her sides. He talked about his rambunctious brothers (he was the youngest of four boys), about his parents, and about his childhood friends' fear of his loving but strict mother. He described the sailing competitions he had won and lost, and the college pranks he and his friends had pulled. And he told her about his adventures running a seafood restaurant in San Francisco's Ferry Building, when his background was in equities trading.

But like clockwork, in the middle of dinner and another hilarious story, Jon would check his watch, say he would be right back, and disappear, returning breathless just as Sonja was finishing her dinner.

After several such dinners devolved into a Jon Perkins disappearing act, Sonja grabbed his hand and asked, "What is going on?"

He smiled sheepishly. "Ute is very particular about the things she likes," he began, referring to Ute Bowes, his business partner at the newly opened Ferry Plaza Seafood. Ute was married to venture capitalist and USVP founder Bill Bowes. "She bought these handmade linens for the restaurant. They're beautiful. They're what you see at the finest restaurants. But we are a fish market.

"When I tried to hire someone to wash the linens," Jon continued, "no one would wash them because they can't be replaced. So I've been picking the restaurants we've been dining at near laundromats. I put the napkins in the wash before we sit down, and I set my timer for when they need to go in the dryer. I run over, put them in the dryer, run back, and then pick them up after dinner. That's where I've been going."

Jon could have told her she was beautiful, or lavished her with gifts, or brought her baskets of her favorite hydrangeas. But somehow Sonja found his explanation more endearing. "Why didn't you tell me?" she asked. "I can help you! I can show you how to take the napkins out of the dryer and run your hand over them, like an iron."

Sonja had met Jon at a wedding in Sun Valley in January 2003, less than a month after she broke off her engagement to the writer she had been dating. She had planned to get married on New Year's Eve at the St. Francis Hotel in San Francisco, but the closer she got to the date, the more uneasy she'd felt. Part of her success as a venture capitalist was her ability to listen to her intuition when something about a deal didn't feel right. And in the weeks leading up to the wedding, her doubts and unease only grew. She realized she was getting married for the wrong reasons. She was in her mid-thirties, with a dream job, family, friends, and a big house, but she felt as if everyone was wondering where the man in her life was. Did she scare potential men away because of her success? Was she married to her job? The pressure she felt to conform to societal expectations seemed to come from all directions. For women, it was more acceptable to be divorced at a certain age than never to have married. While single middle-aged men were seen as playboys or bachelors, single middle-aged women were spinsters or old maids, anomalies in the natural order.

Sonja called off her engagement shortly before the wedding and donated the room for their reception to a nonprofit to host a New Year's party. Her wedding dress went to a consignment shop. But instead of staying home over the Christmas holidays feeling sorry for herself, she took off for Costa Rica with a friend, Anita Weissberg, who lived across the street.

On New Year's Eve, when she was supposed to be walking down the aisle in San Francisco, Sonja sat alone at a picnic table on Tortuga and began to cry. She cried for the loss of the future she had imagined. She cried because she had thought her life was going one way, and now it was not.

But soon enough, like a warm summer rain, the tears stopped. *Snap out of it,* she said to herself, the way Cher told Nicholas Cage in *Moonstruck,* after slapping him. It was one of her favorite scenes in one of her favorite movies.

On their return to San Francisco, Sonja told Anita she intended to ignore societal pressure and embrace being single. She would focus on her own life. She would travel to exotic places, dine by herself, and relish her independence. "I'm going to spend time with my three best friends," she said. "Me, myself, and I."

THERESIA

With the departure of Jim Goetz, Theresia was more than ever at the forefront of Accel's efforts to rebuild, recruiting new stars, chasing new deals, and building team morale.

One of Theresia's first acts since Goetz left had been to hire a new principal, Kevin Efrusy. Theresia and Efrusy had worked together at Bain. After Bain, Efrusy went on to work as a product manager for Zip2, the company founded by Elon Musk, and as an entrepreneur-in-residence at the venture capital firm Kleiner Perkins, where he founded an applications service provider called Corio that went public in 2000. In her new role as managing partner, Theresia advised Efrusy on a new company that he was chasing for Accel as a possible investment. The company, offering free phone calls over the Internet, was called Skype.

Skype went live for the first time on August 29, 2003, and was an instant hit, attracting close to a million users. Efrusy was one of the first on the team to identify the new peer-to-peer Voice over Internet Protocol (VoIP) as a possible game changer.

"The challenge," Theresia told him, "is that there are multiple geographies and multiple complications." For starters, Skype founders Niklas Zennström of Sweden and Janus Friis of Denmark were in hiding somewhere in Europe to avoid being served with court summonses by U.S. lawyers.

Theresia told Efrusy, "You can help us as a principal, but you'll need to let the Europe guys take the lead."

Bruce Golden, who had joined Accel as a partner in 1997 in Silicon Valley, moved to London in the summer of 2002 to help develop Accel's European team with Kevin Comolli. In the summer of 2003, Golden and Accel associate Fearghal O'Riordain made contact with the elusive Skype founders and began negotiations with Zennström, who was based primarily in London, while the Skype development team was in Estonia, in northeastern Europe.

Theresia thought the world of Golden, who had invited her to shadow him on the job before starting at Accel. He was an entrepreneur himself, with several big wins as an investor, including the software companies Support.com, comScore, and Responsys. He was also one of the most principled people she knew. She and Efrusy would support Golden and the London team.

"On the positive side, we are seeing the birth of a new platform,"

Golden told the Accel team. "The growth is very impressive. On the flip side," he admitted, "the issues and risks are *beyond* anything I've ever seen in one company."

Zennström and Friis were defendants in a legal case involving their earlier company, Kazaa, a peer-to-peer music and video file-sharing site. Kazaa had become one of the most downloaded software applications ever while doing basically the same thing as Napster, which was shut down in the United States for enabling the illegal sharing of music files. Zennström and Friis had launched Kazaa without reaching deals with music and film companies in the United States. As a result, they were being pursued by a phalanx of lawyers for theft of copyrighted materials. Zennström was known to hide under his desk whenever an unfamiliar person walked into the unmarked Skype office.

Zennström and Friis had been instructed by their lawyers not to travel to the United States. Golden agreed to the stipulation that he would not reveal the founders' whereabouts at any time.

Part of Golden's job was to evaluate the risks with every deal: What were the risks within the team? Were there technology risks? Were there competitive risks? Were there unique intellectual property risks?

"This company has every one of those risks—and more," Golden told Theresia and Efrusy.

Golden had discovered that the core peer-to-peer technology behind Skype was *licensed* via a company that Zennström and Friis partially controlled. This meant that Skype could not entirely control its own destiny and potentially created conflicts of interest. For Skype not to own or fully control its core intellectual property at this stage was highly unusual for this kind of investment. With any deal, Golden needed to see how a company "invented" or innovated in some meaningful way to solve a problem or create an opportunity. Golden also learned that the creators of Skype's VoIP technology were freelance developers rather than employees where all work was clearly owned by the company. Not only that, the ongoing Kazaa litigation created uncertainty over whether the founders would be able to establish Skype in the United States. It was also uncertain how the FCC would rule on VoIP traffic, including issues such as tariffs and law enforcement intercepts. And finally, Skype was registered as a Luxembourg business entity, something Accel hadn't dealt with before. "This is very unusual and problematic," Golden noted.

Yet emphatic voices in Palo Alto and London were saying that this was just the kind of deal Accel should be doing and desperately needed for its portfolio. Golden tried to understand and mitigate the risks, and he studied up on Voice over Internet Protocol, which began to be developed back in 1975 and saw its first public application in 1995. It had started by emulating the telephone network but gradually evolved to an independent set of software standards for instant messaging, conference calls, and video calling. Skype had created a proprietary protocol suite targeted to corporate customers, a rare case of proprietary protocol dominating the open source alternative.

While remaining uneasy over all the risks, Golden and the London team reached an agreement with Zennström and offered him a term sheet in mid-December. The men shook hands, and Golden believed that Accel had a deal. Not long after, though, Zennström called Golden. The deal had to change. Zennström told Golden that he thought the Accel investment was in *euros,* not *dollars.* Golden was incredulous. Every term sheet, every discussion, every back-and-forth was in *dollars,* not *euros.* Accel's funds were denominated in U.S. dollars. The change would effectively increase the valuation of Skype and the amount of invested capital by roughly 25 percent, given the exchange rate. *This is not happening,* Golden thought.

Golden, who believed that deals were sealed with verbal agreements and handshakes, was forced to go back to the drawing board, creating a new term sheet with the latest numbers. After some discussion at Accel, a new agreement was reached. Golden and Zennström shook hands a second time just before the Christmas holidays.

Exhausted and relieved, Golden told Accel's London and Palo Alto teams that they finally had a deal. He was taking off with his family on a much-needed vacation. They were going on safari in South Africa.

With the Skype deal behind him, Golden and his wife and kids enjoyed the rugged beauty of South Africa and sightings of lions, leopards, rhinos, elephants, and buffalo. Traveling in South Africa's remote southernmost tip, cell phone reception was as elusive as big game. A few days into their vacation, Golden noticed he had an e-mail from Zennström. *Why would he be reaching out now?* Standing in a tropical forest in a patch of rare cell reception, Golden learned that Zennström was changing the terms—again. Zennström told Golden that he was getting better offers from other VCs. If Accel still wanted in on the deal, it would need to compromise on the amount it could invest and alter the terms of governance.

Golden considered his next step: Should he cut the family vacation short and fly back to London? Deal with this upon his return? Or try to connect with Zennström now? He at least needed to talk with Zennström. The next time he had cell reception, he would call him—which was challenging enough with Zennström, who had a reputation for swapping out cell phones the way he changed his clothes. After several attempts to reach him, Golden learned that Zennström was on vacation as well and was unavailable. Golden was conflicted. The deal was likely a moneymaker and maybe even one of those rare Picassos, the splashy brand-name deal that Accel couldn't afford to miss. Part of him wanted to put the deal back on the rails. But he had also reached a point where he could not rely on what he was being told.

Golden worried about the brand risk to Accel, given the possibility of intellectual property lawsuits. He worried about his relationship with the Skype team. Investor-entrepreneur relationships had to last for years and weather lots of ups and downs. Mutual trust and respect were required. Golden needed to know he could sit down with an entrepreneur and have a real conversation about how to work through issues and conflicts. *If this is our honeymoon period, what will it be like later?* Golden thought.

He felt he had done everything he could to establish a good relationship with the founders, particularly Zennström. He had made the case for how Accel would bring their resources to the table to build a dynamic business based on best practices. He jumped through every hoop, made it over every obstacle. Golden held to his belief that early-stage venture was a relationship business. Zennström clearly looked at the relationship as purely transactional. He wanted to make sure that at the end of the deal, he held all the cards. Golden had to acknowledge that Zennström was a formidable entrepreneur and a fierce negotiator. Skype was an outlier company with smart and aggressive founders, and this was their moment to bring in capital. Zennström had a strong hand to play.

When Golden returned to London, he updated the Accel team. In Palo Alto, Theresia understood Golden's desire to build relationships and companies. He was the lead on the Skype deal for Accel, and the final call was his. She knew not to be a Monday-morning quarterback. Golden had mentored her when she was an associate. He was an advocate for women, a team player, and took his responsibilities as an investor seriously. He had told her, "Great partners encourage other partners' moneymaking tendencies and try to discourage them when they have blind spots." It was a philosophy she was passing on to Efrusy.

Theresia also understood the issue of doing well while doing good. For some investors, deals were strictly business, not personal. For others, business was entirely personal. The best founders Theresia knew were those driven to make life richer, better, and fuller.

"I am concerned," Golden finally said of the Skype deal. He wanted to work with "people who will be very focused on doing things the right way and creating durable value for the ecosystem around them."

In the end, after final efforts to find a workable compromise, but facing deal fatigue and far weaker terms than originally negotiated,

Golden decided to pull out of the Skype deal. As he did, a dozen other venture firms continued the chase. It was a financial blow for Accel, as Skype went on to become a valuable and important new Internet platform. Golden would have mixed feelings, including regret that he had let his partners down. He would rehash the negotiations in the months to come. Fortunately, he would soon meet a tiny Scandinavian company called Qliktech, where he would serve as lead investor and board chairman, establishing great relationships over more than a decade. The investment would become the best in Accel London's first fund, returning 80 percent of the fund.

And for Theresia, it was early in the third quarter of a football game, with plenty of time to stage a comeback. She would continue building morale—and figure out her own ways to make the twenty-year-old venture firm shine.

SONJA

On a beautiful weekend in April 2003, Sonja went sailing on San Francisco Bay in a thirty-five-foot J/105 one-design keelboat, *Good Timin'*, owned by Jon's brothers Chris and Phil. Sonja and Jon were joined by Phil as they sailed from the St. Francis Yacht Club in San Francisco past Alcatraz Island and toward the majestic Golden Gate Bridge. Jon and Phil were accomplished sailors who had won major races with *Good Timin'*, and Sonja had done her own share of sailing in college. The wind picked up, the spinnaker was hoisted, and *Good Timin'* sliced through the choppy gray waters. Later that morning, they headed to lunch at the San Francisco Yacht Club in Tiburon, where the Perkins boys had spent almost every day of every summer learning to sail, competing for who was king.

Sitting out on the deck of the clubhouse, they were soon joined by several others. Within a half hour, at least fifteen friends had pulled up chairs. The view was great, the stories salty, but everyone wanted to meet this lovely woman named Sonja and hear how she had met Jon.

Sonja kept a photo of the first time she was with Jon, before they had officially met. Jon had been seated directly behind her at the wedding of Anita Weissberg's daughter in Sun Valley. He was attending with his mother, father, and Phil. Jon and Sonja met at the reception. A clever Anita had seated them together, and they hit it off immediately.

Sonja told Jon she had just ended her engagement. When Jon asked how she was doing, she told him honestly, "I'm okay with it."

The next day, as everyone returned home, Sonja spotted Jon with his family at the airport. They promised to get together when they were back in the city.

A month later Jon asked her to dinner. From the first date—with the beginning of the disappearing acts—Sonja had a great time with him. But she didn't hear from him for several weeks. Then suddenly he'd call out of the blue, and they'd get together again.

Sonja wasn't upset by the infrequency of their dates, as she worked long hours. At thirty-six, she was happily focused on her career. And Jon was putting out fires with his own start-up, Ferry Plaza Seafood.

Sonja began helping Jon out at the restaurant on weekends, selling fish with him behind the counter. She understood sales: Growing up, she had bused tables at a local Chinese restaurant and worked as a sales-girl in the children's section of Leggett's department store, where she had learned the art of upselling, offering a shirt to go with the pants, or rain boots with the coat.

Watching her work behind the counter, Jon was reminded of the wide-eyed Charlie on the Willy Wonka golden-ticket tour. As he turned away, he smiled. Her happy energy was contagious.

THERESIA

Theresia had an idea for a new category of investing, one that related to a few of her favorite things: shopping, travel, and real estate. Having landed the WebCohort/Imperva deal, and with her investment in People-

Support rising from the ashes and now showing amazing growth after moving its call center operations to the Philippines, she was on the trail of what she believed would be the next great investment opportunity for Accel.

Her "proactive investment thesis," as she called it, came from watching Google grow into the most popular way to search the Web. In 2003 Google earned $106 million on sales of nearly $1 billion. About 200 million searches were done through Google daily; it was an amazing success for two computer geeks who liked to Rollerblade and hoppity hop around the office. They had started out with a great algorithm for search, with no idea how to make money off what they'd built.

At an off-site meeting to discuss new investment themes, Theresia, now a managing partner, told her partners, "Google is impressive for making a ton of money, but what's also impressive is how they're pulling ad dollars away from traditional media—from print, from newspapers.

"To be successful, Google has had to optimize its 'one box' search experience. But there are different kinds of searches coming down the pipeline. If you're shopping online, you're better off putting in more specific perameters. You want size, color, images, stores, and availability. You want 'vertical search' or 'specialized search.'"

Theresia had followed Google's December 2002 launch of its vertical shopping search engine Froogle—a pet project of Larry Page's. "It hasn't gotten very big, and I think it is because it shows the classic innovator's dilemma," Theresia said. "Their core business, ninety percent of their revenue, is the one-box search. They have their best people on it. There's a burden in building another brand. What I'm talking about is the antithesis of one box. It takes you deeper into one category. It creates a better place for users. You won't need a new algorithm for this type of search, just a new way to organize all the information that is coming online."

She predicted, "Specialized search engines are going to drive transformational shifts in multiple consumer industries."

The more she researched "vertical search," the more excited she became. She was soon introduced to a couple of Stanford grad students who had spent much of their second year of business school working in secrecy on a vertical search start-up. The Stanford students believed they were onto something that could modernize an industry that was fundamental to the American way of life.

MJ

MJ watched her mother sift the flour, aerating it for lightness, breaking up clumps, and eliminating unwanted particles. Flour compresses in bags and boxes, and humidity makes it denser. There was something soothing about the sifting, something old world, connecting MJ to her family kitchen in Terre Haute, where a cloud of flour had looked magical in the slanted beams of the afternoon sun.

MJ's mother, Dorothy Hanna, had used this cake recipe a hundred times, but today she kept looking at the bowl and back again, confused. She couldn't remember whether she had added the salt and baking soda. MJ and her sisters shared worried looks. MJ's daughter Kate, now seventeen, stepped in to help. When Kate was little, her grandmother had babysat her every Saturday night. MJ and Bill would return from their date night to find them giggling in the kitchen, baking cookies, with flour scattered everywhere.

For the Fourth of July, Dorothy offered to bring homemade cookies to the family get-together. But when she showed up with packaged, store-bought cookies, MJ knew something was wrong. After seeing several specialists, the family learned that her mother had Alzheimer's. The woman who had never had a bad word for anyone, the kindest person MJ knew, was becoming argumentative and agitated. Her descent was rapid. It was as if her mother's personality changed overnight. MJ and her siblings huddled to figure out options for care.

MJ had successfully navigated major crises at IVP, but her family's dilemma was on a completely different level. At first, her dad had insisted on keeping his wife at home. But he was slightly built, and Dorothy was a bigger woman. He simply couldn't help her with physical things. So MJ and her siblings were forced to relocate their parents to an assisted care facility. But before long, MJ started getting calls in the night that her mother had wandered or fallen. Eventually Dorothy was moved to the "memory section" of the care facility. MJ admired her father for being there with her; after all, he had all his faculties. But when MJ visited, she would find bruises on her mother's arms—the staff claimed Dorothy resisted them. At that point, MJ realized she needed to find a better solution for her mom.

MJ, who was approaching her fiftieth birthday, wondered whether her mom had ever been truly happy. Was this horrible disease exposing a latent anger in her for not having achieved her full potential? Eventually her thoughts shifted to the choices she had made in her own life, when things were supposed to be better for women of her generation. MJ had never really asked herself the big questions. *Was she happy?*

MJ had always figured that her mom would outlive her dad, given that she was five years younger and women statistically live longer than men. MJ had envisioned her widowed mother one day in a cute little apartment of her own. In addition to cooking and sewing, Dorothy loved art and poetry and was a talented painter. But she never had time for these things with all her household responsibilities.

One day in early 2004, while cleaning up Kate's room, MJ sat on her bed to look at Kate's pictures. Kate had been an easy baby, and MJ had had an easy pregnancy. She smiled thinking of the night her water broke. It had happened right after her baby shower and five weeks before her due date. She and Bill went to the hospital the next morning and were told to go home and come back a few hours later. While Bill worked, MJ cleaned the house, made calls to IVP, then decided the lawn needed mowing. There she was mowing the lawn while she was in labor. MJ shook her head at the memory. Then she scooped up an armload of laundry and thought, *How much has really changed for women?*

PART
SEVEN

Life, Death, and Picassos

2005–2009

THERESIA

Theresia was in a board meeting for a company called Glam Media when she heard a juicy bit of news from fellow venture capitalist Tim Draper. Like a trader with a hot stock tip, she quickly fished her BlackBerry out of her purse and messaged Kevin Efrusy at Accel.

"Tim Draper just said he met with the Facebook guys yesterday," Theresia wrote to Kevin, who had been rebuffed in his efforts to meet with the founders of the year-old networking platform for college students called Thefacebook.com.

Kevin had been at Accel for two years now as a principal but had yet to land a major deal of his own. In early spring 2005, he had been chasing Facebook but getting nowhere. His calls and e-mails had been ignored; he was told the Facebook team wasn't meeting with venture capitalists.

Theresia's intel suggested that the Facebook guys were indeed meeting with venture capitalists—just not those from Accel. But she saw an opening that she knew Accel needed to seize. With the economy bouncing back, after bottoming out around 2003, Accel was focusing on new projects, instead of talking about which companies to close. The resurgence of consumer Internet companies and rise of social networking was starting to change relationships, dating, and even the way people communicated. Some looked at it as a new era, a Cambrian explosion of start-ups.

The dot-com boom had brought more than its share of overhyped companies that blew up and ultimately went bankrupt, but it had also yielded game changers such as eBay, Google, Amazon, and PayPal. And now new stars were emerging: LinkedIn, MySpace, Friendster, Yelp, YouTube, and Flickr. Yahoo!'s stock was surging. Google had launched

Gmail. Tesla, the electric car company founded in 2003 by Martin Eberhard and Marc Tarpenning, had a dynamic woman, Laurie Yoler, as its first seed investor and founding board member. Elon Musk had started his private space company, SpaceX, in 2002 and joined Tesla as an investor and chairman in 2004. Great deals felt possible again.

After getting the Facebook tip from Theresia, Kevin promptly went to see Peter Fenton, an Accel partner who was friends with Reid Hoffman, the former COO of PayPal, co-founder of LinkedIn, and one of the most connected people in Silicon Valley. Hoffman, an early seed investor in Facebook—he invested $37,500—wasn't sure about making an introduction. As he saw it, about 10 percent of VCs knew their stuff and were "value added." He believed that entrepreneurs needed to be extremely selective in who they partnered with, and Accel was not at the top of his list. But after a second call from Peter Fenton, Hoffman agreed to make an introduction.

On Friday, April 1, Kevin and Arthur Patterson, the silver-haired co-founder of Accel, walked from their offices on University Avenue in Palo Alto to Facebook's Emerson Street headquarters. They hoped to meet with former LinkedIn employee Matt Cohler, now Facebook's vice president of product management. Arriving at the office, Kevin and Arthur found Cohler and Dustin Moskovitz struggling to assemble Ikea furniture. The office was a mess. The men were directed to the conference room, where they were surprised a few minutes later by the appearance of Facebook's co-founder Mark Zuckerberg and its president Sean Parker, holding burritos.

Parker was an entrepreneur with a colorful track record. He had co-founded Napster, the music file-sharing site that had had a spectacular rise before an ignominious fall at the hands of the Recording Industry Association of America on copyright infringement charges. Parker had also founded a company, Plaxo, where his own board forced him out. He joined the Facebook team in the summer of 2004, when Zuckerberg moved operations from Harvard to Palo Alto.

Parker was extremely self-assured, while Zuckerberg came across as shy. Although the meeting was quick, Kevin and Arthur were impressed by Facebook's growth. Thefacebook.com had been launched on February 4, 2004, from Zuckerberg's Harvard dorm room. It was open to students at a growing number of colleges and universities, and it now had more than 2 million users in its first year.

As the meeting ended, Kevin asked Parker and Zuckerberg to come to Accel's Monday morning partners' meeting. The Facebook duo agreed, although they looked at each other in a way that made Kevin unsure of their commitment.

On the walk back to Accel, Arthur urged Kevin to make sure the Facebook guys showed up on Monday. Kevin planned to make it his weekend's work.

At the appointed hour on Monday morning, Zuckerberg, Parker, and Cohler walked into the Accel offices. The twenty-year-old Zuckerberg was dressed in pajama pants, a T-shirt, and Adidas slides. To Theresia, he looked impossibly young and like he had been up all night coding. Soon everyone took seats in the partners' conference room. Zuckerberg casually handed Theresia and the others his business card. It read: "I'm CEO, Bitch."

MAGDALENA

Salesforce had gone public in June 2004, and since then, the stock had been fluctuating, tempting employees to constantly track gains and losses. Marc wanted to get the employees focused back on company building rather than net worth tracking, so he called an all-hands meeting. He asked Magdalena to address the employees.

Taking inspiration from her time spent sailing off Turkey, Magdalena told the group: "The best way to avoid getting seasick in turbulent waters is to focus on the horizon. If you focus on what's nearby, you're going to get sick. Keep your eye on where you want to go, on the horizon as your long-term goal, and steer toward that.

"Just because we're a public company now doesn't mean we do anything differently," she went on. "It's business as usual. One of the most important lessons I've learned is, love your customers more than anyone else. Work for the customer, not the investor, or employees, or your boss."

The IPO had made paper millionaires out of many of Salesforce's early investors and employees. Courtney Broadus was just happy to be able to pay off her car lease. She was amused when she began seeing Marc Benioff surrounded by his own security detail. Months earlier she had seen Michael Dell, founder of Dell Technologies, arrive at Salesforce looking like the president flanked by Secret Service. Now she needed a special badge to get close to Marc at off-site events.

Salesforce's stock, which made its debut on the New York Stock Exchange, had ended its first day of trading with a 56.4 percent gain. Salesforce raised more than $110 million and ended the regular trading session at $17.20 a share, substantially higher than the company's IPO price of $11. Magdalena told Marc later, "We should have priced the stock way higher. If it jumps over thirty percent, you probably priced it too low. The appetite was there, and we were too conservative."

Benioff had wanted Magdalena by his side when he rang the bell on the New York Stock Exchange. But Magdalena couldn't make it. One of her boys was sick, and she opted to stay home in California to take care of him. She watched the proceedings from her home in Atherton.

Walking into USVP shortly after the Salesforce IPO, Magdalena was oddly melancholy. Her $500,000 personal investment was worth millions of dollars on paper—cause for a lifetime of celebrations. But she arrived at work feeling sad that USVP had missed the boat. She knew investors were calling and asking why USVP hadn't invested in a deal brought to them by their own partner. How was it that Magdalena had made a fortune by *personally* investing in the company, while USVP had passed on the opportunity *repeatedly*? Instead, USVP had invested in Tom Siebel's start-up, Sales.com, which went nowhere.

One reason Magdalena loved being a venture capitalist was that it gave her the chance to see an almost unfathomable range of companies in a day, to be intellectually challenged, and to test her judgment and aptitude on which companies to fund. She enjoyed working with entrepreneurs to help them make their dreams come true. The negative, as she saw it, was that venture capital firms were often comprised of lone wolves, individuals working in a partnership with no bosses. They had the *appearance* of cohesion, but equality was an illusion. As Magdalena saw it, there was always a pecking order, always a power dynamic. And she, as a woman, even one who became a partner, was lower in that pecking order.

At the top of the venture-entrepreneur food chain was Tom Siebel, whose company was acquired in 2005 by Oracle for $5.85 billion. As Oracle absorbed Siebel, setting up a fierce competition between former friends Larry Ellison and Marc Benioff, Salesforce continued its astounding growth. In 2005 Salesforce reported $176 million in revenue, an 84 percent increase over the year before, with 227,000 subscribers. In 2006 revenue jumped to $450 million, and the company had nearly 400,000 subscribers.

The terms *SaaS* (Software as a Service), *cloud,* and *cloud computing* were entering the national lexicon. In 2006 Google's CEO, Eric Schmidt—a friend of Magdalena's from her CyberCash days and from his time at Sun Microsystems—popularized the term *cloud* at an industry conference. Schmidt said, "What's interesting is that there is an emergent new model. I don't think people have really understood how big this opportunity really is. It starts with the premise that the data services and architecture should be on servers. We call it cloud computing—they should be in a 'cloud' somewhere."

Marc Benioff's memorable "antisoftware" campaign—coupled with his mantra that software and data should be accessible from anywhere anytime over the Internet—had been all about the cloud, before the term existed. At this point, it was clear that no one would call him Larry Ellison's "Mini Me" again.

Magdalena had watched the gifted former salesman step into the role of founder with assurance, creativity, and persistence. Benioff had come a long way from their exploratory lunch on the country club terrace in San Mateo, when he had asked her, "Should I do this?" and "Can I do this on my own?"

Magdalena, without hesitating, had answered in the affirmative. Long before just about anyone else, she had seen the clouds gathering, pointing to the future.

THERESIA

In the Monday partners' meeting at Accel, Theresia filed away Mark Zuckerberg's "I'm CEO, Bitch" business card without comment and got out her sequentially dated and coded notebook and mechanical pencil in preparation for the all-important sit-down with the Facebook team.

In addition to Theresia, seated around the table on the Accel side were Kevin Efrusy, Jim Breyer, Peter Wagner, Peter Fenton, and Ping Li, who had been hired as a principal six months earlier. Sean Parker took the lead in the presentation. He told the Accel group that two-thirds of Facebook users logged on at least once a day, and that the typical user spent at least twenty minutes a day on the site. Engagement rose as user numbers grew, unlike MySpace and Friendster and other big social networking sites backed in recent months by nearby VC firms. Those sites were losing user engagement as user numbers increased, Parker noted. There was clearly something different about Facebook, the second-fastest-growing site on the Internet. Only MySpace, with a population ranging from adolescents to senior citizens, was growing faster.

Theresia liked what she heard about Facebook. But she worried about who was running the company—was it Parker or Zuckerberg? She turned to Zuckerberg and asked, "How are you rolling out the business?"

Zuckerberg answered softly and articulately, explaining what he called his "velvet ropes" strategy: Colleges were "waitlisted" before they could be "admitted" to Facebook. To be waitlisted, a university had to submit an e-mail petition signed by students, and the petition had to include all the students' .edu e-mail addresses. "Your friends at other schools are on it. You want to have it at your school too—if you're lucky enough to get in," Zuckerberg said. "Everyone wants to be the next college on Facebook." Once Facebook was available, students felt compelled to join because everyone else was using it.

Theresia found Zuckerberg's thinking shrewd. *Quiet but a deep product thinker,* she wrote, adding, *FB the eBay or Amazon of social?* As the meeting went on, she became convinced that Zuckerberg was in charge.

Jim Breyer, who had risen through the ranks of VCs to become one of the masters of the universe—he sat on the board of Wal-Mart and Dell—had been approached by Zuckerberg before the morning meeting. Zuckerberg told him that if they did any deal with Accel, he needed Breyer personally involved.

Listening to the presentation, Breyer was impressed by the numbers and by Zuckerberg's quiet intensity. Breyer had learned that Zuckerberg, whose father was a dentist and mother a psychiatrist, was a psychology major at Harvard and a computer whiz with a reputation on campus as the go-to guy for software programming. Zuckerberg made it clear to Breyer that he wanted to build a business beyond colleges and connect people worldwide. He was proud of the monthly active user numbers, the daily active users, and the amount of time users spent on the site. In the partners' meeting, Breyer zeroed in on the small print at the bottom of one of the slides, where a footnote would be placed. It read "Thefacebook, a Mark Zuckerberg production." *Important detail,* Breyer thought. The meeting lasted about an hour. Kevin promised to get back to the Facebook guys right away.

Trying to get a room full of type A personalities to agree on a deal wasn't always easy. In this case, though, the enthusiasm from the Accel brass was unanimous and overwhelming. Patterson, not prone to superlatives, had called the Facebook numbers "spectacular" after he and Kevin met with the Facebook duo on Friday. Theresia found Zuckerberg compelling, saw the extraordinary growth of the site, and thought the demographic was golden to marketers, who looked at college as the time when brand loyalty took hold. Given its closed network, Facebook also felt different from other networks such as Friendster and MySpace, which had a reputation for fomenting a sleazy element among its users. Breyer, a student of technology and a lover of the arts, thought Zuckerberg was socially reticent but intellectually confident. Breyer intended to make some calls to VCs who had worked with Parker and gather as much information as he could.

The Accel team had been told that Zuckerberg was going to sell only 10 percent of his company, so he could retain control. He reportedly already had a $6 million offer at a $60 million valuation from *Washington Post* chairman and CEO Don Graham. Graham had the advantage of running a privately held company and told Zuckerberg that he would never push him to go public. Any venture firm, on the other hand, had a responsibility to eventually return liquidity to its investors with a sale or public offering. Therefore Accel would need to pay a premium over Graham's offer.

Kevin worked with Breyer and Accel's in-house lawyer on the terms of the offer. Standing by the printer, Theresia and Kevin talked about the best approach. Kevin was thinking about a term sheet that mirrored Don Graham's offer.

Theresia had a different idea.

"Look, the whole partnership believes we should win this deal," she said. "I think you should bring multiple term sheets." Accel had a $450 million investment fund to draw from. "The most we can lose is ten million dollars. That's *if* we're all wrong on this." She believed they needed to offer $10 million for a $100 million post-money valuation. "Mark is a student of technology," she said. "Google's valuation was a hundred million. Mark is going to want at least that."

She added, "If you offer six million and they want ten million, we lose potentially a hundred-million deal over a four-million dollar difference. If we don't get the deal, we make nothing."

Kevin agreed with Theresia's strategy and went with two term sheets. That afternoon Kevin, Theresia, and Ping Li headed the six blocks down University Avenue to Emerson Street. "Strength in numbers," said Theresia, who had cast off the androgynous and unflattering VC uniform of khaki pants and blue button-down shirt in favor of a dress and high heels. "If you want to show love for a deal," she said, "grab your people and go to their office."

She glanced at Kevin, his body seemingly pulled along by his thoughts. Theresia admired his determination. He had a bachelor's degree in engineering and an MBA from Stanford. And his first child was born three months after her daughter, Sarah.

Kevin, too, had been impressed with Theresia. She had established credibility in the world of cybersecurity, not an easy thing, and had developed relationships with key industry leaders, such as Shlomo Kramer. And she had helped mentor Kevin. She told him to dive into new fields of interest without overthinking the subject or its challenges, and not to worry about his first investment in a new space, as it sometimes took a second or third investment to pay off. She urged Kevin to pursue a company, even if everyone was saying no. He had followed her advice, staying close to Facebook when all leads went cold.

"This is it," Kevin said, standing outside the Facebook office. It was located above a sushi restaurant. After being buzzed in, the Accel team headed upstairs. At the top of the stairs was a graffiti-inspired mural of a buxom woman in lingerie riding a fire-breathing animal. The walls of the office were covered with similarly edgy and arresting murals, most depicting women's faces and scantily clad bodies. Theresia did her best to ignore the sexual undertones. But it was clearly a company run by men, and not particularly enlightened men at that.

Theresia, Kevin, and Ping headed into the conference room. Theresia looked at the offerings on the side table. Where most companies stocked bottled water or Power Bars for visitors, Facebook had a two-liter bottle of Jolt Cola and a half-empty plastic gallon of Popov Vodka. As they waited, Kevin and Ping urged Theresia to check out the women's bathroom and report back on the murals. The images in the men's room were apparently explicit. Theresia, who had spent her fair share of time in frat houses at Brown, thought the Facebook office had a fraternity feel.

"I'm not going to the bathroom to look at the murals," she protested. "Besides, the meeting is about to start!" Distractions aside, Accel needed this deal. Facebook, while run primarily by college students and open only to college students, was viral. Theresia and the team had come to present their offer in person to show their love for Facebook.

A few minutes later Parker and Zuckerberg joined them at the table. Kevin opened by talking about the unanimous enthusiasm on the part of the Accel partners, the impressive usage numbers, and the company-building expertise and contacts that Accel could bring to the deal. He had two term sheets and handed over the first, which valued Facebook at $60 million post (after Accel's $10 million investment). Theresia could see that offer was going nowhere. Kevin kept talking, and slid the second term sheet across the table, this one giving Facebook a post-money valuation of $85 million. The reaction from Zuckerberg and Parker was warmer. After some discussion, they said they needed to talk it over and would get back to Kevin.

Returning to Accel, Kevin was relieved he had brought more than one term sheet, as Theresia had suggested. Negotiations had begun.

That night Jim Breyer was at home when he got a call and an e-mail from Zuckerberg and Parker. Accel's best offer was "unacceptable." Breyer was used to such negotiations and set up a dinner for the next night at the Village Pub to talk strategy.

Negotiations continued for several days, as Efrusy and Breyer worked their angles to cement the deal. Theresia supported them both. She had learned a lot from Breyer about the consumer side of the business and respected him enormously. When she joined Accel in 1999, Breyer had been negotiating a deal with Wal-Mart to spin out Wal-Mart.com.

Theresia was made Breyer's second on the deal and attended the board meetings as an observer. She'd met Don Graham through Breyer as well; he and Graham were both on the board of BrassRing, a job listing site.

Everything looked promising for Accel to land the Facebook deal. But Theresia knew from experience that a deal wasn't done until the contracts were signed. Peter Fenton had thought he had a deal to invest in the photo-sharing site Flickr, only to see it snatched at the last minute by Yahoo! And Breyer had recently got close to an investment in the social network Tickle, until Monster.com swooped in and acquired it. And of course, Bruce Golden was sure he had had a deal with Skype, only to be repeatedly disappointed.

On Thursday, Zuckerberg walked alone from the Facebook office to Accel. He and Breyer met one-on-one in Breyer's office, with the door closed. The negotiations lasted for two hours. As Theresia had predicted, Zuckerberg was looking for a $10 million minimum investment that would value Facebook at $100 million. The sticking point in the closed-door meeting was in the ownership stake. Accel wanted to own 20 percent of Facebook for its $10 million investment. Zuckerberg flatly refused. He countered with 10 percent ownership of Facebook shares. Breyer then proposed a compromise: that Facebook give up 15 percent ownership if Accel put in another $2.7 million. Terms of the dilution of the shares were negotiated, with complex stipulations by each side. Breyer, determined to close the deal that afternoon, said he would also invest $1 million of his own money. Zuckerberg had a final stipulation: that Breyer join the Facebook board. Otherwise the deal was off.

The men shook hands on the final details that afternoon, and the news soon hit the street: Accel would invest $12.7 million in Facebook, giving Facebook a valuation of slightly less than $100 million. It would own roughly 15 percent of the company.

Jim Breyer took his seat on the board and began a routine of weekly walks with Zuckerberg. Kevin Efrusy, the principal who had brushed aside rejection and kept after the elusive Parker and Zuckerberg, had landed his first major deal. And Theresia had played a hands-on role. If the original term sheet hadn't been upped—if Efrusy had gone to Facebook with only one term sheet—the conversation could have ended in the Facebook conference room.

Not long after the announcement, Theresia was in a meeting when a visiting VC said to her, "We hear you valued Facebook at a hundred million, and they have only two million users? What were you guys thinking!"

Theresia knew exactly what she was thinking. Maybe, just maybe, Accel finally found its Picasso.

MAGDALENA

Magdalena noticed something wrong with her: her feet and hands tingled with numbness. Initially she dismissed it as a weird anomaly, until it happened again and again. She went to see her doctor, who didn't have an answer for what was going on. He referred her to a specialist. As she made the rounds of specialists, her condition worsened. She would lose consciousness at times without warning.

A number of neurologists misdiagnosed her. It became clear that no one was sure what was going on. The only consensus was that what was good for the heart was good for the brain. She was advised to focus on her health, to exercise more and eat better. Magdalena had always loved food and enjoyed walking, hiking, swimming, and sailing. She had a fast metabolism and was never overweight, but she was aware that she spent too many hours sitting at her desk and in meetings. She also enjoyed USVP's catered lunches and ubiquitous cookies, a huge treat for her boys when she brought them with her on weekends.

As someone who thrived on solving problems, she was desperate to find an explanation. Fixing a computer was a matter of replacing the part that was broken. Fixing a nervous system wasn't so straightforward.

The only thing Magdalena knew for certain was that her health was in decline. Faced with uncertainty, she began to withdraw from work, friends, and even her time at Salesforce. She didn't tell anyone except her husband, Jim, because she didn't have a clear diagnosis. She didn't want to be perceived as weak.

Privately, she worried about who she was without work. She didn't read books, go to movies, visit museums, or watch television. She had attended operas with her mother, who knew every opera by heart, but it was hardly a passion. To Magdalena, work was her life.

Her mother, Selma, had found fulfillment at age sixty-three working in the bakery of a new Whole Foods store in Palo Alto. Up to that point, Selma had played a support role in her family: supporting her husband, her mother-in-law, her children. Magdalena's decisions in her life had been in part a response to her mother. Selma had been a good mother, but she wasn't happy. When Selma landed a job and began receiving a paycheck for the first time, her life had been transformed. She showed up at work so early every day that the manager gave her the keys and suggested she open the store. When Magdalena and Selma walked around town, everyone seemed to know Selma.

Magdalena's symptoms waxed and waned but didn't go away. To get better, she believed she needed to turn her attention to just one project: herself. Over a difficult breakfast with Marc Benioff, Magdalena, without going into details, told him she had health concerns and would need to resign from the Salesforce board. She told him that she would be fine, but the concern in his eyes was clear. They'd come a long way together, and Magdalena was determined to exit on a high note.

As she returned home, she did have one regret in her professional life—and she wasn't one for regrets. She regretted that she had set aside her own needs the day Salesforce went public. She should have gone to New York for the IPO, she realized. Yes, her son had been sick that day, but he would have been fine without her. She should have stood next to Marc during that historic moment when he rang the bell on the New York Stock Exchange. She should have been there to celebrate the company she had helped build and bring to life in that apartment on San Francisco's Telegraph Hill. An IPO, like a birth, happens only once. *Big mistake,* she said as she drove home. *No man in his right mind would have made that decision.*

Magdalena continued to appear confident in public. But in private, the undaunted girl who loved her hammer and nails, the intrepid young woman in her flamboyant costumes at the Stanford computer center, the competent builder of companies, was scared.

THERESIA

In the spring of 2005, the Stanford business school students were still developing their business plan in stealth mode when Theresia met with them as part of her quest to find transformative new vertical search companies. The graduate students were trying to keep a low profile, knowing that their start-up was going to rankle the second most powerful lobbying group in America—the National Association of Realtors.

Sami Inkinen and Pete Flint had spent most of their second year of business school learning everything they could about the real estate industry. Flint, who had an undergraduate and a master's degree from Oxford University and had co-founded a leading European online travel site, had been dismayed by how little information was available online when he began to look for off-campus housing. The process of finding a place to live felt medieval.

There was no consumer-focused site that aggregated data and listings. Searching for a home required scouring individual real estate broker websites, calling the brokers, and scanning newspaper listings. Something called an MLS—a Multiple Listing Service—provided access to residential listings, but its information was available only to agents. Home buyers were not permitted to search the MLS, and the realtors' association held the information closely, working with one aggregator, Realtor.com, in exchange for revenue sharing. But the walls were coming down around real estate listings and housing data. Some agents and brokers were beginning to share the information on their own websites.

Inkinen, who grew up on a farm in Finland, had a master's degree in engineering physics. He had co-founded a software development company in Europe and was an elite cyclist. Their idea for a vertical search site started with the basics, featuring homes for sale online. Flint told Theresia, "We feel that when a consumer searches for information on a property for sale, they should end up on the listing broker's website. That's where there are the most pictures, information, and virtual tools. That's where the contact info is. That's where I would want to go as a consumer."

Inkinen and Flint grew their site layer by layer with user-supplied content, photos, maps, and much more. They believed that making this information readily available to everyone free of charge would modernize an industry that was fundamental to American life and to the American dream. "We will offer the best user experience for home seekers," Inkinen said. They had raised seed money from family and friends and were just starting to look for venture funding for their site, tentatively called RealWide.com.

Theresia, believing real estate was going to be disrupted the way travel had been, met with a dozen start-ups in pursuit of next-generation search in real estate before meeting Flint and Inkinen. Taking ad revenue that traditionally went to print newspapers and magazines and moving it online, the way Craig Newmark had done to classifieds with his online market Craigslist, had huge moneymaking potential, she realized. She thought Inkinen and Flint had the best grasp of how to build a product, set up distribution, move content from brokers to their site, monetize, and brand. She liked everything about their start-up except the name, RealWide.com, which sounded like a motor home. It would need to change.

While being hit with cease-and-desist letters from the realtors' association, Inkinen and Flint had made a key discovery. No longer able to deflect the National Association of Realtors by saying they were Stanford students working on a school project—a line they'd used with success in the past—they researched legalities and loopholes in search and copyright. They discovered that they had the right to use thumbnail photos of homes on their search site if they linked back to the copyright holder. This constituted "transformative fair use." Theresia saw that this was the breakthrough they needed, and that she needed to feel secure as an investor. Inkinen and Flint began meeting with real estate professionals and organizations to convince them of the advantages of promoting their business online rather than in print and on their site rather than on individual broker sites. After prototyping ideas, Inkinen and Flint officially launched in late 2005, with a $5.7 million investment from Theresia at Accel.

Early on Theresia's partners were concerned that Inkinen and Flint were "too much alike," with physics degrees, MBAs, and international backgrounds. They even looked a bit alike. The Accel partners also worried that neither had a computer science background. But the two founders quickly figured out their roles, with Flint as CEO and Inkinen as COO. They dealt with the lack of coding experience by hiring Stanford computer science student Louis Eisenberg. And they came up with a new name aligned with their desire to provide truthful and accurate information: The company would be called Trulia.

As Theresia drove back to the Accel office in her silver XK series Jaguar convertible, she gunned it, luxuriating in the 370-horsepower engine and the XK series' 4.0-liter aluminum cast AJ-V8 engine, forcing 11.6 psi of boost through twin liquid-cooled intercoolers. Just as Theresia knew sports better than a lot of guys, she also knew cars better than most. She grew up with guys who fixed American muscle cars. She had worked at Harrison Radiator the summer after her sophomore year at Brown, and she had watched and learned. She knew how to replace a fan belt with pantyhose, fix a radiator hose clamp with a swimming pool hose clamp, and reattach her car muffler with a coat hanger.

Accelerating down the highway, she cranked up the radio to Gwen Stefani's "Hollaback Girl." It had been ten years since Netscape went public, the seminal event marking the start of the dot-com boom. She had started at Accel at the peak of the bubble. And then the tech bubble had burst; the next three years, from 2000 to 2003, were an extended dry spell.

But now that the economy had rebounded, it was a different ball-game in Silicon Valley. She had received her first million-dollar bonus, allowing her to buy her parents a home nearby—a big deal for the child of immigrants. She also had a financial windfall when two Accel companies went public. Theresia's once-moribund dot-com company, PeopleSupport, which provided online outsourcing and had moved its operations to the Philippines, had gone from burning $1 million a month in cash to generating more than $1 million a quarter in cash, six months later. PeopleSupport founder Lance Rosenzweig took the company public in September 2004—a month after Google's IPO—raising $48 million. It was Theresia's first IPO and a lesson in the importance of a founder's determination. The turnaround by Rosen-zweig taught Theresia that a good founder who cares enough about his or her company can make the tough decisions needed to get through a crisis. The IPO payouts allowed Theresia and Tim to take care of all future college expenses for their daughter and for the sixteen children in the extended family. And Theresia bought a second home on the Hawaiian island of Lanai. Looking back, she realized that the dot-com bust had been tough, but she was that much the wiser—and richer—for having lived through it.

As Theresia eased her Jaguar into a parking spot at Accel, she had a good feeling about entrepreneurs Pete Flint and Sami Inkinen. What a year it was turning out to be. It had been only a few months since the Facebook deal, and now Trulia was on the horizon. She almost had to pinch herself: Could Trulia end up being a Picasso, too?

SONJA

On a beautiful spring day in 2008, Sonja left Menlo Ventures on Sand Hill Road to see her doctor at the Stanford University Medical Center.

She was confident that her physician had good news for her. She planned to do some shopping at the Stanford Shopping Center afterward, before returning to the office for a board meeting later in the day.

The day before she was scheduled to have a mammogram, Sonja had discovered a lump under her arm. She'd had a biopsy and was now meeting with Dr. Jocelyn Dunn to get the biopsy results. But she was confident everything was fine. Years before, her father had had quadruple bypass surgery. He was a naturally happy man and didn't spend a second worrying about his surgery. His motto had always been "Gratitude and a great attitude."

Sonja smiled at Dr. Dunn and thanked her for getting the results so quickly. Dr. Dunn got immediately to the point. There was no easy way to deliver this kind of news: Sonja had breast cancer. And in the pantheon of types of breast cancer, Sonja's was serious.

At first, the news didn't register. Dr. Dunn continued explaining the diagnosis and walking Sonja through the stages and grades. Then Dr. Dunn said something that Sonja understood: Her tumor was *very aggressive*. Sonja's blue eyes, normally placid and good at giving nothing away, blinked back tears. Her older sister, Julie, had been diagnosed with early-stage breast cancer a month before. It was her sister's cancer that had prompted Sonja to make an appointment for a mammogram. *Now I have breast cancer, too?*

A kaleidoscope of images ran through her mind: her parents telling her to take time off to destress; her romantic and beautiful wedding to Jon Perkins; her pitch meetings at Menlo over the years. Sonja searched Dr. Dunn's face for more information. The most devastating and confusing part of the news came in the form of what wasn't said: Sonja and Jon were about to adopt a baby girl, an opportunity presented to them unexpectedly, only weeks before. The birth mother was eight months' pregnant and a week away from moving into their home for the last month of her pregnancy. All Sonja could think was, *I have cancer and am about to adopt a baby.*

THERESIA

It was close to ten P.M. on Wednesday night, and Theresia was still at work. She hated to miss her nights at home and her bedtime stories with Sarah. She had been reading her the illustrated children's book *Strega Nona*, about a magic pot that floods a town with pasta. Wolfing down a Power Bar at her desk, she could think of worse things than a growing wall of macaroni.

As a managing partner, Theresia was spending a huge amount of time working with new hires, even those who weren't her own. She was also dealing with personnel issues, something she had come to see as the invisible work of women managers. She was still the only senior woman investor at Accel, and employees at all levels came to her with problems and questions. Her door was always open, and someone always seemed to be on her couch.

She felt she was constantly choosing between being liked and being respected. When a female employee asked whether she could leave to pick up a sick child, Theresia asked where the babysitter, partner, or husband was. There was a certain double standard here; Theresia was driven in part to protect the female employee. If a man asked to leave to take care of his sick child—something that never actually came up— he would likely be applauded as a great dad. If a woman did it, she was seen as weak or unreliable. Theresia was careful about her credibility with the guys. She was aware that her success at Accel could lead to other women being hired and achieving success in venture capital. She felt that the decisions she made—rightly or wrongly—represented to the men around her how all women managers might respond. So she weighed her decisions carefully. One woman, however dynamic, could not change a culture. But two women, or more, could begin to shift the dialogue and priorities. Two could even make a quorum.

Theresia's assistant, Angela Azem, had noticed subtle changes in Theresia's behavior and management style over the years. Theresia had become more vocal in meetings, talked faster, and tended to interrupt more, like the men. The male investors naturally spoke in deeper tones and thought nothing of interrupting.

But in countless other ways, Theresia was clearly not one of the guys. When she needed to get to the East Coast for a meeting and someone suggested she charter a private plane, she asked Angela, "Do you think that's okay? It's a lot of money." Angela replied, "Are you kidding me? Look at how much you contribute! You're a managing partner. We're a three-billion-dollar firm." Angela had never heard of a male partner questioning the use of a chartered plane. Angela was also struck by Theresia's kindness. She remembered her birthday, surprised her with coffee, asked about her kids, and worried when anyone was sick. This was something Angela had simply never experienced with any other boss.

Before joining Accel, Angela had worked at Wells Fargo. She'd managed twenty people and made peanuts. Plucky and smart, she was the mother of two young boys. She was constantly struggling with how to be there for her sons and not jeopardize her job. She saw Theresia navigating the same challenges, only magnified. Theresia was managing a household, a young child, an extended family, and a multibillion-dollar firm.

Angela witnessed a procession of white, male Ivy Leaguers at Accel and other firms funding companies started by mostly white, male Ivy Leaguers—or even more often, by elite college dropouts, many of them barely socialized geeks. The entrepreneurs repeated the pattern in hiring, creating one homogenous interlocking clique after another. Angela saw how little venture funding went to woman-founded start-ups, despite studies showing that the female-founded start-ups outperformed their male counterparts in terms of revenue. Angela also was aware of how the women founders received pushback during presentations. When a woman's founding team included a man, the man was asked the technical questions. Women founders tended to ask for too little when seeking funding, while men often oversold their company and accomplishments. She even knew of women founders who created fictional male co-founders to communicate with investors and outsiders over e-mail. Responses to the made-up male character were quicker and more serious.

In her seven years at Accel, Angela had met three women she considered to be "badasses": Theresia; Sukhinder Singh Cassidy, a bold and successful entrepreneur of Junglee and the financial technology start-up Yodlee; and Liz Kalodner, the wise, funny, and decisive CEO of SocialNet.

Not easily impressed, Angela had come to see Theresia as someone in a league of her own. Theresia didn't take it personally when visitors to Accel asked her for coffee, assuming she was someone's assistant. Theresia didn't let jealousy-fueled rumors sidetrack her. She brushed them off. From time to time, Theresia and Angela would go out after hours. Theresia, Angela discovered, could drink her under the table. It was Theresia who had inspired Angela to come up with her own definition of what a female badass looked like: She is not afraid to take risks in an industry that isn't female-friendly; she shares the spotlight and empowers other women; she is philanthropic and cares about issues that aren't just related to her world; she builds relationships rather than just networks; and she is an overachiever and high-performer who recognizes she can't get half the things done without a village of people working with her.

Theresia was aware of how far she'd come. But she was also savvy enough to know that in the topsy-turvy world of the tech economy, what went up often came down.

MJ

The venture team at IVP took their seats in the conference room with Evan Williams and Biz Stone, founders of a microblogging start-up called Twitter. The founders sat at the end of the long white conference table in the all-white room, the sun streaming in behind them.

Across town, MJ sat in another white room, but instead of a

conference table, there was a bed with her mother in it. Instead of talking about the future, she was thinking about the past.

In the meeting at IVP, Norm Fogelsong asked what made Twitter special. *How is it different from group e-mail or group texts?* Evan Williams answered in a way that resonated with the investors. When the terrorist attacks took place in Mumbai weeks earlier, Twitter users had reported the news as it was unfolding, faster than traditional news media. There were eyewitness accounts, warnings to stay away from the area, pleas for blood donors, directions to nearby hospitals, and a helpline that would include the list of the dead and injured.

At the hospital across town, MJ talked with her mother's doctor about what to expect. Dorothy Hanna had fallen and broken her hip. Her mind, ravaged by Alzheimer's, suffered another setback while she was under general anesthesia during surgery. She was now hallucinating and refusing to eat or drink.

At IVP, Biz Stone summarized the purpose of Twitter: "It's the pulse of the universe," in real time, in 140 characters.

MJ hated missing IVP partners' meetings. They were a glimpse into a better future. Seated by her mother's hospital bed, she was focused on end-of-life care and on her mother's pulse, on that tactile connection to a heart she loved.

The IVP team ended the meeting with the Twitter founders with an eye toward investing. MJ and her siblings made plans for their mother to be moved to hospice care. MJ looked at her diminished mother and thought, *I'm not ready to lose her.*

SONJA

Sonja emerged from Dr. Dunn's office at Stanford like a sleepwalker. She found her car and got behind the wheel. The springtime sunshine—so glorious an hour before—felt harsh and unkind. She needed to call Jon, who would be at work. She needed to call her parents. She reached Jon first. "I have cancer," she told him. Jon, normally the life of the party, fell silent. They agreed to meet at home.

Today Sonja didn't mind the slow commute from Silicon Valley to San Francisco. She needed time to process. She thought of odd things, like the time she was at Harvard Business School and one of her professors told the women in the class not to wear pastel colors because if they raised their hand and they were wearing pastel, he wouldn't see them. Sonja told herself from that moment on, *All right, I'm wearing navy.*

She thought of the time she was president of Harvard's venture capital club and had scheduled Yahoo! founders Jerry Yang and David Filo to speak. Shortly before the event, Yang called her to say he was worried that no one would show up: The Harvard event was slated to take place the same night as the last episode of *Seinfeld*. Instead of rescheduling, they decided to air the show after the talk and provide snacks. The event sold out.

She recalled the day she became a partner at Menlo, four days shy of her thirtieth birthday, in 1996. Her partners had pulled her into the conference room and surprised her with the news. Her parents had celebrated by buying her a desk chair from her alma mater, the University of Virginia.

Then her mind wandered to her wedding, on December 2, 2006, held at a chapel in San Francisco's Presidio. Sonja, thirty-nine, felt that being older gave her a different vantage point. She didn't need everything to be perfect; she just wanted to be with her friends and family. And most of all, she loved the idea of marrying Jon. Her wedding dress, designed by Dean Hutchinson, was gorgeous. Her twin sister, Lisa, was her maid of honor, and her father walked Sonja down the aisle. The reception had been held on the second floor of San Francisco's Ferry Building, upstairs from Jon's restaurant. Sonja joked that she'd planned it that way to ensure Jon would show up. The night was magical, from the splendor of the newly renovated Ferry Building, with its grand promenade and tiled archways, to the holiday lights and decorations. The after-party moved across the street to a penthouse suite, where they danced until the sun came up.

They had married nearly four years after she and Jon started dating.

Nearly three years into their relationship, Sonja told Jon, "I will marry you if you want to get married. But if you don't want to marry, I'm not going to break up with you, because we're having too much fun."

She remembered a Thursday afternoon in late September 1991—*seventeen years ago*—when she slipped out of her Harvard dorm room to return to her old apartment on Myrtle Street, where her former roommate Anne and friends were hosting a keg party on the roof as a warm-up to the evening's concert. At around seven P.M., they walked together to Boston Garden to see the Grateful Dead. Sonja loved the Dead. She hadn't told her new Harvard Business School friends that she was going to the concert, fearful she'd be falsely labeled a pothead the first week of school—though she could have made the business point that the band raked in more money on the road than any other touring group. All their stadium shows were sellouts. But the truth was, Sonja had gone for the sense of joy and release, the positive energy that fed and mirrored her own. The band opened that night with "Jack Straw," and Sonja sang and danced and lost herself in a sea of tie-dye and patchouli.

Now, driving on Interstate 280 heading into San Francisco, Sonja hummed the lyrics to the Dead's "Box of Rain"—"Look out of any window, any morning, any evening, any day / maybe the sun is shining, birds are singing . . ."

MJ

MJ's husband was in Antarctica starting a nine-month sabbatical, in which he planned to travel across the globe. Her son, Will, was home for winter break from Colgate University, where he was a freshman. The little boy who used to love to ride his BMX bike and play T-ball was now an offensive lineman at the academically challenging Colgate. He weighed in at 260 pounds; MJ was half his size. He had grown into a smart, emotionally intelligent young man and a leader among his friends. MJ's elder daughter, Kate, had graduated from Stanford and was living in San Francisco's

Mission District, looking for her first job and finding her way. Hanna, her youngest, was a high school sophomore excelling at a top private school that she loved. As the kids got older, MJ felt that her ability to intervene in their lives and help solve their problems was diminished. Instead of diaper rash and playground mishaps, their issues revolved around boyfriends, girlfriends, partying, cliques, mental health, academic pressure, and peer pressure.

MJ had stayed on at IVP as an adviser, but she had stepped back from full-time work for the second time, to take care of her family and to be more present for her husband. Her mother was also requiring more of her attention.

At a hospice care center in Redwood City, MJ and her dad and her siblings spent time with Dorothy, shared stories, and kept one another company. MJ pulled out a journal she had kept from childhood and found the page where she had written about the newspaper route that she and her sister Shirley had had as kids:

> *Since I was so young—I was six—I had about thirty customers that I could walk to. Every week I would have to go and collect thirty-five cents from my customers. . . . The profits and the tips from the route really added up, and Shirley and I spent it on sweets, gifts for Mom, and trips to the town trampoline park. Most Saturdays we would go downtown to the soda shop and take turns proudly treating each other to our hearts' desire of sundaes, banana splits, cherry cokes, root beer floats, or cherry phosphates. It was a great feeling sitting on those stools with pockets full of cash. We would then walk over to the Rexall Drug Store and buy a gift for Mom. She had a favorite red Revlon lipstick called Fire and Ice that we loved to get her. . . . We loved treating her because she gave so much to make a nice home for us, and Dad was not the type to spoil her in any way. So, we took on that task. It was easy enough to show her our love.*

The room at the hospice center took on a heavy amber light. MJ had asked the pastor from her church to come to see her mother. As the pastor stood over Dorothy and prayed, her mother suddenly woke up, looked at the man, and said, "I don't know you!" It was a moment of clarity that MJ hadn't seen from her mother in years.

The pastor smiled and placed his hand on her arm. "That's right, Dorothy, you don't know me."

MJ's father, Michael, cheered by this moment of lucidity, asked the pastor to pray again. But as the room dimmed with the winter light, the pulse of life in her mother was fading. Later that night, MJ's mother, always in motion, was finally still. Dorothy Wilson Hanna, born August 28, 1929, a graduate of Gerstmeyer High School, a catalogue supervisor at JCPenney, a seamstress and baker, a wife of fifty-nine years, a mother of five and grandmother of ten, had died.

That summer, still grieving her mother's loss, MJ went to meet her husband on his sabbatical. Bill had come home briefly for Dorothy's funeral in March, then set out again. MJ had supported his sabbatical idea—she thought it would be good for him. She had originally planned to meet him in London a month earlier but had to scrap her plans because Kate was having challenges and had moved back home. Will and Hanna were also home for the summer.

MJ was reluctant to leave the Bay Area even now, but she felt she needed to spend some time with Bill. Her marriage wasn't in the best of shape, and she knew she needed to work on it. So she flew to France to begin an eight-day Tour du Mont Blanc hike that started at the base of the mountain. Their walk would take them from France into Italy, into Switzerland, and back to France. The company that organized the tour transported their luggage from one hotel to the next. Accommodations ranged from the luxurious to the equivalent of a youth hostel. At night, ravenous from hiking, they feasted on fondue, stews, raclette with potatoes, and tarts. The scenery was gorgeous, from snowy spires in the Alps to meadows filled with colorful wildflowers, from narrow paths through coniferous forests to a long suspension bridge that crossed a plunging valley. But while the others enjoyed the serenity of the hike, MJ found herself stepping off the path regularly to deal with issues at home nearly six thousand miles away. Bill seemed annoyed at the interruptions. He had been acting strangely to MJ, but she figured it was because of the amount of time they had been apart.

At the end of the eight days, MJ flew home. Bill was expected home in a month. Back in Palo Alto, she focused on caring for Kate, who was having stomach problems, and setting up appointments with doctors. Fortunately, IVP was thriving, returning huge and consistent profits to its investors. It had invested $14 million in Twitter as a part of the company's third funding round, and made other later-stage investments in Dropbox, HomeAway, and Zynga.

Finally, Bill returned from his sabbatical. So much had happened in the months that he had been away: the death of MJ's mother, their children's various victories and crises, MJ stepping back from the job she loved. Everything had changed, and nothing had changed.

SONJA

When Sonja arrived home, she found flowers from Jon. *Jon never gets me flowers,* she thought.

She gave herself time to settle in before calling her parents. Now two of their daughters had breast cancer: Julie, two years older, had always been the animal lover in the family, taking in strays, dreaming of becoming a vet. Sonja's twin sister, Lisa, was the creative one in the family, the talented artist. Sonja was the peacemaker, always sitting in the middle seat, helping her sisters to get along.

After sharing the news of her breast cancer with her parents, Sonja called two close friends, one of whom was involved in biotech and life sciences. Thinking she was being helpful by being direct, the friend in biotech told Sonja, "You have a fifty-two percent chance of survival. You should not adopt a baby."

Hearing her friend's words, Sonja began to hyperventilate. A day that had started like every other day had brought Sonja to tears. At work, she was on ten company boards. She was in the middle of investing a $1.2 billion fund. She had a baby coming into her life in a month. The birth mother, not ready to be a parent, was the niece of a family friend.

When Sonja had been asked if she would consider adopting the baby, she and Jon hadn't hesitated. But now Sonja wondered whether she could welcome this new life into a home where the future was so uncertain. She kept hearing her friend's words: *"You have a fifty-two percent chance of survival."* In other words, *"You have a forty-eight percent chance of dying."*

As she struggled to fall asleep that night, she thought about how and when she would tell her Menlo partners. When a prominent male venture capitalist let it be known he had cancer, the rest of the industry had treated him as if he were already dead. *If a man is quickly written off like that, what will happen to a woman?*

PART
EIGHT
The Days of Reckoning

2008–2013

SONJA

Sonja sat in a large cushy chair in the chemotherapy room at the University of California San Francisco Medical Center. Her gloved nurse, whom she referred to as Bruce the Almighty, hooked a bag of chemotherapy onto the IV pole next to her. A catheter was inserted into a vein in her arm; the drip infusion began delivering the potent chemicals to her bloodstream. The process was terrifying because it was so unknown. It could save her, and it could send her to her knees.

Sonja had opted to take her chemo treatments for breast cancer on Mondays, the day she'd always had her partners' meetings at Menlo. She was used to a Monday schedule, so this would be her new routine. She faced a daunting eight sessions of chemotherapy, one every other week, followed by thirty days of radiation. Chemotherapy, as she saw it, was both modern and primitive—a cell-destroying bomb instead of a guided missile, wiping out the good cells with the bad.

Shortly after her diagnosis, a friend gave her a book on what to expect from chemotherapy. The title and cover were so grim that Sonja took a Thomas Jefferson Monticello newsletter she had at home and used a page of it, devoted to discussing life, liberty, and the pursuit of happiness, to fashion a new jacket for it. The book was filled with tips about what to do before starting chemo, from going to the dentist for teeth cleaning to using towels for bed pillows—it made it easier to clean up the clumps of hair when your hair began to fall out. A minor infection or fever could turn serious quickly, and she should expect to feel worse with each treatment.

Sonja's health crisis had come at a time when Silicon Valley—and America—was having a life-changing crisis of its own. It was 2008, and

Bear Stearns had collapsed in February, followed by the bankruptcy of Lehman Brothers in September, the largest bankruptcy in U.S. history. Then the Fed had had to bail out insurance giant AIG. Home mortgages and values were in a complete meltdown.

Sonja had made a career of navigating the economy in good times and bad. Indeed, her life as a venture capitalist had been about taking calculated risks on unproven companies. But in the grand scheme of things, risk taking in Silicon Valley was circumscribed and safe. She was now facing an altogether different type of risk.

A natural optimist, Sonja decided to invest in life. She asked Bruce the Almighty for a warm blanket. Compact and muscular, he was as kind and doting as a grandmother, yet as dishy and interesting as the latest issue of *Vanity Fair*. She had to undergo four hours of chemo and, Bruce told her, could have as many warm blankets as she wanted.

Sonja had informed the mother of her soon-to-be-born adoptive daughter that she had breast cancer. The birth mother was calm and reassuring—she told Sonja that everything would be fine. The adoption plans should proceed. Sonja met with her doctors, Hope Rugo at UCSF and Jocelyn Dunn at Stanford, and the dire diagnosis she'd received from her well-meaning friend turned out to be off, in her favor. Her chances of survival were better than 52 percent. She had triple-negative stage 2 cancer, but it hadn't metastasized. Dr. Rugo told Sonja, "You should absolutely adopt—we've got this." The message was both a hug and a call to action. Sonja believed her doctors wouldn't tell her to commit to the future with the life of a newborn baby if they didn't think she'd get through this. She told her partners at Menlo that she needed six months off for treatment.

Throughout that first morning of chemo, Bruce the Almighty came by countless times to ask Sonja whether she needed her feet propped up, a pillow adjusted, or another warm blanket to battle the chills. He told her about his love for *Sex and the City* and how much he liked the newly released *Sex and the City* movie. The protagonist, Carrie Bradshaw, the chronicler of adventures in the Big Apple, was his you-go-girl hero, the fashionista who mixed vintage finds with Manolo Blahniks.

"You *absolutely* must see the movie," Bruce the Almighty said.

"I am *absolutely* going to see the movie," Sonja told him, as soon as Jon returned from sailing overseas.

Sonja had actually met Candace Bushnell, the author of the book *Sex and the City,* in New York in the summer of 2001. Sonja had been with her fiancé at the time, and Candace was with her boyfriend, a game designer for the Lara Croft Tomb Raider series. The foursome went to a small Italian restaurant where waiters greeted them by name. Sonja remembered Candace's outfit: a suede triangle halter top paired with preppy East Coast pants. Candace had taken to Sonja, as much as Sonja did to her, telling her she knew too few women who made their own money. Serving room-temperature champagne at two A.M., she announced that Sonja was a Norwegian superhero and gave Sonja a superhero name: White Sonja.

Sonja smiled thinking of this now. She would need all the superhero powers she could muster to fight off the cancer cells invading her body.

THERESIA

Theresia was having a late breakfast with Sheryl Sandberg at Hobee's Restaurant in Palo Alto. Compared with Buck's see-and-be-seen restaurant in Woodside or Il Fornaio in Palo Alto, Hobee's was a low-key meeting choice near the Stanford campus. It was where Theresia had come as a grad student to study and indulge in Hobee's "world famous" blueberry coffee cake, or an early-morning or late-night super veggie scramble. At one point, the restaurant offered an omelet called the Dot Com Ommie.

Sheryl was about to share a secret with Theresia that would make news in Silicon Valley and beyond. "I just got back from telling Eric Schmidt that I'm going to Facebook," the Google executive said.

Theresia grinned. "Well, then, this just turned into a business meeting. And breakfast is on me."

It was March 2008. Sheryl had been vice president for global online sales and operations at Google, and now she was leaving to join Mark Zuckerberg at Facebook as chief operating officer. Theresia was one of the first to know.

Theresia and Sheryl had become fast friends after being introduced by Sheryl's husband, Dave Goldberg, who knew Theresia from their days working at Bain in Boston. Goldberg, a year ahead of Theresia at Bain, was a peer of Theresia's husband, Tim, and her friend and fellow VC Jennifer Fonstad. Everyone loved Dave. When Theresia ran into Goldberg at a recent event, he said, "I've got to introduce you to my wife, Sheryl. She runs a part of Google," and he added, "We have too few women in tech—and too few moms in tech."

The women also shared overachieving pasts: Sheryl, whose father was an ophthalmologist and whose mother was a teacher, had a 4.64 grade-point average in high school and had earned undergraduate and graduate degrees at Harvard. By twenty-nine, she was chief of staff to Treasury Secretary Larry Summers, who had been her professor at Harvard and thesis adviser when she wrote about the economics of spousal abuse. Like Theresia, who had founded a women's engineering group at Brown, Sheryl had started a student organization, Women in Economics and Government, to inspire more women to major in those subjects.

Sheryl and Dave had a one-year-old son, Nate. Theresia's daughter, Sarah, was now five. Both of their husbands were entrepreneurs, and both were between jobs. Goldberg had built and sold his company, Launch, a music site, to Yahoo! He was now an entrepreneur-in-residence at Benchmark Capital, looking for his next start-up. Tim was not working, having closed his company.

Theresia immediately liked Sheryl, who she thought was smart and a lot of fun. Sheryl looked at Theresia the same way: whip smart and a genuine geek with a thing for the latest Manolo Blahnik pumps and sandals and Jimmy Choo boots.

The women talked about the challenges of balancing demanding full-time careers with husbands who were entrepreneurs. The life of an entrepreneur tended to fall into one of three patterns: working at all hours to build a company; figuring out the next deal; or "vesting in peace" and doing very little after a start-up was acquired. Right now, for both husbands, it was the latter—and the two men had ample free time.

"All of a sudden I'm getting e-mails or texts at six P.M. asking when I'm going to be home!" Theresia said. Sheryl laughed, as they had over stories of pumping breast milk during conference calls.

Facebook was emerging from a maelstrom of controversy over a project called Beacon, which allowed companies to track users' actions and purchases on sites other than Facebook. Zuckerberg had publicly expressed regret for Beacon, saying, "We simply did a bad job with this release, and I apologize for it."

Sheryl had been heavily recruited by Zuckerberg and by Facebook board member and Accel managing partner Jim Breyer. Breyer used the Beacon fiasco to convince Zuckerberg it was time to bring in a strong chief operating officer. Zuckerberg and Sheryl had met at a Christmas party in 2007 and had several lengthy talks afterward. All the finalists for the COO position were male except for Sheryl. Breyer was particularly impressed by Sheryl's focus on results. She also was different from the male candidates in a key way. The men he interviewed for the job thought of the COO position as a two-year stint on the way to being CEO. Sheryl got the complexity and importance of the COO position and zeroed in on that, without looking beyond. She understood she would be working in lockstep with Zuckerberg. Breyer and Zuckerberg fretted that they might not be able to land Sheryl, given her success at Google. After more talks, Breyer invited Zuckerberg and Sheryl to his home in Woodside for lunch. Over salad and sandwiches, the three talked about Facebook's economic model, Sheryl's personal goals, how she would work within the culture of Facebook, how she would scale the site, and what the immediate areas for improvement were. After several hours of discussion, Sheryl agreed to join the company.

From the VC side, Theresia could see that Zuckerberg, now twenty-three, was maturing into his role of CEO. He had come a long way from his pajama pants and Adidas slides days when Accel made its initial investment. Even a year later, in 2006, Theresia had seen Zuckerberg struggle in social situations. Accel invited him to its annual limited partners' meeting in San Francisco, where the firm liked to trot out an impressive start-up or two. Mark, in jeans and Facebook hoodie, was scheduled to speak to the group of roughly one hundred investors. Before his speech, he was sheet white, sitting with his head in his hands. Worried he was going to faint, Theresia offered him a glass of water. She told him this was no big deal, that no one was going to ask follow-up questions. "They are here to applaud you," Theresia told him. "We've chosen you as a standout company and founder in the Accel portfolio." Theresia wasn't sure if it was her words or the water, but Mark soon began looking more at ease, and the color returned to his face. Facebook had grown to more than 66 million users and had a recent valuation of $15 billion.

Theresia recounted a story Breyer had told her. He had invited three senior executives from Wal-Mart to Palo Alto to meet Zuckerberg. The team from Wal-Mart wanted to learn more about Facebook. Zuckerberg, without saying so much as hello, had asked Doug McMillon, "Why would anyone shop at Wal-Mart and not Amazon?" It was Zuckerberg being Zuckerberg. McMillon became Wal-Mart's CEO and president.

Theresia was happy for Sheryl. Both of their careers had taken off meteorically, at a time when the economy was tough. Sheryl had joined Google when it had fewer than three hundred employees. She helped build AdWords and AdSense into a multibillion-dollar revenue stream, and her department went from a handful of employees to thousands. She wanted to help Facebook grow into a global leader as well. As

Theresia and Sheryl finished breakfast, they made plans to meet along with their husbands for dinner in Woodside.

Shortly afterward Theresia was off to *Fortune* magazine's Most Powerful Women Summit, where the conference theme was "Extraordinary Talent." Toward the end of the summit, the *Fortune* team unveiled to great fanfare the year's Most Powerful Women issue. Copies were distributed to attendees and the press. The cover featured Sheryl Sandberg, Gina Bianchini, Sukhinder Singh Cassidy, and Theresia, against a simple gray background, looking fashionable and formidable in beautifully tailored black suits. The title of the issue was "The New Valley Girls."

The article included vignettes about each of the four women. Theresia talked about her partners' meetings at Accel: "You can imagine Monday morning meetings. Nine guys, all used to being in charge. I'm absolutely conscious about speaking up more frequently and interrupting people—even though we were taught not to interrupt. Damn it, I'll repeat myself! I'll say it louder! I'll lean forward in my chair." Theresia noted, though, that she had a different role at board meetings, including the board meeting of her alma mater, Brown University. In those meetings, she was an adviser instead of a partner, allowing her to show her feminine side, her *real self.* "Having a more female style works there. You're playing more to the male ego. Though that doesn't mean that I won't take the men on."

Theresia had Sheryl Sandberg to thank for being included in the *Fortune* cover. The magazine had wanted to feature Sheryl alone and write about the salons and dinners she hosted for women at her home in Silicon Valley. But Sheryl wanted other women to share the spotlight and suggested Theresia. Sheryl said, "When women celebrate each other's accomplishments, they're seen as more professional and accomplished as well. Supporting other women helps each other, helps women as a group, and also helps the woman that does it."

When Theresia returned home after the *Fortune* conference, she received congratulations from Accel co-founder Arthur Patterson, from the staff at Accel, who had the cover framed, and from her parents. The only person who said very little was her husband.

MJ

MJ remembered every detail of the night she first met her future husband in 1973 at Purdue. She wore blue-and-white-checked bell-bottoms, a halter top, and white clogs. Her hair was almost down to her waist. Her hand was newly stitched up and bandaged following a mishap earlier that day in the chemistry lab. MJ, a freshman, needed a last-minute date for her sorority pledge dance. Her older sister Shirley, a member of Alpha Xi Delta, asked around and was told there was "only one nice Beta left," referring to the fraternity Beta Theta Pi. That one nice Beta was Bill Elmore.

So MJ, who had the use of only one hand, relied on a fellow sorority pledge to help her get ready and do her hair, before meeting Bill at a pre-dance dinner at the Beta house. As the dinner progressed, toasts were made and quickly grew louder and livelier. At the end of the toasts, Betas picked up water glasses and lightly doused the table and diners. The dousing escalated, and soon a kitchen worker appeared with an industrial hose, hosing down the group as if the house were on fire. Pandemonium ensued, with shrieking, laughter, and food flying. MJ and Bill, thoroughly soaked, dove for cover. From that night on, the two were a couple.

Now, four decades later, Bill had moved out and rented his own apartment. They had separated and were getting a divorce. When Bill had returned from his nine-month sabbatical, the relationship had gone from unhappy to untenable. MJ had been hit with certain painful realities that she wouldn't share even with her siblings or closest friends. After months of counseling, they began divorce mediation. It was one of those times when her experience in venture capital paid off in her personal life: She knew how to negotiate with men.

Driving to his apartment, MJ thought about the early years, when Bill had looked at her as if she walked on water. At Purdue, they would hop into his little orange Fiat convertible and head to nearby towns to discover dive bars with jukeboxes that played MJ's favorite country music. When they were newlyweds, Delta Airlines ran a special deal where travelers could buy an inexpensive pass and fly anywhere in the world over a three-week period. Wherever Bill and MJ flew during those three weeks—whether to Dayton, Ohio, or to the Bahamas— they always seemed to go through Atlanta, something they laughed about afterward. In the early days of their marriage, they continued to travel together on backpacking trips to Yosemite, and ski trips to Tahoe. At Intel, one of the men told MJ, "We all know you are *very* married."

But with the arrival of Kate, their first child, MJ's attention had been pulled away from her husband. Then Will was born, leaving less of MJ's time and attention for Bill. And then came Hanna. Three kids in nine years. Questions about each other's day turned into questions about the kids. Though they both worked full-time, MJ was the "on call" parent.

MJ had regrets about her marriage and knew she had made her share of mistakes. But as she saw it, her mistakes were of omission rather than commission. She should have talked more with Bill when they first had kids and delineated their parenting responsibilities. Instead, she had tried to do it all, to work full-time *and* parent full-time. It felt easier to do it by herself than to ask for help. She made sacrifices that she felt Bill never considered for himself: cutting back her work hours, and stepping away from a lucrative job she loved, to be with the kids and try to improve her marriage. In doing so, she realized, she made a subconscious decision that her career was less important than Bill's—and neither one of them suggested otherwise. She had given up her job to save her marriage, and it had failed anyway. She knew the statistics: Women who become chief executives divorced at a higher rate than men; winning a best actress Oscar portended a divorce, while winning best actor did not; and winning elections for women increased subsequent divorce rates. One female CEO she knew hinted that it was the spouses at home who often helped install the glass ceiling at work. MJ had felt supported by her husband as a venture capitalist but unsupported at home. She believed that if Bill had supported her more as a person, she could have stayed at work.

To be sure, Bill had never asked her to cut back at work; he was proud they were a two-VC family. He was married to one of the first women to make partner at a venture capital firm in the United States. MJ's investments in enterprise software solutions, such as Clarify and Aspect Communications, changed the way businesses and customers interacted. The legacy of these companies was seen in later-enterprise software companies, including Salesforce, WorkDay, and PeopleSoft, which had been acquired by Oracle.

Arriving at Bill's apartment, MJ studied her hands; she was still wearing her wedding ring. When they were first engaged and had no money, Bill had asked his brother, an aspiring jeweler, to make an engagement ring with a tiny chip diamond. Years later Bill got MJ a new ring, a beautiful emerald-cut diamond with a solid gold band. MJ had added yellow emerald-cut side diamonds. She loved her wedding ring.

Before going in, MJ took a few deep breaths. Their conversations together were not easy. As the two began to talk, MJ felt something strange in her hand. Her left thumb felt the back of her ring finger. As Bill continued to make his point, MJ turned her hand over. She could not believe what she saw. The solid gold band of her wedding ring had broken in the back, down the middle. Her wedding ring had literally cracked in two. Holding the two pieces of her ring, MJ mumbled something to Bill and rushed out the door.

MJ was a spiritual person. To her, the universe was confirming what she already knew. Her marriage, once so treasured, was irreparably broken.

THERESIA

Theresia was in a Glam Media board meeting near the San Francisco Airport when she began to feel back pains. She was almost nine months pregnant, and it had been a difficult pregnancy. She had been to her ob-gyn the day before and the ob-gyn had scheduled a C-section for the following week, still two weeks before her due date. The doctor told her everything looked fine.

But this morning, Theresia felt increasingly not fine. At first she told herself, *This is because I'm huge and fat.* She did what she'd seen a lot of guys with back pain do in meetings. She got up and paced. But the pain kept returning. Finally, she told everyone: "Look, guys, I know the board meeting is supposed to go until noon, but I'm not feeling well. Can we do the formal board approvals and complete finance and sales updates by ten, and I'll leave and dial in for the rest of the call?" After the sales updates, she gathered her things and called her doctor from the car.

"I'm feeling pain I haven't felt before," Theresia told the nurse's assistant, who asked whether the pain was steady or intermittent. "Intermittent," she replied.

"Okay, so I want you to time the pain," the assistant said. Theresia sat in her car and watched the clock. It was another six to seven minutes before the pain returned. The assistant said, "I think you're in labor. How quickly can you get here?" Theresia remained strangely calm. She figured it would take twenty minutes to drive to her ob-gyn's office next to the Stanford Medical Center. She looked at the clock: 10:10. She should be at the hospital by 10:30. As she drove, the pain came in waves, but that didn't stop her from getting on the conference call for her board meeting.

As soon as she walked into the ob-gyn office, her doctor took one look at her and said, "Theresia, you are one hundred percent in labor. Go straight to admitting. They have your paperwork. The baby is coming."

By the time she got over to Stanford and was admitted, it was 10:50.

Tim arrived at 11:00, at which point Theresia had to hang up from the conference call, telling the group, "I have to drop off early. I'll catch up with you this afternoon." Her son, Luke, was born at 11:30.

Once again, Theresia was called back to Accel within a matter of weeks. This time, she had her support group of family and her nanny around her, and was making new deals and mentoring new investment hires at Accel. Nothing could slow her down—at least that's how she felt at the time.

SONJA

Sonja's second chemo session fell on the same day her daughter was born. The birth mother had gone into labor that morning. Sonja had shared her news with Bruce the Almighty, who couldn't contain his excitement. She was eager to get through her chemo session so she could go to the hospital and be there for the birth of her daughter. They had decided to name her Tess. When Sonja was finished with the chemo—it was not something that could be rushed—she drove straight to California Pacific Medical Center in San Francisco's Pacific Heights. Tess made her entrance into the world that night, healthy and weighing seven pounds. She had blue eyes, fat cheeks, and a smile that immediately won Sonja's heart. Sonja thought Tess's smile was somehow wise and knowing, with a hint of *Hee hee—I am exactly where I want to be.*

Not long afterward, Sonja faced a glaring dichotomy: She was struggling with her health while her baby was thriving. To compound the situation, Jon went to Europe. He was on a competitive sailing team and had signed up for the races months earlier. He had also been working nonstop at the restaurant and was eager for time off. Sonja understood—to a degree. But she needed him to be with her and intended to take the issue up with him when he returned. For now, she couldn't deal with another crisis.

Not knowing how her body would handle the chemo sessions to

come, Sonja set up around-the-clock backup care for Tess. She found two Irish nannies who worked as a pair. They seemed ideal at first, but before long, one of them arrived hungover and grumpy, more than once. She took naps when Tess took naps instead of cleaning and helping out with the house. Finally after her eighth chemo treatment, Sonja had to fire them. She gave them two weeks' severance but asked them to leave immediately.

She put an ad in Craigslist: "Nanny position available for upwardly mobile business professionals." With the economy still in a recession and the unemployment rate rising, Sonja received more than two hundred applications. She hired two nannies, each to work three days a week. She wanted them to have time to pursue their own careers. One young woman she hired would go on to attend Harvard, and another would work her way through medical school.

The nanny crisis behind her, Sonja felt lonely. Life had been reduced to the joy of her baby and the pain of chemo. She spent most of her days in the house, alone with Tess. She couldn't wait for Jon to return.

While a few close friends did little to help her, other friends who were not as close stepped up in amazing ways. Jenny Saling, who had started at Menlo as her executive assistant but was rising through the ranks, came to see her every week, bringing notes from the weekly partners' meetings and taking her on walks. Jenny proved to be a lifeline, strong, constant, and cheerful. Sonja's parents helped as well, and she had support from her former mentor, Tom Bredt, and his wife, Polly. Tom had left Menlo in 2004 after suffering a mild heart attack.

The chemo took a toll on Sonja. She grew weaker with each treatment, and she had trouble sleeping. One day she fell and broke five ribs. She landed in the hospital on several other occasions as well. Shots of Neulasta, a synthetic protein that was supposed to stimulate the growth of white blood cells, made her feel pain she had never experienced before, deep in her bones. She tried to look at chemo the way she viewed taxes: It wasn't fun, but it needed to be done. But this was brutal. She focused on healing and was careful with what she ate, eliminating sugar and red meat. She went to acupuncture, chelation therapy, and massages, and she tried to walk every day.

Brought up Presbyterian, Sonja became interested in Buddhism. She was friends with the Tibetan monk Orgen Chowang Rinpoche, who taught the importance of finding happiness within rather than linking happiness to outcomes. Rinpoche liked to ask, "We exercise our bodies, we fix our hair, but do we do anything to enhance the mind?" The storm clouds would soon pass, he told Sonja, and blue sky would be revealed. Sonja adopted a Buddhist prayer and recited it daily:

May our lives be long and may all of our wishes come true;
May obstacles not impede us but arise as allies;
May purpose, fortune and abundance occur naturally without effort; and
May the light of Manjushri, the Buddha of Wisdom, enter our hearts.

Jon finally returned home, for good. Later, when Tess began crawling, he and Sonja came up with a game called Teddy Bear Tag. Sonja would put two teddy bears at the end of the L-shaped couch, and Tess would have to crawl as fast as she could to touch one of the bears. If Tess was caught before reaching a bear, Sonja could tickle her. Tess's giggles were Sonja's anodyne. They had a way of easing her pain. Beautiful Tess seemed to know what those around her needed. She was a happy and easygoing child, and she somehow understood when her mom was too sick to get out of bed.

During her six months at home, Sonja had time to reflect on who she was and what was important in her life. She was a mother *and* she had breast cancer.

THERESIA

After appearing on the cover of *Fortune,* Theresia became a fixture in top-ten-women-in-tech lists of the most powerful women, the most influential women, the most successful women, the women to watch. She was featured in *Time* alongside Susan Wojcicki at Google, Meg Whitman at Hewlett-Packard, Virginia Rometty of IBM, Marissa Mayer of Yahoo!, Safra Catz at Oracle, and Sheryl Sandberg. Theresia was one of only two women on the *Forbes* Midas list of top one hundred venture capitalists, where she was lauded for "bringing in more than a billion dollars in capital gains through her savvy investments."

She had hit one home run after another. In 2011, Shlomo Kramer's data-security-software company, Imperva, went public, raising $90 million. Theresia, with Kramer and the team on the floor of the New York Stock Exchange, was reminded of the days when she and Kramer went around to Wall Street banks to market-test his idea. Theresia looked at IPOs as graduations that sent companies on to their next phase of life in the public markets. A year later Trulia, which had grown to more than 22 million users, went public. Again, Theresia was there for the ringing of the bell on the NYSE. As Theresia stood on the dais with founders Pete Flint and Sami Inkinen, she realized that one of the things she loved the most was seeing entrepreneurs mature and succeed. Flint was there with his wife, who was holding their baby girl. When she met him, he was a graduate student. Theresia knew the sacrifices required to build a company from idea to IPO and to keep going from there. For many founders and employees, an IPO was a life-changing event, a before and after, when they knew they could buy that house they always wanted and make important strides in their lives and contribute to the lives of others.

Theresia was invited to speak on a panel at the World Economic Forum at Davos, Switzerland, where she talked about trends she saw in mobile and the Internet. She noted that she was seeing more and more companies bypass creating websites to go straight to mobile apps. After the talk, Theresia was approached by a man who asked for examples of companies doing mobile apps rather than websites. As she looked down at the man's nametag, she was stunned to see it was Tim Berners-Lee. The inventor of the World Wide Web was asking *her* about Internet trends.

Not long afterward she was interviewed by Willow Bay for a new hour-long Bloomberg TV show called *Women to Watch,* along with Jessica Herrin, CEO of Stella & Dot; Carolyn Everson, VP of global marketing for Facebook; and Selina Tobaccowala, VP of product and engineering at SurveyMonkey.

When Theresia returned home after the show aired, Tim was not happy. The show had used photos of Theresia and their daughter, Sarah, but none of him. Theresia explained that she had submitted a bunch of family photos, but the selection had been up to the producer. They probably picked the images they did because the show was about women, she said.

Theresia and Tim had been in and out of couples therapy for several years. Unfortunately, it didn't seem to be working. Tim, who was still between start-ups, routinely told her, "I'm married to Don Draper. You travel 150 days a year!" referring to the character from the television series *Mad Men.* Although Tim was the one who had made their first million, Theresia had been the primary breadwinner for years.

The growing divide between them was impossible to ignore. She eventually stopped asking Tim to any work dinners and events. Then she stopped mentioning the awards and recognition to Tim altogether. On one occasion when he attended an event with her, he said to her afterward, "No one asked me the entire night what I do!" It was what women said all the time when they were written off as a man's armpiece. Tim still served as the family CFO, managing their money, except for the 10 percent of her bonus that she gave herself so that she didn't have to smuggle new shoes into her closet. Theresia had handed the running of their finances to him as a peace offering, a way to affirm that he was the man of the house. But she realized it had been a mistake. There was even a phrase for Theresia's gesture: "manning up and womaning down."

Theresia and Tim had been peers when they started out together after college. They had been Stanford MBAs with similar dreams and career goals. They had both worked in the world of finance and start-ups. But along the way, it was Theresia who became the star; it was Theresia who made the family millions. She felt like he had tacitly been keeping score. She realized that after all their years together, she should have looked at his own family upbringing. She was asking Tim, who grew up in a traditional family where the man worked and the woman stayed home, to be happy in a nontraditional marriage. The wives of his three brothers had given up significant careers when they had children. Theresia was the square peg in a round hole, unwilling to be knocked off the professional ladder because she had children.

After twenty years of marriage, Theresia and Tim filed for divorce. Sarah was nine and Luke was three. Theresia's greatest fear was that if this headed to court in a custody situation, she would be seen as an absent Don Draper. She didn't anticipate a battle—Tim was a good guy. But she wasn't taking any chances. Without a job, Tim could be home all the time, even though they always had a full-time nanny. Theresia was clear that she needed to show she could pick up the kids and drop them off and do all the traditional mom things. She had never been one to volunteer at Sarah's school, and she had been on only one of Sarah's school field trips, to Intel. She couldn't love her kids more—but she also loved her job. And she knew her male colleagues worked similarly long hours without being questioned.

As Accel co-founder Jim Swartz acknowledged in an interview, he worked "six and a half days for sure" and said his "normal routine was Monday through Friday traveling and dinners in New York three, four nights a week, and on Saturday for half a day or three-quarters of a day. Then you'd start again Sunday afternoon reading and preparing."

The looming custody questions put Theresia in crisis mode. Moreover, her imminent divorce made her feel like a failure—she had failed herself, Tim, her family, and his family. Her mother would probably tell her she worked too much. Theresia regretted that she hadn't tried harder to remain close to Tim over the years. He had claimed to be happy as the at-home parent, but she could see he really wasn't. She was a perfectionist, she knew. She had made the mistake of trying to manage how

Tim managed the kids. She should have relaxed more and worried less. She needed to rethink how she spent her time. Everywhere she turned, she felt as if society were telling her she needed to be less of a success at work to be more of a success at home.

SONJA

Sonja returned to Menlo Ventures six months after going on medical leave, with thirty days of radiation ahead of her. She now had a new routine: She left her home in San Francisco early, received radiation treatment, and then made the hour-long drive to Menlo. Outside of a small circle at work, no one knew she had cancer. She didn't want to compete for a deal only to have another VC whisper to the entrepreneur, *Oh, you didn't know? Sonja has cancer.*

Being back at Menlo was wonderful in many ways: The work was rewarding, and having a routine felt good. But there were unsettling elements. Sonja was struck by how few women there were at work. This, of course, was hardly a news flash, but she felt it more acutely now.

She returned to her seat at the partners' table on Mondays, a world away from her time in the hospital with Bruce the Almighty. A series of impressive companies came in to pitch. Ellen Levy—who met her future husband at Sonja's fortieth birthday party—brought LinkedIn to Sonja. LinkedIn co-founder Reid Hoffman, long a champion of women and diversity in tech, told Ellen that he hoped to have a woman investor for this round of funding. Sonja loved LinkedIn but failed to get the support of her partners, who had questions about the market and thought the company's valuation was too high.

Palo Alto Networks, a network and enterprise security company, was brought in by Menlo partner John Jarve. Sonja knew Palo Alto Networks' co-founder and CEO, Dave Stevens, from the University of Virginia, and thought he ran a phenomenal company. Stevens's co-founder was Nir Zuk, who had been an early employee of Shlomo Kramer's at Check Point. But again, Sonja couldn't convince the Menlo partners of the merits of the deal.

Diapers.com was pitched to Menlo at around the same time. Again, Sonja loved the company and thought co-founder Marc Lore had brilliantly figured out shipping logistics. He had set up warehouses around the United States close to post offices to ensure that items reached customers within a day. But Sonja's partners weren't convinced of the market for Diapers.com. She was 100 percent convinced, as she used the company every day for diapers, wipes, baby clothes, and more.

Sonja began hearing of another start-up called Uber, which was launched in June 2010 in San Francisco. The company was already being studied by her partners Shawn Carolan and Shervin Pishevar, who had been newly hired as a managing director. Sonja told Carolan and Pishevar that this was a deal to take seriously. While some of the other Menlo partners questioned whether people would get into a car with a stranger, Sonja, who regretted not having been more aggressive with LinkedIn and the other start-ups, said, "You should really pound the table on this one."

Sonja had spent countless hours under the tutelage of her father, who had been a professor of civil engineering and the director of the Center for Transportation Studies at the University of Virginia. Sonja told Carolan and Pishevar, "Point-to-point public transport is the holy grail of public transportation. Uber enables point-to-point public transport using existing resources and creating jobs." She was relentless this time in sharing her views of the importance of the company. Menlo succeeded in landing a deal with Uber and led the Series B investment with $26 million of the $39 million round. (Other Series B investors included Jeff Bezos and Goldman Sachs.)

Around the same time, Sonja helped engineer the sale of one of her earlier investments, Q1 Labs, to IBM. Q1 had been preparing to go public when it was acquired, and it extracted a hefty purchase price.

Sonja had been on Q1's board since 2003. She had also made investments in Flurry, a mobile analytics company, and in Minted, an online marketplace for independent artists and designers, which was started by one of her favorite entrepreneurs, Mariam Naficy, who had co-founded Eve, the first major online cosmetics company.

In 2011, the year after she returned from battling breast cancer and adopting a child, Sonja was named Menlo's Investor of the Year. The recognition was based solely on returns on investments. While she appreciated the recognition, and the pitch meetings were exciting, she found herself missing Tess. And no matter how much Sonja liked work, it was stressful, and stress wasn't good for her, given her health. Her prognosis was good, but cancer was slippery. She didn't know how far into the future to plan. She had to have her blood tested every six months and await the results.

She loved the deals, ideas, and entrepreneurs. But as she sat in the partners' meetings and scanned the room, looking from one investing partner to the next, she couldn't shake the memory that while she had been home alone, fighting cancer while caring for Tess, she had never heard from a single one of them about her illness. They hadn't called, they hadn't visited. Not once.

THERESIA

In the fall of 2012, Theresia shared with her partners at Accel in Palo Alto the news that she was getting divorced. She told them she needed to take a sabbatical starting in the first quarter of 2013. Accel offered three-month sabbaticals to employees who had been partners for at least seven years. Theresia had been a partner for thirteen of her fourteen years at Accel and had never taken a leave of any kind. She had taken only three weeks of maternity leave with each child. Accel co-founder Jim Swartz had taken a four-month sabbatical and joined a master's ski racing program. Swartz called sabbaticals "a great concept" and a "very healthy thing to do every five or ten years." Jim Breyer had taken a sabbatical, and Kevin Efrusy, who had brought in the Facebook deal, was out on a yearlong sabbatical, traveling the world with his wife and kids.

Theresia was on a record number of boards—fifteen—including her two newly public companies, Trulia and Imperva. She and fellow Accel partner Sameer Gandhi, with Arthur's direction and support, had single-handedly pitched and raised the firm's new growth fund.

And because of Accel's past mistakes in not bringing partners up through the ranks and sharing economics fast enough, Theresia made sure that the newer partners were given equity stakes much sooner than in the past. She also sent great deals their way and made time to attend important meetings with them.

So now, when she told the new partners—the very men she had hired, mentored, walked through their first term sheets, and teed up deals for—that she needed to take a sabbatical, she was entirely unprepared for the response. "Well, there's no sabbatical policy," she was told. "What do you mean there's no sabbatical policy?" she responded. *Kevin is out on a sabbatical now!* She showed them a Word document on Accel's sabbatical policy written by Jim Swartz.

"That was years ago. We're not going to honor it," the new partners responded. In addition, they argued that although Kevin Efrusy was indeed out on sabbatical, he had given everyone proper notice. Theresia agreed that Kevin had done everything right: He had set up the sabbatical far in advance and told investors what would be happening in the next fund-raising cycle as he stepped away for a year. And the partners had told him it was fine for him to take a year instead of three months.

Theresia shot back, "I couldn't tell you a year ago that I'd be getting a divorce and dealing with issues around young children. I'm taking the time."

Because they were now away from day-to-day operations, Jim Swartz and Arthur Patterson were not involved in the conversation, and Theresia didn't feel she could ask them to intervene. Jim Breyer was also stepping away, shedding his seats on boards of Wal-Mart, Dell, and even Facebook, with plans to focus more on his personal investment fund. The new partners soon sent another partner—another guy Theresia had mentored—to again tell her that she would not be getting a sabbatical.

Theresia saw the irony: She had empowered this cabal by flattening the management structure and making the partners more co-equals. Now that same cabal was attacking her. It was like boys playing dodgeball, thinking nothing of hitting someone in the head. Theresia had become a veteran over the years at handling the off-color jokes, handsy guys, and suggestive comments. She could brush off being overlooked, outtalked, and mistaken for an assistant. But this was different.

The partners' decision was that a sabbatical was not an option—but she could take *family leave*. Theresia questioned the intent of the offer. If she were granted a sabbatical, her job and her income would be secure, because there was a precedent for sabbaticals. But family leave was untested—no one at Accel had ever taken it. So her position would not be guaranteed upon her return. She was sure that the same guys who had benefited from her guidance and deals would go after her job, her companies, and her equity.

What followed, though, went beyond avarice or apathy. Theresia was asked to do something that no man in her position would have been asked to do. She was told that if she wanted to take family leave, she would have to call Accel's top investors and tell them one by one that she was going on leave *because she was getting a divorce*. Knowing her children needed her—she would do anything for them—she reluctantly began making the calls. Whenever the calls seemed unbearable, Theresia closed her eyes and thought of her kids. They gave her the strength to get through the humiliation.

MAGDALENA

Magdalena set out on her early-morning walk on Mount Tamalpais in Marin County north of San Francisco. After coming down with her mysterious ailments, Magdalena had turned her considerable energy and brainpower to what she called Project Magdalena. She walked, hiked for hours, ate well, and lost weight.

For a woman who thrived on finding solutions, it had been a puzzling time, with few answers. She didn't go to Sand Hill Road much anymore, though she always had at least one assistant working for her. Her boys, Justin and Troy, had grown up; they were now twenty and eighteen, respectively. Justin was graduating from Duke University with a computer science degree and had accepted a job as product manager at the video game company Zynga. And Troy was at Duke getting his bachelor's degree in economics.

Magdalena didn't feel the empty nest angst that many parents feel, as her boys had established their independence as teenagers. Her time was now taken up by her mother, by her aging extended family, and by her nonprofit and civil society work. She had joined public policy and international diplomacy boards at Duke and Stanford, and the engineering board of Santa Clara University. International diplomacy was a brand-new field for her, and she was especially interested in working on efforts to open the border between Turkey and Armenia. Her work in Silicon Valley consisted of coaching young investors and entrepreneurs.

She had slowly shed her USVP boards, reducing them from eleven down to three. She missed the camaraderie of going to the office and working with her partners, especially the very wise Rabbi, Irwin Federman. She had recently got a call from Sonja, who asked whether she'd step in and coach one of her entrepreneurs, Tim Young, who had a start-up called Socialcast. The company was based in San Francisco and provided enterprise social collaboration tools. Magdalena was happy to do the favor and was now counseling Young on how to develop a sales cycle and an enterprise sales organization.

Heading up the winding path near the top of Mount Tamalpais, she thought about her exit from Salesforce. There was no doubt that she had jumped the gun by leaving the Salesforce board. She could have waited to see how her health progressed. But at the time she was worried she might die or become disabled. At the very least, she would be less than perfect. And she hated to disappoint anyone. Now she was realizing that perfection was her enemy.

Magdalena had been away from Silicon Valley long enough now to see that her whole technology career could be summed up in one sentence: She was good at projecting how people would use technology in the future. When she arrived at Stanford, she had fallen in love with the West, with the spirit of the Gold Rush and being a part of a frontier town. At Advanced Micro Devices, her first job out of Stanford, she had been responsible for getting local area networking chip sets designed into computers before anyone had really heard of the concept. When she joined Fortune Systems, the first Unix desktop computer company, she had seen the perils of the frontier life. Computer dealers couldn't support such sophisticated machines, and the machines went unsold on dealers' shelves. When she became a pioneer in electronic commerce, the Internet had just opened for business.

She wrote a book in 1997, *Creating the Virtual Store,* but few people then bought what she was saying. A section in the book called "Johnny, Turn Off the PC!" had stirred derision. She wrote, "The PC has brought new complexities to these unsuspecting parents. . . . Children have become the systems operators of the PC, having the ultimate say in its configuration and content." Her prediction that kids would one day be more hooked on computers than on television was also met with skepticism.

As Magdalena navigated the rocky path of the trail, she passed a steady stream of dog walkers, joggers, and women with babies snuggled into front carrier packs. Magdalena smiled. The years had flown by; her sons had grown up. One constant in her life, though, was her family unit. After all these years, she was still married. She had never made the relationship the kind of priority some women did, with date nights and weekends away. To her, marriage was cultural. It was about belonging to a tribe. Growing up in Turkey, she never knew anyone who was divorced. You married, and that was that. She had never looked for reasons why her marriage was working or wasn't working, but she also hadn't invested in it the way she should have.

She had met Jim when she was twenty-two; he was thirty and had just returned from Brazil. Her first impression of him was that he talked too much. His intricate stories captivated everyone except Magdalena, who listened with an engineer's approach. When Magdalena was invited to a picnic party at Jim's ranch, a pipe broke and there was no running water. Many of the guests appeared scandalized by the lack of water. Magdalena merely watched with amusement. She had grown up in a country where water was cut off three to four days a week throughout the summer.

Magdalena had liked Jim's values and found him pure in many ways. Their biggest fights over the years had been over trivial things, like how to stack the dishwasher and clean the kitchen. And Jim was impressed by Magdalena's calm. He fell in love with her because she was on a mission of her own.

But these days, having been sidelined by health complications and assorted family health issues, Magdalena wasn't as directed anymore. So she was intrigued by a recent call from Sonja, who mentioned that she had an idea she wanted to run by her. She hadn't heard Sonja this excited in a long time. Sonja had said part of the inspiration for her idea had come from their all-women boondoggle weekends in Hawaii. The two made plans to meet at Sonja's house.

As Magdalena gazed out from the trail, looking at the spectacular waters of San Francisco Bay, she marveled at the natural beauty. The fog was still dense, spread out like a down comforter surrounding the brick-red cables of the Golden Gate Bridge. If she looked far enough, she might be able to make out the site where Salesforce was discussing taking over a development under construction at the former Transbay Terminal. Salesforce, which had nearly died a thousand deaths, had recently reported annual revenues of $1.3 billion. If plans went through, the company's headquarters would be called Salesforce Tower, and it would be the tallest building in San Francisco and, in fact, in the western United States.

At the moment, the tallest things near Magdalena were the redwood trees towering above her. But as she walked through the redwood forest and took in the fresh air, she was finally getting a better sense of her future: She needed to get back and apply herself fully to Silicon Valley.

SONJA

Between work, home, and health concerns, Sonja sought more balance in her life. She was worried that she would not be able to complete her work and family obligations while staying cancer-free. To stay healthy, she needed to reduce her stress. She made the decision that she would not be investing in Menlo's next fund.

The Menlo partners were starting a new fund—Fund XI—which was often a time of transition, when younger partners moved up and were given more equity, and older partners sometimes pulled back and reduced their percentage of the profits. Sonja needed to make her health her top priority.

She proposed to the Menlo partners that she work part-time. From her viewpoint, the timing was ideal: Venture firms and tech start-ups were opening offices in San Francisco almost every day, turning areas like South Park, in the bustling South of Market neighborhood, into mini Sand Hill Roads.

Sonja also thought she could save time on the commute—more than two hours a day—by working remotely. She had been with Menlo Ventures for nearly seventeen years. Her investments had brought hundreds of millions of dollars to the firm and created a number of legacy companies. McAfee Associates, which she had cold-called when she was an investment analyst at TA Associates, had recently been acquired by Intel for $7.68 billion.

Sonja's friend and former mentor, Tom Bredt, while no longer at Menlo and with no oversight responsibilities, followed the developments at Menlo from the sidelines. He had heard rumblings from some of the partners, after Sonja returned, saying that she couldn't be counted on to do the work she had once done. She now had a baby to look after *and* was battling cancer. He knew that one partner thought Sonja was "pushy" and too aggressive.

In weighing Sonja's decision, a partner told Bredt he didn't like the idea of her working part-time. He wanted people in the office. It was quite a statement coming from a guy who was a member of the all-male Bohemian Club, who spent half the summer away at the Bohemian Grove. A behind-closed-doors meeting was called, where a vote was taken. The partners—all men—decided not to allow Sonja to work part-time. In effect, they were telling her there was no longer a place for her at Menlo. The girl who had believed obstacles were her allies had finally hit an obstacle that was not her ally.

Sonja could have stayed on at Menlo full-time, but ultimately decided to begin her transition out. She would continue with her board seats and investments made through Fund X, and she would continue to come in for Monday partners' meetings during a lengthy period of transition. But she would not be involved in Menlo's future investments. She had expected to stay at Menlo her entire career and now cycled through a range of emotions. She was frustrated by how few women there were in such an important industry. At the same time, she hadn't forgotten the lack of support from partners during her months of chemotherapy. One day she arrived at Menlo and found that Shervin Pishevar had moved into her office.

Tom Bredt described the denial of Sonja's part-time status as "really misguided" and said the decision to let her walk away was "dumb and stupid." Before joining Menlo in 1986, Bredt had worked at Hewlett-Packard for nearly a decade; HP was a model of diversity. Many of the managers were women, including Carolyn Morris and Nancy Anderson, and they were outstanding executives. He backed women CEOs for companies he invested in and had done hugely successful deals with MJ at IVP. He had watched Sonja grow into a formidable thinker and investor.

As Bredt told Sonja in the aftermath, "You can't be partners with someone who doesn't want to be your partner." Sonja, trying to remain positive, adopted a saying of her own: "The best revolutionaries are not the people who hate the dictators but [those] who empathize with the victims."

Andy Ory, the founder of Priority Call Management and Acme Packet, was upset when he heard that Menlo and Sonja were parting ways. He had arrived at Menlo as an awkward and exhausted young entrepreneur, just as Sonja was starting out as a Silicon Valley venture capitalist. She had believed in him when everyone else turned him down. He'd recently gone with Sonja to one of her radiation sessions in San Francisco, as it fell on a day they had been scheduled to meet. Sonja had suggested they continue their conversation after she had her treatment. In those moments at the hospital—as Sonja talked business with her usual clarity and optimism—the normally loquacious Ory was speechless. What her Menlo partners apparently thought was a weakness, Ory saw as a strength. She was stronger and more determined than ever.

In the end, Sonja felt as though the universe had staged an intervention. She had been outed as a woman—and turned into a feminist, overnight.

MJ

Months after MJ's divorce became final, MJ and her ex-husband, Bill, took their youngest daughter, Hanna, to Duke University for the start of her freshman year. When MJ had first considered what it would be like to be divorced, she thought about her own pain and worried about the kids. What she didn't think about, what hit her now, was how divorce destroyed a family unit. This wonderful thing called the Elmore family no longer existed. To her, that felt like the biggest loss of all.

Hanna loved her dad and knew he was an impressive man in the business world and a successful venture capitalist. But she looked to her mom as her guiding light and the family glue, the one who had taught her to ski and got her through acne, braces, and boys. Her mom had set the rules around her first boyfriend in middle school, saying she could see him only in groups. It was her mom who—despite Hanna's refusals, protests, and slammed doors—had insisted on getting her help for her teenage stress. It had put her on a successful track for high school and now for Duke. Her mom always appeared so composed and calm, even in this awkward and emotional situation, as her parents were together in her dorm room, saying goodbye to her. But they were no longer together as a couple.

When MJ returned home, she made a detour to Whole Foods. Emotionally drained, she began piling things into her cart: bagels and cream cheese for the kids, bread, bagel dogs, chocolate chip cookies for Bill, veggies, and salad mix for the "mommy salad" that Hanna loved.

As she neared the checkout, MJ stopped herself and stared at her cart. *What am I doing?* She didn't know whether to laugh or cry. For the first time in decades, she had no one to shop for but herself. As shoppers pushed past her, her eyes welled with tears. She didn't need any of this food. She thought, *God, I don't even know what I want for myself at the grocery store.* Then she asked herself, *What on earth do I want for myself?*

PART

NINE

The Awakening

2010–2018

SONJA

On her rooftop deck in San Francisco, Sonja looked up as the navy's Blue Angels buzzed the sky in their F/A-18 Hornets. It was the city's annual Fleet Week; Sonja was hosting a party to give her friends a front-row seat for the dazzling air show.

But Sonja had much more on her mind than jet plane maneuvers. She was still saddened by her parting of the ways with Menlo Ventures. Menlo's website now featured a picture of five guys, including one palming a basketball. Investing teams at other top VC firms in the Valley were the same, with row after row of interchangeable men in plaid untucked shirts, dark denim jeans, and the occasional puffy vest. It wasn't just that the men of Menlo Ventures had moved on, she realized; women were being written out of the history of venture capital—and the history of so many key industries. Something had to change. Women needed to come together to be heard.

As the F/A-18 pilots roared overhead, Sonja and fellow venture capitalist Jennifer Fonstad ducked downstairs to have a private conversation.

"You'd think there are no women in venture," said Jennifer, who was considering leaving Draper Fisher Jurvetson, where she was a partner.

Sonja shook her head in frustration. "We've been at the top of our field for a long time, and no one has even heard of us! We need to showcase the top women in venture. We need to be unified. Instead of hiding the fact that we are women, we should celebrate what we do. We need to inspire women and girls to become venture capitalists."

That day the two women hatched a plan that could make them

money, create more networks for women, and begin rewriting the history of venture capital.

Not long afterward, Sonja sat down with Magdalena to talk about starting an all-women's investing group. The organization would feature the most successful women investors in Silicon Valley, women who had founded and funded companies that employed hundreds of thousands of people and shaped industries. Women who had made a mark in the Valley, even if they weren't always being included in the history books.

Magdalena, standing in Sonja's kitchen, knew that Sonja was not participating in Menlo Ventures' new fund. After a period of soul searching, Sonja was intent on founding a VC investment platform with other women.

"If we inspire people and fund great deals as a venture group made up entirely of women, there will be more women who want to be venture capitalists," Sonja said. In turn, she went on, those women will fund more female entrepreneurs, who will then hire more women, changing the power dynamic in Silicon Valley once and for all.

Sonja told Magdalena, "You don't have a platform for the investing you are doing."

Magdalena replied, "I have enough of a brand name that I really don't need one. Why do I need a platform?"

Sonja stressed the advantages of an all-women investing group. There was strength in numbers from a financial standpoint. The women could rely on one another to source deals and do due diligence. There would be an all-female "debate society," as Magdalena had called the partners' meetings at USVP. As a bonus, they would enjoy the female camaraderie they'd experienced during their Hawaiian weekends.

"You will still write your own checks," Sonja said, "but we can share our experiences with each other. I may be good at one type of investing, while you're good at another. We can capitalize on each other's strengths."

Sonja had come up with a name for the group—the Broadway Angels—because of the neighborhood where she lived.

The more Magdalena thought about Sonja and Jennifer's idea, the more it made sense. Now out on her own, she missed the camaraderie of USVP. Angel investing was more difficult without others to bounce ideas off. And she had to admit, she had loved the Hawaiian getaways with experienced, like-minded women.

And so Magdalena agreed to be a co-founder, with one caveat: "I want to do things that will make money. I don't just want to sit there and socialize."

Sonja grinned. There was no danger of that. Like the Blue Angels pilots, she intended to run the Broadway Angels meetings with military precision.

THERESIA

In February 2013, Theresia reluctantly agreed to co-host an "Un Valentine Valentine's Party" with one of her best friends. Theresia and Tim had filed for divorce, she was on family leave from Accel, and friends were telling her to start looking to the future. But Theresia had no interest in a relationship. She was comfortable with her life of kids, friends, and career.

She told everyone who tried to play matchmaker that she had "zero interest in dating anyone who has anything to do with my world." She also questioned her interest in dating, period. She was recently in a swanky hotel bar in San Francisco with two girlfriends when a group of guys came and sat down with them. It was happy hour on a Saturday night and the guys proceeded to set their Google ID badges on the table *face up,* in an apparent effort to impress.

Theresia figured that if she did eventually start dating, years down the road, she'd have to find a talented starving artist. Several of her women friends in business and academia found that their successes at work caused problems at home. American men, she decided, were raised to be the breadwinners and had a hard time adjusting when a woman made more money or was more successful than they were professionally. When Theresia returned to work at Accel, she had no intention of becoming any less successful.

The "Un Valentine" party took place at the San Francisco home of a business school friend, Laura Sanchez, a managing director at Goldman Sachs who was going through a divorce herself. Sanchez and Theresia hosted the event with a couple of divorced friends from Stanford. Theresia, wearing a red dress and high heels, noticed a tall, good-looking guy in jeans and a gray sweater walk in. He was holding a bottle of rose champagne, her favorite drink.

The two struck up a conversation, and as they talked, Theresia kept thinking, *Handsome, very handsome.* His name was Matthew McIntyre. When she got past his good looks, she was even more impressed by what he said to her. He told Theresia he had to leave the party early to pick up his daughter and ex-wife at the airport. They were flying in so that the three of them could attend a mutual friend's wedding. His daughter was the flower girl. Theresia thought, *Maybe someday my ex-husband will pick me up at the airport.*

Theresia was almost afraid to ask Matthew what he did for a living. Anything in tech or finance would be the kiss of death. She took Xerox CEO Ursula Burns's comment, made at a tech conference, to heart: "The secret to success is to marry someone twenty years older." Burns's husband had retired as her career was ascending. Meg Whitman, former CEO of eBay and Hewlett-Packard, was married to a neurosurgeon. *Totally different careers.*

"I'm a firefighter," Matthew said, bringing a smile to Theresia's face. Before he left the party, she learned he was a fire captain in San Jose. He was on FEMA's Urban Search and Rescue Task Force, specialized in large building collapse rescues, and had been boots on the ground following the attacks of 9/11. Before departing, Theresia and Matthew made plans to see each other again.

Theresia returned to Accel from family leave in the spring of 2013. She told her partners she wasn't going to be a part of the next fund. She felt as if she'd given Accel fifteen years of blood, sweat, and tears, only to be bullied into calling investors—many of whom she barely knew—to tell them she was *getting a divorce*. She admired Accel's founders, Arthur Patterson and Jim Swartz, and remained friends with her London colleague Bruce Golden. She would always be grateful for the opportunities the firm had given her and impressed by the outstanding work of many of her colleagues. But she couldn't forgive the actions by some of the newer partners at the firm, at the very time when she had most needed their support. *They would never have asked a male partner to do the same.*

Theresia's exit from Accel involved a final negotiation session in San Francisco. Matthew offered to take her to the meeting. By this time, the two were dating casually. The negotiations at the downtown office tower started in the late afternoon. Theresia told Matthew that it would probably last a couple of hours. At eight P.M., she texted him to apologize that things were moving slowly and that he should head home if he hadn't already. She could take Lyft or Uber.

"I'll wait for you," he insisted.

The mediation went on past nine P.M. Then ten P.M. Then eleven P.M. Then midnight. Theresia hadn't had time to look at her phone. She figured that Matthew was long gone. Emerging from the building exhausted, she stopped in her tracks. There, still waiting in the car, was Matthew.

MJ

MJ looked at her life in stages, in terms of lessons learned. During her childhood in the Midwest, she was free to roam and explore creeks, trees, and cornfields. As the middle child, she was often called upon by the other kids to be the tiebreaker. Her opinion mattered.

In her years at Purdue, she was defined in part by her aptitude in math. That fluency gave her the confidence to solve problems in other fields. It had helped her when she was hired at Intel, where she learned to perform under pressure and work in close, cohesive teams, under the direction of visionaries Andy Grove, Bob Noyce, and Gordon Moore.

During her graduate years at Stanford business school, she had met trailblazers like Steve Jobs and Sandy Kurtzig, who arrived driving a Ferrari and carrying a pink briefcase. She still remembered Kurtzig's parting words: *"You can't play the game if you're not in it."*

Then she'd landed a dream job as a venture capitalist working for Reid Dennis. The people-loving, bow-tie-wearing Dennis set a tone of ethics and decency at the firm that continues today. Dennis, like his peers Bill Draper, Pitch Johnson, Dick Kramlich, Arthur Rock, Larry Sonsini, and a handful of leaders in the Valley, looked at talent rather than gender. It was at IVP that MJ learned to analyze the most important things about a business and a market. Her judgment became her greatest skill.

And now she was in a new phase of learning: divorced, living alone, with three grown children. She was trying a new approach to life, one that was not based on assumptions. She had begun to tell herself, *Don't muscle your way through every problem.*

She wanted to tell the bright young entrepreneurial women she met some of the lessons she'd learned over the years: *Don't be a martyr; be more selfish about your own needs; keep your foot in the door of a job you love; and whatever you do, don't leave to make someone else happy.* The ecosystem of entrepreneurs and venture capitalists of Silicon Valley was a creative wonderland, she would say. Despite its faults, it was a place where an invisible economic hand rewarded those who worked hard, had great ideas, and wanted to make a difference in the world.

MJ had begun to think about starting her own company or raising a venture fund herself. She no longer had to juggle husband, kids, and job. She hoped to work for another thirty years. She had been one of the first women to make partner at a U.S. venture firm, along with Jacqui Morby, Patricia Cloherty, Ginger More, Nancy Schoendorf, and Annie Lamont. Maybe she would now challenge Silicon Valley's assumptions about age.

For those who knew her, this was a new MJ. She soon joined Sonja, Magdalena, and Jennifer Fonstad at Broadway Angels.

SONJA

As Sonja had promised, Broadway Angels meetings ran like clockwork. Entrepreneurs were introduced by a sponsoring Broadway Angels member, and the founders had twenty minutes to pitch, followed by ten minutes of discussion.

Before the group found a permanent meeting spot at Comcast Ventures in San Francisco, it moved from place to place: in the women's homes, at an office in San Francisco's historic Presidio, on a boat. The group was a who's who of Silicon Valley women, from MJ to Ellen Levy at LinkedIn; venture capital partners Kate Mitchell, Maha Ibrahim, Emily Melton, Robin Richards Donohoe, Jesse Draper, Claudia Fan Munce, and Karen Boezi; serial entrepreneurs Sukhinder Singh Cassidy and Kim Polese; Laurie Yoler, the tech veteran who had helped start Tesla; Amy Banse of Comcast Ventures; Katie Rodan of Rodan + Fields; Katherine August de-Wilde of First Republic Bank; and Leah Busque, founder of TaskRabbit, among others. The women had MBAs, PhDs, and stellar track records. They were entrepreneurs, investors, and moms.

At one of the first meetings, Sonja laughed when a male founder walked into the room, saw all the women, and said, "Whoa!" At another meeting, Sonja refrained from rolling her eyes when a male founder insisted on explaining technical details to his female co-founder.

The Broadway Angels' early investments included Rocksbox, a jewelry subscription service founded by Meaghan Rose, a mother, math whiz, and scrappy entrepreneur; Debbie Sterling, an engineer who founded the toy brand GoldieBlox to introduce girls to science and engineering; and UrbanSitter, co-founded by Lynn Perkins, a mother who wanted a better way than word of mouth to find a babysitter. Other investments included Hint Water, a beverage company founded by Kara Goldin, who started the company because she wanted to lose weight and get away from diet soda. Hint was now a $100-million-a-year business. Sonja invited Brad Stephens, a pioneer in blockchain technology investing, to talk about opportunities in the sector.

Sonja slowly reduced her time at Menlo and stopped attending partners' meetings. In addition to Broadway Angels, she had started a nonprofit to support at-risk teenage girls. The nonprofit, Project Glimmer, was inspired by the online beauty site Eve, and gave gifts of jewelry and makeup at Christmas, reaching more than 125,000 girls and women a year.

Broadway Angels was Sonja's platform to bring recognition and opportunity to women and to amend the history books to include more of her peers. Project Glimmer was her way to inspire the next generation, by making young women feel valued and loved.

MAGDALENA

The giant steel doors opened slowly as lunch recess ended. As the other students returned to class, Magdalena, in first grade and wearing her Catholic school uniform, stared at the open entranceway to the school. She thought, *I'll just go across the street to the chocolate man and get a chocolate bar.* The doors had never opened during the school day. Magdalena headed out and across the street.

The man who owned the shop across the street was surprised to see Kevork Yeşil's daughter before him. Magdalena told him, "I would love to have some chocolate." The shopkeeper, friends with Kevork, sold radios and fans and other electrical appliances. He smiled at the precocious girl with her chubby cheeks and big hazel eyes. He reached into his stash of chocolate bars.

Magdalena thanked the kind shopkeeper, peeled back the wrapper, and devoured the chocolate. Walking back through the big open doors at the school's entrance, she was intercepted by a nun, who didn't look happy. Magdalena was led straight to the office of the head nun.

"Why did you escape?" the head of school demanded.

Magdalena analyzed the question. "I didn't escape from school," she replied. "I came back to school."

The nun asked the question another way: "Why did you think it was okay to leave school without permission?"

Magdalena answered, "The door was open. The chocolate man works across the street. I went to get chocolate."

Magdalena's father was summoned to the school. She was being dismissed from school early—another bit of good fortune, to her mind. Her father arrived and apologized to the nuns. He looked sternly at his daughter.

Out on the street, Magdalena tried to explain to her father that she had seen the open doors as a good opportunity to get some chocolate. It made perfect sense to her.

Today, so many decades later, Magdalena stood across the street from the school where the shop had stood. She could picture her father: smiling, squarely built, with white hair. He always had candy in his pockets for kids who cried on the ferry and for orphans who called him Keyif Amca, "Uncle Joy" in Turkish.

The school looked far more impressive than she remembered. It was now a cultural institute, offering theater and music. She had toured inside the building earlier in the day, returning to the classrooms she remembered, and the upstairs room where she and the other students had taken naps in small chaise longues. The beautifully carved marble trough she remembered was still in place.

Magdalena spent a few more minutes studying the exterior of her school. In her youth, the draw of America had been undeniable, more magnetic than a thousand chocolate bars. But recently she'd felt the tug of home. She loved this mystical, imperial, and cosmopolitan land with its intricate history that was both Christian and Islamic. The smells and sounds were engraved in her mind. If growing up here had a sound, it was the sounds of boats. Ferries were a feature of everyday life, like taxicabs in New York. Her father had taken the ferry across the Bosporus twice a day. The horns of the ferry announced arrivals and departures and sent commuters scurrying to the docks. Small boats sputtered with one- or two-stroke motors. The other sounds she remembered came from the street vendors who made their way through her quiet neighborhood. The cry of the yogurt man was different from the harsh yell of the vegetable vendor.

The smells tended to be seasonal, though the smells of saltwater and seaweed were omnipresent. In the fall there was the smell of roasted chestnuts, and in the summer, fresh corn on the cob boiled and sold at the beach. Not all the smells were good, however, in a dense city where people lived flesh to flesh without deodorant. Magdalena remembered getting onto crowded buses as a girl and trying not to breathe.

On this trip back to Turkey, Magdalena went to Fethiye, a port city in the south, before returning to her neighborhood of Moda, on the Asian side of Istanbul. Her cousin still lived in the same house, five minutes from where Magdalena grew up. Magdalena wandered into the bedroom where the two had once played. The flower and animal stickers they'd put on her dresser were still there.

She visited the ice cream parlor she used to go to as a child, and ordered her favorite ice cream, sour cherry. And she stopped by the church her grandmother attended. Her father had passed away decades earlier, but to her, his presence remained strong here. Magdalena's older sister had been her mother's to mold and shape; Magdalena was her father's daughter.

She walked over to the public beach in Moda, where she once swam and played. It was where the other kids threw sand in her face after learning she was Armenian. But even when those kids pushed her away, she hadn't run away and cried. She'd said to herself, *How can I play their game? How can I get them to make a seat for me?*

Today, much of the beach had been turned into a promenade. But for Magdalena, it would always be the place where she began to understand the game of life.

THERESIA

Theresia and Jennifer Fonstad sat down at the café of the Cantor Arts Center on the Stanford campus. The terrace overlooked the Rodin Sculpture Garden, featuring the French sculptor's various interpretations in bronze of the male nude form. Theresia and Jennifer had met what felt to both like a lifetime before, when they'd worked at Bain in Boston after college. Jennifer, another woman who was becoming a voice for change in Silicon Valley, had announced she was leaving Draper Fisher Jurvetson, the venerable firm where she was a managing director.

Theresia and Jennifer talked about angel investing opportunities. As Theresia was stepping away from Accel, she would now be free to join Broadway Angels.

But Jennifer had her own idea to float. "Instead of just doing angel investing," she said, "we should join forces and start a firm of our own."

By the end of lunch, Theresia was sold. Jennifer was someone she knew and trusted. Like Theresia, Jennifer was a divorced working mom who embraced the importance of career and kids. She believed it was possible to excel at both. As Theresia had always said, "If you want to get something done, hire a working mom. They feel guilty about everything and are hyper efficient." The two women had other things in common as well: Jennifer had landed on the *Forbes* Midas list, climbed Mount Kilimanjaro, and closed a deal while in labor. And they both had demanding fathers who had driven them to succeed. When Jennifer was twelve, her dad had asked her to write out a five-year plan and goals and explain how she'd accomplish them.

Theresia left the lunch feeling excited about her work for the first time in far too long. Much that she had cherished in her life had ended. Now something important, something worthwhile, was about to begin.

In 2014 Theresia and Jennifer announced the formation of their new firm, Aspect Ventures. Combined, the two women had created $10 billion in public market value, helped lead fifteen merger and acquisition transactions, and raised more than three hundred rounds in follow-on capital for their portfolio companies. Trulia, one of the more recent companies Theresia had invested in, was in the news as it was being acquired by Zillow for $3.5 billion. Theresia and Jennifer planned to start by investing their own money, then raise funds from limited partners. They opened offices in San Francisco's South of Market district and in Menlo Park.

When the story on the founding of Aspect broke, Theresia told a reporter she wanted to invest in great companies, regardless of whether they were founded by men or by women. But she also said she wanted to be a part of creating more stories of successful women who raised capital and built companies. At Accel, about 20 percent of the pitches had been from women founders. Aspect aimed to double that, with a goal of one day seeing entrepreneurs and VCs look more like the general population.

In 2015 Aspect raised a $150 million debut fund, focused on Series A investments in software companies. And Theresia remained invested in one of her longtime companies, the cybersecurity firm ForeScout, which was finally looking to go public and getting attention as a possible unicorn—one of those rare start-ups that achieve a billion-dollar valuation. She had worked with co-founder Hezy Yeshurun and the ForeScout team from their beginning in the summer of 2001, and the company had pivoted and persevered and become successful.

She also invested in a new cybersecurity start-up, Cato Networks, founded by her friend and entrepreneur Shlomo Kramer of Check Point and Imperva. Before long, Theresia and Jennifer began attracting high-profile investors, including Melinda Gates, wife of Microsoft co-founder Bill Gates and co-chair of the Bill & Melinda Gates Foundation. Gates had quietly turned her attention to the world of venture capital after learning about the dismal numbers of women in venture and in tech.

Theresia and Melinda Gates met for breakfast at the Rosewood Hotel on Sand Hill Road. Melinda wanted to apply what she had learned from the Gates Foundation's work in global health to improving conditions for women in tech.

The boys' club of Silicon Valley, as Melinda saw it, was both harmful to society and bad for business. If tech and Silicon Valley shaped the future, Melinda asked, what happened when there were so few women?

As Gates began to study the issues, she had to decide whether to put her money and energy into helping to advance entrepreneurs or venture capitalists. She decided to focus on venture because it was the start of the food chain. If venture didn't diversify, tech couldn't diversify. She believed that women were more likely to fund other women and that more women were needed at the decision-making table.

Once she defined the focus on venture, Melinda wanted to understand what was keeping women out of the industry and what were the pathways in.

Melinda had been drawn to tech personally because of an outstanding woman math teacher who was able to get ten Apple II computers into her Catholic girls' school. She remembered the teacher asking the girls whether they wanted to learn to code in BASIC. Melinda took to coding immediately, finding it like solving a puzzle, something she'd always loved. She then got a summer job teaching kids how to program in LOGO. She attended Duke because the university had a grant from IBM for two big computer labs. She had worked at Microsoft for nine years and loved her job.

"I've always been interested in how tech serves *all* of society," Melinda said. "I am a big believer in disruptive innovation. But if we want more innovation and better products, we've got to put more money behind women and minorities."

Theresia was impressed by Melinda, finding her engaging, impassioned, and down-to-earth. Theresia offered her ideas on how to increase the number of women in tech in general as well as women investors and women founders. The two women talked about what it's like when a firm only has one woman, and that woman is under pressure to assimilate into the boys' club rather than change it. Melinda said, "When you put several women on a board, the questions asked of the business become different. Change begins. VC firms have to wake up to that."

The two parted ways that morning with an eye to working together to shake up the status quo.

When Aspect raised its second venture fund, it surpassed its target with $200 million, and Melinda was in as an investor through her company Pivotal Ventures. In an ironic twist of fate, Aspect moved from Menlo Park to the office in Palo Alto where Facebook had been located when it first got funding, where Theresia had presented the Series A term sheet and listened to a twenty-year-old Mark Zuckerberg talk about his cool college start-up.

SONJA

At a Broadway Angels meeting in 2017, Sonja and the group grappled with some ugly news about endemic harassment and sexism in Silicon Valley. The subject had come up in a more isolated way in 2012, when venture capitalist Ellen Pao sued her former employer, the venture firm Kleiner Perkins Caufield & Byers, alleging that she was discriminated against and sexually harassed. She lost the case but became an activist for equality.

Now a flurry of stories, allegations, and lawsuits filled the news and was spreading from industry to industry. Female entrepreneurs in Silicon Valley were coming forward to say they had been afraid until now to report the misconduct of certain venture capitalists. Susan Fowler, an engineer at Uber, accused her company of fostering a toxic culture of sexism. Uber CEO Travis Kalanick had quipped to a reporter in an interview years earlier that he should call the company "boober" for all the women he gets "on demand."

New allegations of abuse and bad behavior seemed to make headlines every day. Everyone at the Broadway Angels table knew someone who was accused of misconduct or worse. Shervin Pishevar, the Menlo partner and Uber investor who had moved into Sonja's old office, was being accused of sexual harassment and assault by a handful of women.

He has denied the allegations. Steve Jurvetson, a wunderkind venture investor who had funded Theresia's start-up, Release Software—and was a friend—had left his firm DFJ (where Jennifer Fonstad was a partner) following allegations that he hosted sex and drug parties and had multiple affairs, including with female entrepreneurs. (Jurvetson has also denied the allegations.) Maha Ibrahim was seated on a plane next to a well-known male VC who confided to her that his firm would never hire another woman as an investing partner. The man told Maha that his firm didn't want the trouble. As he put it, they didn't want to be "Paod"—a reference to the lawsuit by Ellen Pao.

The problems in tech mirrored problems in the broader American workplace. But Sonja had a hard time reconciling the Silicon Valley she knew with the Silicon Valley in the news. She could still remember her first day in venture capital, January 2, 1989, when she'd started at TA Associates in Boston and thought, *This is the best job in the world.*

There had been a time when Sonja would do anything to prove herself. When she applied to Harvard Business School, she wrote about a lifeguard certification class she'd taken at the University of Virginia, with members of the UVA swim team as classmates. Every day she swam until her body shook from exhaustion and she felt like she was drowning, but she kept on swimming. Every week another woman dropped out. At the end of the class, she had to take the certification test. She was blindfolded in the dive pool, and a UVA swimmer nick-named Moose—a huge guy—got into the pool to simulate a person drowning. He grabbed onto her, pulling her under. Sonja dug her nails into Moose, pulled his hair, and got him off her before "saving" him. She was the only woman in her class to pass the test.

Now, looking back, Sonja wondered if her efforts to gain approval from her male colleagues had been misguided. But she concluded that she did what was right to stay in the game and succeed, and now to pave the way for other women to enter the field. It had been almost two years since she had walked away from Menlo Ventures, but a more important anniversary was approaching.

MJ

MJ had returned to Stanford as a fellow at the university's Distinguished Careers Institute, a yearlong program offered to successful individuals "rethinking the concept of a life journey." The fellows created a customized lesson plan and attended whatever combination of classes interested them. MJ signed up for a course taught by social psychologist Rod Kramer called Lives of Consequence: How Individuals Discover Paths to Meaningful Engagement.

Students in the program were asked to think about finding purpose. They focused on something Kramer defined as "flow," activities that make you lose track of time. The idea was the more flow, the greater your happiness. Students listed the things that made them lose track of time. MJ hadn't thought of this before, but wrote: "For me, flow comes from music. I like almost all genres, but with a nod to my mom, Dorothy, and her one LP, *Hank Williams' Greatest Hits,* a country music lover was born."

She continued, "So flow happens to me through music, drawing and painting, making jewelry, watching Giants baseball, hiking, spinning, working out, cooking, having a great meal with people I love."

On another day, Kramer instructed the students, "Grab friends and talk about how to pick a mate, a partner, a spouse, of consequence." MJ, decades older than the students in this second-year graduate-level business class, joined a group of three women and four men. They had to come up with ten traits they wanted in a partner. MJ looked at the group and thought, *I'm not really doing this with twenty-somethings, am I?* When it came time to reveal the top traits, all three women in MJ's group listed "emotional intelligence." When all four men asked, "What's that?" MJ laughed.

The class made MJ think about the future rather than dwell on the past. She wrote, "Lately I am on a new trajectory. I am evolving from a human *doing* to a human *being.* I believe in the power of the now and in living in the day and the moment."

She wrote out her "axioms to live by":

Love is a verb. Make your top relationships your top priority.

Be more than generous in your dealings with others, like Reid Dennis was with me. Give people more than they ask for.

Be an inclusive, big tent kind of person.

Approach each day with thankfulness, savoring the small moments of joy. Keep a joy journal. It might surprise you what gives you those moments.

Be a person of your word.

Be yourself, everyone else is taken (Oscar Wilde).

Be "everyday brave" (MJ) and "do one thing every day that scares you" (Eleanor Roosevelt).

Be kind, for everyone you meet is fighting a hard battle (Plato).

It doesn't cost anything to be nice (Mom).

God is great, beer is good, and people are crazy (Billy Currington).

In addition to reevaluating her life journey, MJ was taking a new approach to investing. She had first heard of Broadway Angels over lunch with venture capitalist Aileen Lee, a Broadway Angels member who had founded her own firm, Cowboy Ventures, in 2012 and co-founded an important new nonprofit called All Raise with Jess Lee, the first woman investing partner at Sequoia Capital, to bring more women into venture capital. MJ knew Sonja and many of the other members of the group. As soon as she joined Broadway Angels, she found herself gravitating to companies that were aligned with her hobbies and passions, with those things that felt like "flow." Instead of enterprise software, semiconductors, and networking, she began investing in food, fashion, travel, art, and music.

MJ invested in The RealReal, a high-end consignment shop founded by Julie Wainwright. MJ admired the resilient Wainwright, who started The RealReal in her early fifties and figured out how to grow the business from zero to $500 million in six years. Wainwright had been the CEO of Pets.com, and became a pariah when the dot-com boom went bust. By Wainwright's own admission, she became "totally unemployable." Her solution was to start her own company to control her own future. MJ also invested in FoodyDirect, which offered door-to-door delivery of iconic regional specialties such as Chicago's deep-dish pizza and New York bagels and lox. And she was impressed by the young women founders of Argent, a company reimagining clothes for working women with the tagline: "Finding workwear you love shouldn't be revolutionary. But it is. Kind of like equal pay." MJ loved seeing Argent founder Sali Christeson at her shop in San Francisco, juggling work, meetings, and calls while holding her baby boy.

When MJ came in to San Francisco for a Broadway Angels meeting, she never tired of seeing a big group of women investors seated around the long glass conference table. Many founders who came to pitch admitted that they rarely saw a woman VC, let alone a whole group of women VCs.

Inevitably, the Broadway Angels meetings set aside some time to discuss relevant news of the day. When allegations of sexual harassment and assault against film producer Harvey Weinstein filled the news, the women again talked about living through a moment in history when they hoped life for women would change for the better. They discussed the importance of the Me Too and Time's Up movements, which were implicating hundreds of high-level executives in every industry around the globe. All Raise would be the political arm of the women's VC movement, while Broadway Angels remained the investing platform. Men who behaved badly were being put on notice, and many firms in Silicon Valley were hiring more women as principals and partners. That marked progress. But the real work, the heavy lifting, was more challenging. It was the deeper problem of bias.

MJ knew that the "bro culture," and stories of sexual harassment in Silicon Valley, were an everyday reality, but she also knew that was not the entire story. She had worked with ethical partners at IVP and elsewhere who looked past gender and always treated her respectfully. She had found Silicon Valley an amazing place to work. She had blazed trails and built game-changing companies. Her problems around gender had been closer to home. Even when she was working full-time, she didn't ask Bill to step up and do more. She didn't ask him to reduce his work hours. No one in her life told her to keep her foot in the door at IVP instead of walking away.

Returning home from her latest Broadway Angels meeting, she smiled when she saw the sign for the Sand Hill Road exit. She was older and wiser than when she'd first arrived in Silicon Valley and seen that sign. She was now driving a BMW X1 instead of a rusted-out Ford Pinto, and she had the latest smartphone instead of a CB radio. But she still had the spirit of that adventure-seeking girl looking at a future full of promise.

As she told Sonja at the meeting, "I feel like I have something big still to do." Whizzing by Sand Hill Road, she cranked up the music. Tim McGraw was singing "My Next Thirty Years":

I think I'll take a moment, celebrate my age
The ending of an era and the turning of a page.

The lyric captured MJ's feelings perfectly. It made her reflect on her own path and think about how to make her journey even more rewarding. In 2016 she had attended the memorial service of Intel CEO Andy Grove. The focus had been on Grove not as a hard-charging and brilliant manager but as an adoring husband and father. MJ had wrongly assumed that because of his intensity at work, he was less of a family man.

For years, she had convinced herself that it was impossible to balance a demanding career with a satisfying home life. Her mother had always chosen hamburger while everyone else enjoyed steak. MJ, despite her own best efforts, had, at times, opted for hamburger, too. Her adult life was far too often about being a martyr and tamping down her expectations, just as her mother had. The truth had washed over MJ in that moment of reckoning in the aisle of Whole Foods, when she realized she didn't know what she wanted. Finally, for the first time in her life, the girl from Indiana realized she needed to invest in herself.

THERESIA

Theresia felt like celebrating again. As 2018 approached, Aspect, her new firm, was thriving. Forty percent of Aspect's investments were in women-founded firms. And she and Matthew were engaged. After showing up that night for the Accel mediation, he'd never really left. Now, whenever she was receiving an award or speaking at an event, he was front and center. And she remained close with her ex-husband, Tim, who had remarried and lived four blocks away. In fact, she and Matthew attended his wedding. And they all celebrated the holidays together with their kids.

In late 2018 Theresia was recognized by *Forbes* magazine as "America's richest female venture capitalist," with an estimated net worth of $500 million. She had hesitated when asked to be a part of the story but realized that she could use the exposure as an opportunity to shine a light on things she cared about. She also felt that women needed to do a better job of owning their success. The reaction to the story was particularly effusive among the men in her industry. The article's focus on money seemed to give her a sort of street cred she hadn't had before. For years, she had heard guys talk about a certain measurement that mattered: getting into the "three comma club," a Silicon Valley term used to refer to those who had made a billion dollars. Theresia was halfway there.

Always a networker, Theresia was helping to build a network for women in the Valley, with Aspect Ventures, Broadway Angels, and All Raise, and through her role in advancing women in tech. In the past, when the women who worked in Silicon Valley had gathered at small dinners, salons, or Hawaiian getaways, they had returned home to their silos. Not anymore.

Theresia and her friends Emily White and Sukhinder Singh Cassidy had a tradition of taking turns hosting an all-women's Christmas cocktail party. Seventy-five women had attended the first year in 2011. This year three hundred women—including MJ, Sonja, Magdalena, Robin, Kate, Laurie Yoler, and Maha Ibrahim—gathered at Theresia's house.

The party was about networking and fun, but it also benefited several charities. This year's beneficiaries were DonorsChoose, an education website connecting individuals to teachers and classrooms in need, where Theresia served on the board, and Project Glimmer, the nonprofit started by Sonja to inspire and embrace teenage girls.

That night, as music played and drinks flowed, the women took turns posing in the photo booth, donning costumes and holding signs like I LIKE BIG BUCKS, I'M WITH HER, and NAUGHTY OR NICE.

Theresia's daughter, Sarah, a freshman in high school, had expressed interest in attending the party. Theresia was half convinced that the draw for Sarah was not her mom but her mom's friends, such as Emily White, the COO of Snapchat, and Susan Wojcicki, the CEO of YouTube.

But Theresia noted a deeper change in her daughter. When Sarah was in elementary school, she had asked her mom why she wasn't a room parent or a field trip chaperone. Theresia was the mother who would buy baked goods and put them in a homemade container to pass them off as her own. But recently, when she and Sarah were in the car together, Sarah had asked whether the stories about gender discrimination in Silicon Valley were true: "So basically you worked with all guys?" Theresia nodded. Sarah had chosen to attend an all-girls middle and high school after seeing how the boys around her acted—the way they raised their hands far more than girls, the assumptions made around who would lead, who liked sports, and who was good at math and science. It alarmed her that she might be seen as a second-class citizen at school. Sarah said to her mom that day in the car, "I'm really proud of you."

In another moment she would not soon forget, Theresia received an e-mail from the principal at her son Luke's school. Luke was now eight. The e-mail read:

> *Dear Luke,*
>
> *I just wanted to say thank you. This afternoon I had the opportunity to pop into your classroom and listen to your class conversation about what makes an invention. When the discussion turned to the term "human-made" rather than "man-made," [your teacher] asked the class to explain the difference. You quickly raised your hand and shared that human-made made more sense because, "Not only men make things, women can make inventions as well." This sparked a conversation about how women create and innovate. Thank you for thinking with an open and inclusive mind, Luke!*

These moments with her children brought Theresia enormous joy, and these days she made sure to savor them. She wanted her kids to have a better life, just as her parents had wanted for her.

Her days at Accel and her divorce from Tim had changed her. She no longer felt the need to check every box, to take every meeting, to speak loudly and interrupt often. In establishing Aspect, Theresia had found her comfort zone: She was doing the work because she loved it.

SONJA

On March 26, 2018, Sonja reached an important milestone. She had been free of cancer for ten years. She celebrated with a girlfriend, who treated her to dinner at Zuni Café in San Francisco. She began putting together a presentation that she called "The Girls' Guide to Winning." She had winnowed her lessons learned down to ten points, ranging from "Don't look for discrimination" and "Do the work that men do" to "Own your story" and "Have thick skin."

The girls' guide made Sonja think of pioneering women in different fields. Marissa Mayer had developed a specialty in artificial intelligence and mapping at Stanford, became Google's twentieth employee, was hired as Yahoo!'s CEO, and left to run her own tech incubator. Taylor Swift, at fourteen, had convinced her parents to move to Nashville because she was determined to be a music star. Malala Yousafzai, the Pakistani activist and Nobel Prize winner, had been shot in the face but refused to back down from her belief that girls should be educated.

In May, Sonja organized a birthday party for her daughter, Tess, who was turning ten. Sonja's own birthday was approaching; inevitably, she was asked what she would change in her life. Her reply: "I wouldn't change a thing. You don't know if the one thing that was negative made you who you are."

But when she looked to the future, she had a guiding image: a group of smart, fun, engaged trailblazing women taking seats around the Broadway Angels table, a table that stretched across the globe, like a strong and beautiful banner too large to ignore. To date, 50 percent of Broadway Angels' investments were in companies founded by women.

Sonja, the southern belle and eternal optimist, had always seen the world the way she wanted to see it. Where others saw bias, she had seen opportunity. For most of her adult life, she had refused to believe that men and women were different at work. Success trumped gender, she was convinced, and merit was what mattered. People were people.

That view of reality had shifted when she was diagnosed with cancer and began to juggle work and family. For the first time, she was bumping up against the challenges so many working women faced. As she struggled, she imagined what it must be like for women who didn't have her resources. If she could lose her professional footing in a moment when she was vulnerable, what did other working women face, who lived paycheck to paycheck? It made her feel a new sense of empathy and urgency.

Sonja had spent her career investing in companies that touched people's lives. Her investments had helped make the Internet safer and more secure. But along the way, she had also become a feminist. And even more to her surprise, an activist.

MAGDALENA

Magdalena was in Istanbul in the summer of 2018 to see friends and family, including her cousin and last surviving uncle. She spent two glorious weeks sailing in the Turkish waters off Datça, Bozburun, and Göcek with her younger son, Troy. Then she returned to Istanbul for several days of meetings with local entrepreneurs and venture capitalists.

She had a book out, *Power Up*—Marc Benioff contributed the foreword—and she was back in familiar start-up terrain, having co-founded an auto-financing company called Informed with her tech-savvy son Justin. One of her investors was Aspect Ventures. Magdalena had found her way back to her intellectual home, Silicon Valley.

She headed out to meet with Dilek Dayinlarli, a woman venture capitalist whom she had advised from time to time over the past six years. Magdalena's schedule was packed, so the two women met while Magdalena was commuting from the Asian side of Istanbul to the European side, and then back again.

Dilek, thirty-six, lived in Istanbul with her husband and daughter. She had a résumé tailor-made for venture capital: a bachelor's degree in mechanical engineering, where she was one of five women in a class of 450 men; an MBA; and she was once a professional women's basketball player, playing point guard. She also had worked as a director at Groupon. Dilek, who traveled back and forth between Turkey and Silicon Valley, had found Magdalena by asking investment bankers and entrepreneurs for names of successful men or women in the venture industry. Magdalena's name came up repeatedly.

The women hit it off right away. Magdalena shared her stories of juggling children and work and how she had to cut out everything else to do those things well. Dilek knew Magdalena was a great mom; she'd met her sons Justin and Troy.

"Take it easy for a while, but *don't leave your job*," Magdalena told Dilek when Dilek became a mother. "Keep yourself in the loop. Work is a blessing. I hate hearing from women who have been blessed with the best education in the world say, 'Well I don't *need* to work.' I say, 'Okay, so you don't need it financially, but maybe you need it for other things. Maybe you need it for you.'"

The two women discussed the fact that women worked harder and were often paid less. As Magdalena told her, women in the United States earn eighty cents for every dollar earned by a man, a gap that widens when broken down by race. "This is reality. Don't be upset. Don't go off and die on the corner fuming with anger. Go and push for equality."

Magdalena had met Dilek not long after starting Broadway Angels. She had found that working with a group of women with similar experiences was transformative. Before, while Magdalena hadn't hidden her gender, she hadn't focused on it, either. She had done what she needed to build a career and win. Now she wanted to help the Dileks of the world win.

This new direction had made her think for the first time about what it meant to be a feminist. To her, a feminist was someone who wants equal pay and equal opportunity for women. It didn't mean demanding that women capture 50 percent of management jobs and 50 percent of board seats. She didn't believe in quotas.

Magdalena was getting her second wind in her career. Walking along the streets in Istanbul, she passed a Salesforce office. The company she had helped build was now global, with about thirty thousand employees, and her friend Marc Benioff was a billionaire many times over. Salesforce Tower in San Francisco had officially opened a few months earlier and was now the tallest office building west of the Mississippi. The company had reported $3 billion in revenue in its latest quarter, with $20.4 billion in future revenues under contract.

As Magdalena headed back to Moda—her childhood home—she felt she had delivered on her father's dreams for her. It was he who had set her on this journey of discovery, telling his young daughter that she could like hammers and nails and be a carpenter if that's what she chose.

Magdalena smiled, remembering something her father had said to her on that wonderful day when the doors of her elementary school opened and the chocolate beckoned. When she and her father were out of earshot of the Catholic nuns, Magdalena was about to explain her actions when her father stopped her. He knelt and said, "You saw an opportunity and you took it. You must decide in life what is right for you." Then he told her, "You don't have to obey all the rules."

Magdalena, and many women in tech and venture capital, had lived by this credo. She had told Dilek: "What I enjoy is what I don't know."

In engineering class at Stanford, Magdalena had discovered the joy of the unknowable—the scary yet exhilarating notion that she could not rely on her brain alone with absolute certainty. The inscrutable had always been reassuring, even if it was beyond her perception and her sense of reality. One of the few times she hadn't embraced the unknowable was when she'd left the Salesforce board too early. She had set unreasonable, perfectionist standards for herself. That decision, made out of fear, had been a mistake. It had gone against the grain of who she was: an explorer, an adventurer, a risk taker.

All the Alpha Girls—Magdalena, Theresia, Sonja, and MJ—in their own ways had adopted the unknowable. That was the only way they could survive and thrive in the competitive, high-stakes world. They had arrived in Silicon Valley as young women, seeking opportunity from uncertainty. Always outnumbered as women in a man's world, they tallied victories more numerous and greater than they'd ever imagined. They had sacrificed and suffered setbacks, but they had never given up. The Alpha Girls had created their own paths, had made their own history. And as Magdalena knew, they'd only just begun.

AUTHOR'S NOTE

The idea for *Alpha Girls* has roots in my last book, *How to Make a Spaceship: A Band of Renegades, an Epic Race, and the Birth of Private Spaceflight.* As I traveled around the country talking to groups of engineers, entrepreneurs, and scientists, I kept asking myself one question: Where are all the women? In crowds big and small, there would be only a handful of women.

I began to research the many fields where women are underrepresented, and I soon homed in on venture capital as an industry that is not well known but has enormous influence. Venture capital matters more than just about any other part of tech, and the people who control the cash are men. Venture capitalists invest in the ideas of entrepreneurs. Successful start-ups shape and change how we live, from the way we communicate to the technology we use, from the cars we drive to the breakthrough medical treatments we may one day need.

When I started my research in late 2016, just 6 percent of investing partners at venture capital firms were women, and about 2 percent of venture dollars went to companies founded by women. Of the $130 billion that venture capital firms invested last year, a paltry $2.6 billion went to women. I wanted to know: What do such hidden inequalities mean for the rest of the world?

Melinda Gates put it most succinctly when she told me, "If venture doesn't diversify, tech won't diversify." Gates, an engineer and co-chair with her husband of the Bill & Melinda Gates Foundation, recently turned her attention to improving diversity in tech. Her focus on diversity came after doing extensive work in the developing world, where she saw how empowered women transform societies. She began to wonder, "How far has the United States come on these issues?" The answer was "not far enough." In her mind, reforming tech would have to begin with venture capital.

In the cloistered good old boys' club of Silicon Valley, male VCs invite other male VCs in on deals and fund male founders. The male founders go on to hire men who look like them. When big companies acquire start-ups, the male-heavy workforce is absorbed into a bigger male-heavy company. This means that the software, hardware, apps, social media, AI, and more are being created, funded, and run by men.

But improving the gender balance is not only about equality—it's also about a better bottom line and a thriving global economy. Women represent half of the world's population and half of its potential. Research shows that companies with more diversity, particularly with more women in leadership, offer higher returns on capital and greater innovation than firms without this leadership. Companies with more women at the executive and board levels perform better. Start-ups with at least one female founder see a better return on their investments. Companies that do the best with gender diversity on their executive teams are statistically more likely to have above-average profitability.

Before I tracked down the women of venture capital, I wanted to understand the industry itself. Much has been written about Silicon Valley, and I was a journalist at the *San Francisco Chronicle* for two decades, so the Valley was hardly foreign to me. But I wanted to see for myself how this dynamic entrepreneurial ecosystem came into existence. I wanted to learn how it took root along a quiet stretch of land known as Sand Hill Road. I wanted to form my own opinions about how venture capitalists and entrepreneurs have changed the world. I started out by meeting with many of the founding fathers of venture capital—yes, they are all men. I spent hours talking with industry legends, including Arthur Rock, Bill Draper, Pitch Johnson, Reid Dennis, Irwin Federman, and Don Valentine (years ago, I also had the pleasure of interviewing Tom

Perkins, co-founder of Kleiner Perkins Caufield & Byers). I met with lawyer Larry Sonsini, who has been the consiglieri to the tech world for decades. I talked with many younger male VCs, including John Fisher of Draper Fisher Jurvetson, who began to point me in the direction of the real unicorns of his industry—the women who succeeded. Remarkably, I found that their stories had never been told. In this way, though, they are like women everywhere whose contributions have been underplayed, diluted, or simply overlooked. (Even Frida Kahlo was referred to as "Diego Rivera's wife" in her *New York Times* obituary.) I talked with Reid Hoffman, a venture capitalist at Greylock Partners and the co-founder of LinkedIn. I interviewed historians, gender experts, and entrepreneurs. Slowly, I began to find my trailblazers, my "Alpha Girls," the women of venture who worked in silos as the only female general investing partners at their firms. They were among the first women in the United States to become partners at major VC firms. They succeeded in a world decidedly stacked against them.

My reporting for this book was already under way when the Me Too movement began, outing men in Hollywood, Silicon Valley, and just about every other industry imaginable. An international dialogue was stirred around gender, bias, power, abuse, and bad behavior in the workplace. The Me Too movement had an interesting effect on my reporting. My Alpha Girls became braver in sharing their important stories. There is power in the collective.

Still, it was at times excruciatingly difficult to get the women of this book to be candid about their failings and vulnerabilities, and about their betrayals at work or at home. These women made their careers by being strong and unflappable, by wearing their Teflon suits and playing by rules established by men. They were brilliant in navigating the minefields of being a woman in an all-male field: knowing when to ignore an off-color joke or when to take it seriously, when to join a networking event and when to pass, when to be a team player and when to compete for a deal. There are so many lessons learned in this book.

I realize now that I asked these women to take big risks in sharing their successes, failures, and regrets. They shared painful chapters in their lives; this wasn't easy for them. Venture capital is an industry where connections and relationships matter. Today, while there has been a bump in the hiring of women, about three-quarters of U.S. venture firms still have zero women investing partners. Of the firms that have hired women as check-writing partners, most have just one woman partner, not multiple. It is rare to find top VC firms with more than one female investing partner.

You may wonder how I chose my primary characters. Certainly, there are other female trailblazers who were entrepreneurs and venture capitalists, and many of their stories are told in part in this book. I wanted to find a small group of women who had deals that were irrefutably theirs; who had played a key role in shaping an industry, whether hardware, software, e-commerce, cybersecurity, or social media; and I wanted women of different generations, personalities, and backgrounds. I wanted to tell their stories at work and at home, as women live complicated lives. I wanted to explore questions such as: How do men support us or hold us back? How do we women limit ourselves? I wanted to see how Silicon Valley looks from a woman's point of view.

This may be unexpected, but as I was writing *Alpha Girls,* I often thought of the television series *Sex and the City,* based on the book by Candace Bushnell. Just as readers and viewers personally identified with either Carrie, Miranda, Samantha, or Charlotte, my hope is that readers of *Alpha Girls* will find commonalities with Theresia, Magdalena, Sonja, or MJ. They will say, "I'm just like MJ" or "I'm just like Theresia." The women of *Alpha Girls* just happen to be great at math, engineering, finance, computers, and business. But like the fictional characters of *Sex and the City,* the real-life Alpha Girls were also trying to find their way in the world.

When women see other women in positions of leadership or success, it reframes what they think is possible for them. *Alpha Girls* gives us the female phenotypes we need. These are regular women: daughters of immigrants, dentists, teachers, and merchants. They are women who invented, funded, and helped build companies that changed industries. They are women who made bucketloads of their own money. Now they are working to rewrite the rules for women in venture and beyond. A rebellion is under way in Silicon Valley, but it is just beginning.

While there are men in this story who behaved badly, there are also wonderful men who were great allies to women and never considered gender an issue. They have much to teach. Overall, I look at the venture industry as one of the most important and dynamic around. It is where the future takes shape. It's a great place for men and women, but I can now see how women are particularly well suited for venture. Women are the most powerful consumers in the world economy, driving up to 80 percent of all consumer purchases. The women VCs I know are smart, data-driven, and intuitive.

Finally, I wanted to share my thinking around the term "Alpha Girls." Yes, these are *women* I'm writing about. But I love the word *girl*. In my mind, the word has power, pluck, and determination. Girls are formidable, caring, hopeful, brave, smart, and strong. Look at Theresia Gouw, Sonja Perkins, MJ Elmore, Magdalena Yeşil, and many of the other women in this story. My research also inspired me to revisit stories of well-known Alpha Girls, women such as the tennis player Billie Jean King, the jurist Ruth Bader Ginsburg, and the activist Malala, to name a few. I researched the Alpha Girls of history, whether the first black woman elected to the U.S. Congress, the young black girls of the civil rights movement, or the formidable peasant woman in World War I who became Russia's first female army officer.

Today, there are Alpha Girls everywhere, and their stories need to be told. These are the first women to command assault ships in the Persian Gulf; an all-women's drumming group in Brazil that is breaking gender boundaries; the female farmworkers fighting sexual abuse and discrimination; the Citadel's first female regimental commander; the Iranian women who are breaking the law by shedding their head scarves; the millions of women in South India who stood shoulder to shoulder on New Year's Day to protest sexism and oppression.

As I see it, an Alpha Girl is a woman of any age who refuses to give up on her dreams. She ignores what others insist is impossible and shows what is possible. As Magdalena Yeşil, the girl who loved her hammer and nails more than any doll, was told by her father in Istanbul, Turkey, "You must decide in life what is right for you. You don't have to obey all the rules."

I am excited to meet the rule-breaking Alpha Girls of the world, to hear your stories and stir discussions around how we succeed, why we fail, how we get back up again and make things better for the women around us and for the next generation of boys and girls.

I hope you will share your stories with me, and let's make sure Alpha Girls past, present, and future get their place in the history books.

Connect at:

julianguthriesf.com

E-mail: alphagirlsbook@gmail.com

Twitter: @JulianGuthrie

Facebook: https://www.facebook.com/AlphaGirlsStories/

ACKNOWLEDGMENTS

My mother, Connie Guthrie, is an Alpha Girl. She was twelve years old when she watched the first United States Women's Open Golf Championship held at the Spokane Country Club in Spokane, Washington, in 1946. She was inspired watching the female trailblazers of golf who established the Ladies Professional Golf Association: Mildred Ella "Babe" Didrikson Zaharias, Patty Berg, Betty Jameson, and Louise Suggs.

After taking up golf at age twelve, Connie won the Spokane Area Women's Golf Championship for the first time at age sixteen in 1951. (She was runner up at age fourteen, the first year she played, losing in sudden death on the thirty-seventh hole.) She went on to win the Spokane championship *fifteen* more times, "retiring" from the competition on her sixteenth win.

She won the Idaho State Women's Amateur Championship in 1951 and 1952, and the Washington State Women's Golf Association Championship in 1951 and 1980. Her wins in 1951 were especially remarkable given she was sixteen years old. In 1953, she was the first—and last—woman to play on the men's varsity golf team at Gonzaga University, where she had a full scholarship.

At the time, opportunities for women in sports were limited, so she went out for the men's team and easily made the cut, having already won the city and state championships. There were occasions when men on competing teams walked to the first tee, learned they were matched against Connie—who was as gorgeous as she was talented—and declared, "I'm not competing *against a woman*." These wins against disdainful men were especially satisfying. But the National Collegiate Athletic Association (NCAA) declared the same year that women were not allowed to play on men's teams. The NCAA banned my mother from playing on the men's team, leaving her with no other options, as there were no women's college sports teams. She thought the decision was "pretty rotten."

My mother was also named Miss Spokane in 1953 and served as the city's official hostess. She then took time off to raise her family, returning to golf decades later. She returned because she missed the challenges of competition, and she wanted something that was just for herself. In 1984, she refocused her energies on the sport she loved and staged a storybook comeback. She pulled off extraordinary wins, becoming the top senior amateur golfer in the United States, winning the United States Golf Association Senior Women's Amateur championship in 1984 and in 1986.

She also won the Pacific Northwest Golf Association (PNGA) Women's Amateur championship in 1984, the Western Senior Women's Amateur Championship in 1986, and the PNGA Senior Women's Amateur in 1993. She found her age was an advantage, saying, "Being older helps in some ways because your attitude and mental toughness are better." She was named by *Golf Digest* as one of the best-dressed women in golf. She was inducted into the Gonzaga University Hall of Fame; the Inland Northwest Hall of Fame; and the Pacific Northwest Golf Association Hall of Fame. That's my mom—my best friend, a great role model, and an original Alpha Girl.

Finally, I extend heartfelt thanks to my literary agent, Joe Veltre; my talented editor at Crown, Roger Scholl; and my friend and editor David Lewis. Thank you again to Theresia, MJ, Magdalena, and Sonja for trusting me with your important stories. Thank you to Martin Muller, to my brother, David Guthrie, and to my son, Roman.

Roman, you are my pride and joy. Remember that strong people stand up for themselves, and stronger people stand up for others. I know you will always do both.

ABOUT THE AUTHOR

JULIAN GUTHRIE spent twenty years writing for the *San Francisco Chronicle*, where she won numerous awards and had her writing nominated multiple times for the Pulitzer Prize. She is the author of three nonfiction books: *The Grace of Everyday Saints*, *The Billionaire and the Mechanic*, and *How to Make a Spaceship*. She lives in the San Francisco Bay Area.